MW00658275

TRANSLANGUAGING WITH MULTILINGUAL STUDENTS

"Not only does this book draw on classroom research, but it lays out the issues of what it means to teach from a translanguaging perspective. It shows what translanguaging looks like, how it can be taken up pedagogically, and why this matters for teachers, students and researchers."

Alastair Pennycook, University of Technology Sydney, Australia

"Offers a unique set of windows into the theory of translanguaging that is both theoretically and practically needed. I'm very excited about this project, and will be among the first to purchase the book and use it with my students."

Deborah Palmer, University of Colorado, Boulder, USA

"An important step in the development of translanguaging pedagogies in bilingual and multilingual education, this book brings together theoretical and empirical contributions based on actual translanguaging practices in New York schools that certainly apply to situations in other parts of the world."

Jasone Cenoz, University of the Basque Country, Spain

Looking closely at what happens when translanguaging is actively taken up to teach emergent bilingual students across different contexts, this book focuses on how it is already happening in classrooms as well as how it can be implemented as a pedagogical orientation. It extends theoretical understandings of the concept and highlights its promises and challenges. Using a Transformative Action Research design, six empirically grounded ethnographic case studies describe how translanguaging is used in lesson designs and in the spontaneous moves made by teachers and students during specific teaching moments. The cases shed light on two questions: How, when, and why is translanguaging taken up or resisted by students and teachers? What does its use mean for them? Although grounded in a U.S. context, and specifically in classrooms in New York State, *Translanguaging with Multilingual Students* links findings and theories to different global contexts to offer important lessons for educators worldwide.

Ofelia García is Professor in the Ph.D. programs of Urban Education and Hispanic and Luso-Brazilian Literatures and Languages at the Graduate Center of the City University of New York, USA.

Tatyana Kleyn is Associate Professor in the Bilingual Education and TESOL programs at the City College of New York, USA.

TRANSLANGUAGING WITH MULTILINGUAL STUDENTS

Learning from Classroom Moments

Edited by Ofelia García and Tatyana Kleyn

Marguerite –
Thank you for all
your work with
translanguaging –
& the Internationals
Ofelia

Routledge
Taylor & Francis Group
NEW YORK AND LONDON

First published 2016
by Routledge
711 Third Avenue, New York, NY 10017

and by Routledge
2 Park Square, Milton Park, Abingdon, Oxon, OX14 4RN

Routledge is an imprint of the Taylor & Francis Group, an informa business

Library of Congress Cataloging-in-Publication Data
García, Ofelia, editor. | Kleyn, Tatyana, editor.
Title: Translanguaging with multilingual students : learning from classroom moments / Edited by Ofelia García and Tatyana Kleyn.
Description: New York : Routledge, [2016] | Includes bibliographical references and index.
Identifiers: LCCN 2016002747 | ISBN 9781138906976 (hardback) | ISBN 9781138906983 (pbk.) | ISBN 9781315695242 (ebook)
Subjects: LCSH: Applied linguistics.
Classification: LCC P129 .T734 2016 | DDC 418—dc23
LC record available at https://lccn.loc.gov/2016002747

ISBN: 978-1-138-90697-6 (hbk)
ISBN: 978-1-138-90698-3 (pbk)
ISBN: 978-1-315-69524-2 (ebk)

Typeset in Bembo
by Apex CoVantage, LLC

Printed and bound in the United States of America by Publishers Graphics, LLC on sustainably sourced paper.

For the teachers who transgress and for the CUNY-NYSIEB team who had the courage to do so—Ofelia and Tatyana

Y para Ricardo que me da el valor—Ofelia

And to баба Gita and тетя Polya: My Yiddish, Latvian, Russian, and English speaking grandmother and great-aunt whose examples of strength and love are a constant source of inspiration—Tatyana

CONTENTS

FOREWORD

Ricardo Otheguy

The volume you are about to read is based on work done for a project on the education of emergent bilinguals that originated with, and is run by, educators and linguists at the Graduate Center of the City University of New York (CUNY). The project is led by CUNY faculty and doctoral students, and includes the active participation and support of teachers, bilingual coordinators, principals, and district administrators from throughout New York City and New York State. The project is named for its financial sponsorship by the New York State Education Department, the New York State Initiative on Emergent Bilinguals, and is usually called "CUNY-NYSIEB." The Initiative is built around the notion of translanguaging. Participants in CUNY-NYSIEB recognize multilingual students and their teachers as natural translanguagers and engage them in the development of an approach to teaching and learning centered on translanguaging.

Readers of this book are probably the type of people who like words and have long recognized in the prefix *bi-* in the word *bilingual* the meaning of two, and in the prefix *multi-* in the word *multilingual* the meaning of more than one. They will also recognize, in the word *translanguaging*, the prefix *trans-*, meaning to go beyond (as in *transcend*). In this case, the thing that one goes beyond in translanguaging is language boundaries. The term was first used in Welsh by Welsh educators. (It is interesting, isn't it, that the word should come from Wales, one of the world's English-speaking societies where bilingualism prospers and emergent bilinguals thrive?) Beyond Wales, we think that the joining of "trans" with "language" can be useful and productive to educators of emergent bilinguals everywhere. This book tells you how participants in CUNY-NYSIEB have found it to be useful and productive in New York.

The term translanguaging makes reference to a particular conception of the language of bilinguals, and to a particular set of student behaviors and teaching approaches that follow from it. It is a conception that sees the bilingual as having a single, or unitary, linguistic competence, as opposed to a dual or bifurcated one. To take the example of the two biggest languages in our multilingual city and our multilingual state, the familiar, dual conception of the linguistic competence of New York bilinguals sees the linguistic features of their English as collected in one box or compartment and the linguistic features of their Spanish as collected in another one. In contrast, the unitary conception of translanguaging takes it that all the features are in the same box. To be sure, the box is structured and ordered, but the partitions are not along the lines of English and Spanish; it is a single-language box.

Thinking of bilinguals as having a dual, two-box linguistic competence is the familiar idea. The single-competence, one-box idea is the innovation behind translanguaging. But now notice this: the old idea and the innovative idea are not opposed. They are meant to be a happy couple who live well together. The new idea that the linguistic competence of bilinguals is unitary is actually quite compatible with the familiar idea that their competence is dual. When it comes to the bi- of bilingual, one can have one's prefix and eat it too. The trick is to understand how. The trick, that is, is to be able to see bilinguals, in the traditional way, as having two languages, but to be able to also see them, in the translanguaging way, as having a single one.

The familiar idea of a dual linguistic competence regards the bilingual from the social vantage point, from the outside. The new idea of translanguaging sees the bilingual from the individual vantage point, from the inside. All that educators interested in translanguaging have to do is to learn to alternatively adopt one vantage point or the other, depending on what they are doing and on what they want to accomplish. Just take two chairs and put them one in front of the other and put your emergent bilinguals in the middle. Sit on one chair (the social vantage point) and look at the bilinguals. Get up and go around. Sit on the other chair (the individual vantage point) and look at them again. Rise. Repeat. Get good at seeing bilinguals sometimes from the familiar outsider point of view and sometimes from the new translanguaging, insider point of view.

In other words, the point the case studies in this book make is that educators can become very good at recognizing the social demands of treating the two languages of emergent bilinguals as separate, but also very good at recognizing the individual demands of seeing the two "languages" of these bilinguals as unitary. Emergent bilinguals have two languages only from the social point of view. From their own point of view, they have only one. Good teachers of emergent bilinguals know when to sit on one chair and when to sit on the other, when to take the social perspective of the society with two languages and when to take the perspective of the translanguaging individual with a single one.

Grounded on psychological and sociolinguistic research, the single-competence conception of bilinguals at the heart of translanguaging has inspired a new way to understand what bilingual students and teachers are often doing with language. And it has inspired a new way to engage them in an approach to teaching that takes what they are doing into account. This book gives the details. In brief, what bilingual students are doing sometimes (when we see them keeping their "two languages" separate) is carefully looking at themselves from the perspective of the outsider, taking into account the social exigencies that separate one language from the other and minding their linguistic steps. The separation between, say, English and Spanish is not to be found in the bilingual's unitary linguistic competence inside. But emergent bilinguals do well to be aware (and their teachers do well to make them aware) that many social settings, some parts of the school included, sometimes want the separation observed. The way to observe it is to engage in feature selection. Take these linguistic features of my unitary repertoire that the society says are English and use them here, take these other ones that society tells me are Spanish or French or Swahili and use them there.

In other words, what teachers and students do when they keep their languages separate is to inhibit the deployment of part of their unitary competence, doing so artificially, for the sake of social rules that, in certain settings and at certain times, are important to observe. It is an exercise that is not reflective of their single linguistic repertoire. But it is what many settings in society call for, and it is good to know how to do it.

These language boundaries that guide the inhibition of part of the bilingual's single repertoire are exactly what gets transcended in translanguaging. To translanguage is to speak naturally and freely, without regard for the restrictions established by the boundaries of named languages, without heed for the constraints that give dual names and borders and limits to the bilingual's unitary competence. While it is good for emergent bilinguals in schools to sometimes inhibit part of their linguistic repertoire, it is definitely and decidedly also good for them sometimes, perhaps most of the time, to deploy it fully and naturally and freely, that is, to translanguage. As in all teaching, which starts where the student is and builds on what the student brings, translanguaging approaches engage the complete repertoire of emergent bilinguals, recognize it, celebrate it, and use it to good advantage (use it sometimes, in fact, as the best way to learn to inhibit translanguaging and to separate the languages). As CUNY-NYSIEB participants have come to understand, the path to growth in content learning and linguistic development in emergent bilinguals goes through translanguaging.

Now, look again at your emergent bilinguals. See, they are not code switching. Or at least they are code switching only when you're sitting on the outsider's chair, the one that takes the social vantage point. Get up and come around and sit on the other chair. Now they're not code switching. They are translanguaging, which means that they are speaking naturally and freely. The teachers in the case studies in this book are doing the same, adopting the insider's perspective of translanguaging.

Once we understand that to translanguage is to make use of one's repertoire without undue consideration of outside boundaries and constraints, we realize something surprising, namely that translanguaging is what is done all the time also by . . . monolinguals! Sure, monolinguals too have to do some feature selection, some inhibiting of their linguistic repertoire; they too have to pick this to say here and that to say there. Say to a child a booboo, say to an adult a cut; say it bugs me at home, say it bothers me at work (there are better examples, but they are not appropriate for this piece of writing, which is the point). But now consider that the inhibitory demands on monolinguals are minimal. In schools, monolinguals are allowed to translanguage, to speak at nearly full competence, suppressing a very small part of their repertoire. In contrast, bilinguals are frequently asked to inhibit half of their repertoire! No wonder that societies around the world report such different degrees of school success between monolinguals and bilinguals. It is in this sense that the translanguaging approach calls, quite simply, for a treatment of bilingual students that parallels the treatment of monolinguals. Teach emergent bilinguals on the basis of an approach that is not solely centered on feature suppression. Teach them in such a way as to take advantage of their full repertoire. The approach is amply documented here. The school authorities, the project director, the professors, graduate students, teachers, principals, bilingual coordinators, and bilingual students working under CUNY-NYSIEB think they are getting it done. Here some of them tell you how.

Ricardo Otheguy, Principal Investigator,
CUNY-NYSIEB

ACKNOWLEDGMENTS

We want to acknowledge the support given to us by our editor, Naomi Silverman, and Sara Vogel's careful reading of some parts of the manuscript. Ofelia also acknowledges the support of the University of Cologne during the writing of some of the chapters.

INTRODUCTION

Ofelia García and Tatyana Kleyn

This book describes the ways in which one project attempted to transform the theory and practice of language and bilingualism in education by taking up translanguaging theory. We call the project CUNY-NYSIEB (City University of New York-New York State Initiative on Emergent Bilinguals). What makes the CUNY-NYSIEB project unique is that it was funded and supported by the New York State Education Department (NYSED) at a time of shrinking spaces for bilingual education in the state (see Menken & Solorza, 2014) and as education standards that did not take into account the growing diversity of U.S. students were imposed.

When officials from the New York State Education Department[1] originally met with Ofelia García, Kate Menken, and Ricardo Otheguy—who became the Principal Investigator (Otheguy) and Co-Principal Investigators of the project (García and Menken)—the state was mostly concerned with the poor results in standardized tests of those students designated as "English language learners." Unlike other states, New York State had, from the beginning, supported bilingual education to improve their education (see Carrasquillo et al., 2014). The New York State educational authorities had also been forward-looking in authorizing the use of languages other than English to ensure that language minoritized students had equal educational opportunities.

García, Menken, and Otheguy started to put elements of a developing translanguaging theory (García, 2009) alongside the existing policies and practices observed in New York State. How, they wondered, would translanguaging theory reshape the ways in which "English language learners" were being educated in the state? How could viewing them as "emergent bilinguals" instead of "limited English proficient" or "English language learners" reshape the ways we teach them? (for a discussion of the use of "emergent bilinguals," see

García & Kleifgen, 2010). How could translanguaging strengthen the use of these students' home languages and their bilingualism? They were also curious about how the practices of educators, as well as the regulations and policies of the educational authorities, would influence a developing theory of translanguaging.

Chapter 1 describes the meaning of translanguaging and the development of our translanguaging theory. We put our own understandings alongside how other scholars see translanguaging, identifying the commonalities, as well as points of difference. We also include in chapter 1 elements of a pedagogical practice that takes up translanguaging.

Chapter 2 describes the work of CUNY-NYSIEB at greater length and how we have gone about transforming both education practices in schools and teacher education. We also describe the educational policies in which the project operated, as well as the political economy to which the policies responded. This context is important, for it turns out that despite the theoretical vision and positioning of CUNY-NYSIEB, translanguaging practices are often constrained by the socioeducational and sociopolitical circumstances in which schools operate. Chapter 2 ends by describing the research project that led to the case studies that we include in Part II of the book.

We then bring together in Part II the voices of some of the members of the CUNY-NYSIEB team[2] as they worked alongside teachers to take up translanguaging in their practice. Chapters 3 to 8 make up the core of the book. These chapters contain six case studies of work done by individual CUNY-NYSIEB team members with teachers of emergent bilingual students in different contexts. Rather than describe work done over time, the authors of these chapters describe how translanguaging is used in a *specific lesson or lessons* that they designed with the classroom teacher. By providing readers with *specific moments* of how the educators and the students both took up, as well as resisted, translanguaging theory and practice, the chapters describe in detail how teachers and students use translanguaging in making sense of their teaching and learning. Furthermore, these chapters give evidence of how translanguaging has the potential to transform how we presently educate multilingual students of all types.

The case studies are purposely varied by age group, type of students, subjects, programs, and teachers. Two of the chapters are situated in elementary schools (Kleyn; Woodley), three in middle schools (Collins and Cioè-Peña; Ebe; Espinosa and Herrera) and one in high school (Seltzer and Collins). Four of the case studies are in classrooms where almost all students are Latinos (Collins and Cioè-Peña; Espinosa and Herrera; Kleyn; Seltzer and Collins), and two are in classrooms with students who have a wide diversity of language backgrounds (Ebe; Woodley). The students in all the case studies, except one, are developing English and designated in schools as "English language learners." However, although all Latinos, students in Espinosa and Herrera's case studies are developing Spanish.

The subjects taught through translanguaging also differ: three of the lessons portrayed in this book are English Language Arts lessons (Ebe; Kleyn; Seltzer and Collins), one is science (Espinosa and Herrera), two are social studies (Collins and Cioè-Peña; Woodley). And these subject lessons take place in different types of programs—transitional bilingual education (Collins and Cioè-Peña; Kleyn), dual language bilingual education (Espinosa and Herrera) and mainstream English classes (Ebe; Woodley).

The teachers in the case studies are also different. Teachers in three of the case studies are bilingual in English and Spanish (Collins and Cioè-Peña; Espinosa and Herrera; Kleyn), three others are considered "monolingual," although the teacher in Ebe's chapter is Jamaican American and is comfortable with Jamaican Creole, and the one in Seltzer and Collins chapter was born in the Philippines and speaks Filipino. Only the teacher in Woodley's case study was born in the United States, although he also has been learning Spanish and American Sign Language.

We decided to organize these chapters based on the settings where we would find more emergent bilingual students. Thus, we start with the English-medium classrooms with a broad range of multilingual students (Ebe; Woodley), followed by transitional bilingual classrooms with Latino students (Kleyn; Collins and Cioè-Peña; Seltzer and Collins), and finally the dual language bilingual classroom for Latino students who were reclaiming their bilingualism (Espinosa and Herrera).

To ensure that these chapters are relevant to educators who read this book, we include questions and activities for further reflection. We hope that these will help practitioners reflect on how lessons from these chapters apply to their own context and students.

In Part III we consider the implications of the case studies and of our work. Chapter 9 reviews the case studies as they relate to each other. In so doing, we identify what we call a translanguaging education policy as enacted in the different settings in which teachers and students operate. We describe how this translanguaging education policy disrupts traditional understandings of bilingualism and educating emergent bilinguals and opens up spaces for equal educational opportunity and social justice. But because we deeply believe that in the implementation of translanguaging teachers are paramount, chapter 10 describes the implications of our work for teachers and teacher education. Teachers cannot learn to do translanguaging on their own, behind closed doors, or only in professional development after they are already teachers. As we discuss throughout the book, taking up translanguaging theory and pedagogy requires a stance, a philosophical belief, which cannot be acquired *after* teacher professionalization. Translanguaging must then be part and parcel of teacher education. As readers will see, the efforts of CUNY-NYSIEB were never limited to just those schools that were part of the project. By involving teacher education faculty in the transformation of the schools, we also set out to transform the education of teachers, and especially of those who work with bilingual students. We end by discussing the role of teacher education in ensuring that translanguaging becomes part of teachers' understandings.

We bookend our work with a Foreword and an Afterword by three people who have been central to the work that we are describing in this book. The Foreword, by Ricardo Otheguy, the founding Principal Investigator of CUNY-NYSIEB, is an important account of the role that translanguaging has in the lives of the students and teachers with whom we work. The Afterword is authored by Kate Menken and María Teresa (Maite) Sánchez. Kate Menken, founding Co-Principal Investigator, has been involved with the project since its inception. María Teresa (Maite) Sánchez came in as the Project Director after an initial 6-month development period. Under Sánchez's relentless leadership, CUNY-NYSIEB has become institutionalized. This book is a testament to the hard work of a large team of people who have had the vision and the energy to make changes in the education of bilingual students so that they achieve the social equality and opportunities to which they are entitled.

Our work is sometimes controversial, and often misunderstood. For some, those who believe that education in the U.S. should be in English only, there is too much attention to multilingualism. For others, especially some traditional bilingual educators, our translanguaging theory does not protect sufficiently either English or the Language Other Than English (LOTE). Some teachers complain that it requires too much work, whereas others see it as essential to students' learning. Bilingual students themselves are often conflicted about taking up translanguaging in schools, where their own language practices had formerly been excluded. This book describes all the tensions in our work, but also the potential of translanguaging in providing better learning opportunities for emergent bilingual students and in fostering justice and equity for these minoritized students and their communities.

Notes

1. We wish to acknowledge the important role that Arlen Benjamin Gómez from the New York State Education Department played initially in the launching of CUNY-NYSIEB. We also want to thank Angélica Infante-Green, present Deputy Commissioner for the Office of P–12 Instructional Support who was Associate Commissioner for Bilingual Education and Foreign Language Studies during the time of our project, for her continued support. Finally, we thank Lissette Colón-Collins, the present Assistant Commissioner for Bilingual and Language Education of the New York State Education Department, for her guidance and support.
2. Members of the CUNY-NYSIEB team since its inception are Ricardo Otheguy, Ofelia García, and Kate Menken (Principal Investigators and Founders); María Teresa (Maite) Sánchez (Project Director), Nelson Flores (founding Project Director); Laura Ascenzi-Moreno, Brian Collins, Ann Ebe, Cecilia Espinosa, Meral Kaya, Erin Kearny, Tatyana Kleyn, Dina López, Kate Mahoney, Vanessa Pérez-Rosario, Zoila Tazi (Associate Investigators); Kathryn Carpenter, Ivana Espinet, Luz Herrera, Sarah Hesson, María Cioè-Peña, Liza Pappas, Kate Seltzer, Cristian Solorza, Luis Guzmán Valerio, Sara Vogel, Heather H. Woodley (Research Assistants); and Christina Celic (Field Assistant).

References

Carrasquillo, A. Rodríguez, D., & Kaplan, L. et al. (2014). New York State policies, mandates and initiatives on the education of English language learners. Retrieved on March 16, 2016, from: http://www.nysieb.ws.gc.cuny.edu/files/2014/05/CUNY-NYSIEB-Report-NY-State-Policies-to-NYSED-04-30-2014-Final.pdf

García, O. (2009). *Bilingual education in the 21st century: A global perspective.* Malden, MA and Oxford, UK: Wiley/Blackwell.

García, O., & Kleifgen, J. (2010). *Educating emergent bilinguals: Policies, programs and practices for English language learners.* New York: Teachers College Press.

Menken, K., & Solorza, C. (2014). No child left bilingual: Accountability and the elimination of bilingual education in New York City schools. *Educational Policy,* 8(1), 96–125.

PART I

Translanguaging Theory and a Project

1

TRANSLANGUAGING THEORY IN EDUCATION

Ofelia García and Tatyana Kleyn

Introduction

In this chapter, we discuss the theory of *translanguaging* that undergirds our understandings of language and bilingualism, and how it can transform education, especially the education of bilingual students. This chapter presents the theoretical framework for the educational project and the Transformative Action Research that we describe in chapter 2, as well as the classroom lessons and moments that we present in Part II of this book. We consider our own interpretation of translanguaging theory, as well as that of others. In so doing, we draw distinctions between how we understand translanguaging theory and how other scholars understand it. To understand our theory of translanguaging, it is important to first draw distinctions between the concept of a "named" language and that of the language system of individual speakers. The second part of this chapter then examines how our translanguaging theory has the potential to transform instruction, assessment, and programs for emergent bilinguals.

Language, Bi/Multilingualism, and Translanguaging

Scholarship on language education has increasingly focused on what Conteh and Meier (2014) and May (2015) have called *the multilingual turn*, a recognition that those involved in language education are, or are in the process of becoming, multilingual. At the same time, poststructuralist approaches to sociolinguistics (Blommaert, 2010; Makoni & Pennycook, 2007; Pennycook, 2010; see also García, Flores & Spotti, forthcoming) have emphasized not only the very diverse language practices of people in a global world, but also the sociopolitical effects that the construction of *named languages* like English, Spanish, Arabic, Chinese, and so on have had on language-minoritized populations.

The phrase "construction of named language" is used to emphasize the fact that the terms "English," "Spanish," "Arabic," "Chinese," "Swahili," "Russian," "Haitian Creole," etc. name *socially invented* categories. These categories are *not imaginary*, in the sense that they refer to entities that exist in the societies that have coined the terms and have had real and material effects (like the terms "White person," "Black person," "alien," "immigrant"). But these terms for named languages do not necessarily overlap with the linguistic systems of individual speakers. While someone may be recognized in society as a speaker of a particular language, each individual uses what amounts to his or her *own* language, which differs in ways big and small (i.e., vocabulary, pronunciation, and structure) from that of every other person who is said by the society to also speak "English" or "Spanish," for example (for more on this, see Otheguy, García & Reid, 2015). One matter is the named language, quite another is the linguistic system of words, sounds, constructions and so forth that permits a speaker to speak, understand, read, write, communicate, and do other linguistic work. Every human being's linguistic system is shaped by and evolves through social interaction. In some cases, when people are very close (relatives, colleagues, friends), their linguistic systems are similar because they have been impacted through their constant interaction. In many cases, the linguistic system of people who are said to speak the same named language are close enough for them to understand each other pretty well. But in others, two people who obviously have very different linguistic systems are also said to speak the same named language. For example, people from Ireland and the southwestern United States are both said to speak the named language "English," but we know that their linguistic systems, the words and rules in their linguistic repertoire, are so different that sometimes they do not understand each other when they speak. That is why when speaking on an American TV show, an English speaker from Ireland usually gets subtitles. Notwithstanding the fact that society thinks of the two English speakers as speaking the same named language of English, their linguistic systems are so different as to preclude understanding.

Now what about bilinguals? Well, societies usually say that they have two linguistic systems, one for each named language. But is this really true? Does the person who is said by society to speak the named language English and the named language Spanish or Russian really have two linguistic systems? In the developing movement in language education that goes under the name of *translanguaging*, and in our interpretation, the answer is "No!" Bilinguals, to be sure, have two named languages, but that is only when seen from the social or outsider point of view. But when seen from the point of view of their own linguistic system, it is more accurate to think in unitary terms, and to assume that they have a single system. The term translanguaging should be taken in the sense of *transcending*, "going beyond," the two named languages of bilinguals (English-Spanish, English-Russian, Zapotec-Spanish, etc.), or the three of trilinguals, or the many of multilinguals, and to think of bilinguals/multilinguals as individuals with a single linguistic system (the inside view) that society (the outside view) calls two or more named languages.

Origins of Translanguaging and Our Meaning

It is by now well known that the term translanguaging was coined in Welsh (*trawsieithu*) by an educator, Cen Williams, who developed a different approach to bilingualism in education (García & Li Wei, 2014). To deepen the students' use of Welsh and English, students were to recast understandings received in one language in the other language. Instead of having students always use Welsh in one situation and classroom space and time and English in another, as traditional bilingual education programs do, Cen Williams's translanguaging (1994) provided Welsh students with opportunities to change the language of the input and the output (see Baker, 2001). For example, students were asked to read in one language and write in another or to discuss in one language and read in another, and so forth.

In many ways, this original sense of the term translanguaging went beyond the ways in which practitioners had interpreted Cummins's interdependence hypothesis (1979). Early on, Cummins posited that there was an underlying Common Underlying Proficiency between the languages of bilinguals that allowed for transfer to occur. It demonstrated how learning academic content, no matter the language of instruction, enhanced the general knowledge base of the student. Cummins's hypothesis was interpreted in those early days as supporting bilingual education, because not everything taught through one language had to be retaught through another. Cummins's very influential hypothesis provided the impetus for the expansion of all types of bilingual education in the 20th century, especially in North America, where immersion bilingual programs in Canada and developmental maintenance and transitional bilingual programs in the United States flourished.

At the same time, Cummins's early work was used by educational authorities and educators to legitimate practices that were in effect, those of double monolingualism (Grosjean, 1982; Heller, 2007). The bilingual education programs that were developed towards the second half of the 20th century were either *sequential*, meaning that instruction was solely in one language until two or three years later, or *simultaneous*, meaning that both languages were introduced at the same time. Regardless of whether the introduction of the additional language was sequential or simultaneous, the two languages were always taught at separate times, for separate subjects, and/or with separate teachers who were in separate rooms. In Canadian immersion bilingual programs, Anglophone language majority children were taught exclusively in French initially until English was introduced a year or so later, eventually maintaining a 50:50 relationship with French. In Canadian immersion programs, two classrooms and two different teachers were used (Lambert & Tucker, 1972). In the United States, in the developmental maintenance programs and the transitional bilingual education programs that became prevalent after the Bilingual Education Act was passed in 1968, educators, for the most part, allocated the languages to different times, subjects, places, and/or teachers. National languages were reified as autonomous, were taught in isolation of students' home languages, and speakers simply had to make the transfer from one language to the other. The legacy of language separation lives on in contemporary forms of bilingual education.

In effect, the translanguaging practices that were proposed by Welsh educators at the end of the 20th century were exceptions to the common practice of separating languages strictly. Within one space, children were encouraged to use the two languages in interrelationship, building a bilingual Welsh identity that did not conceive of the child as two monolinguals, but rather as one integrated bilingual. This was not the first time, of course, that educators advocated for practices other than the double monolingualism that language education programs legitimated. Rodolfo Jacobson, for example, had proposed what he called a "concurrent approach to bilingual teaching" (1990). Jacobson developed the idea that bilingual teachers would use intersentential code-switching to teach bilingual children; that is, alternating languages but only at the end of sentences. But Jacobson's code-switching conception of alternating languages had more to do with enabling comprehension than with supporting and developing bilingualism, which was precisely the Welsh idea behind a translanguaging pedagogy.

Since Gumperz (1976), the sociolinguistic literature has increasingly shown how code-switching represents the agency of bilingual speakers to use two separate languages that represent two linguistic systems (Auer, 1999, 2005; Myers-Scotton, 2005). And educators, especially those working in post-colonial contexts, have shown how code-switching is a common practice among educators to make comprehension possible, especially in Africa and Asia where the medium of instruction is often one that is different from the language spoken by the children (see, for example, Lin, 2013a; Lin & Martin, 2005). Arthur and Martin (2006) speak of the "pedagogic validity of codeswitching" in situations in which students do not understand the lessons.

No matter how positively code-switching is conceived, both in the sociolinguistic and the language education literature, it still endorses what García (2009), following Del Valle (2000), called a *monoglossic ideology of bilingualism*, one that takes an external viewpoint of language and that only takes into account two named languages that are said to constitute two linguistic systems. A translanguaging theory, however, takes *the point of view of the bilingual speaker himself or herself* for whom the concept of two linguistic systems does not apply, for he or she has one complex and dynamic linguistic system that the speaker then learns to separate into two languages, as defined by external social factors, and not simply linguistic ones. Translanguaging, García (2009) says: "is an approach to bilingualism that is centered, not on languages as has been often the case, but on the practices of bilinguals that are readily observable" (p. 44).

Figure 1.1 displays the differences between a traditional model of bilingualism, Cummins's model of interdependence, a model of code-switching, and what we are naming translanguaging.

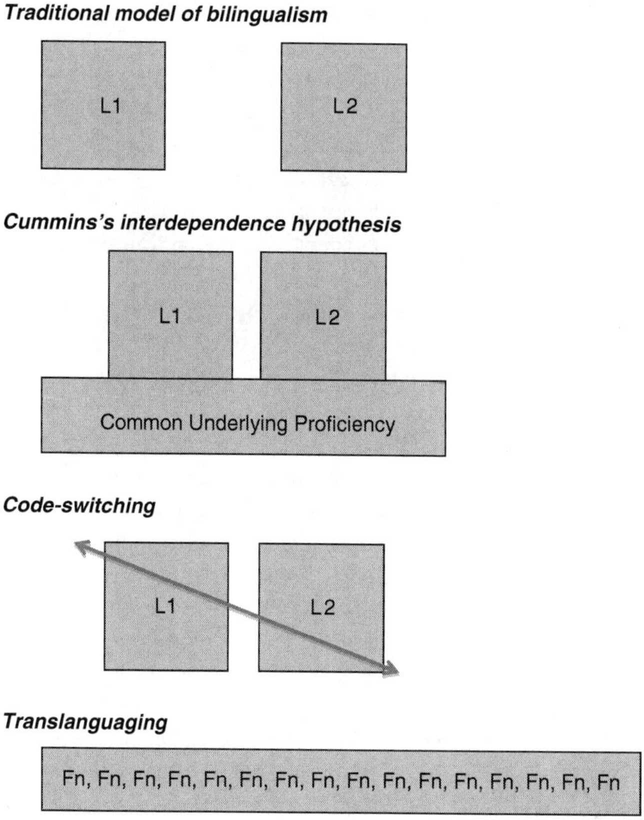

FIGURE 1.1 Different Models of Bilingualism

Source: Extended from García and Li Wei, 2014, Figure 1.1.

Traditional models of bilingualism consider speakers as having a first language (L1) that is separate from the second language (L2). A language education program would then require students to simply add a second language to their first, but always keeping them separate. It was this model of bilingualism that enabled Lambert (1974) to talk about "additive bilingualism" and "subtractive bilingualism." The conception of additive bilingualism responds to two language systems that are always separate. Today many educators still refer to these types of bilingualism and their corresponding educational models, using these terms.

Cummins's interdependence hypothesis brought the two languages closer together by positing a Common Underlying Proficiency that enabled students to transfer concepts (both academic and linguistic) from one language to the other. Cummins's model supported the idea that bilinguals possess two separate linguistic systems, although they feed each other and are interdependent because speakers have one linguistic and cognitive behavior.

Code-switching also relies on the idea that there are two language systems, but indicates that bilinguals transgress these all the time by alternating languages that are still seen as autonomous, closed systems with their own linguistic structures. Even though the recent literature on code-switching refers to this ability of bilinguals as an important and creative resource (see especially Auer, 1999), it is still viewed as exceptional transgressive behavior. Code-switching relies on the notion of named national languages (the external view) rather than on the ways in which bilingual speakers deploy their own linguistic resources (the internal view).

In contrast, for us, *translanguaging refers to the deployment of a speaker's full linguistic repertoire, which does not in any way correspond to the socially and politically defined boundaries of named languages.* That is why we annotate the features (F) of the speaker's linguistic repertoire with a nominal number (n), and we do not designate L1 or L2. The features of a bilingual's repertoire simply belong to the bilingual speakers themselves who have one language system, and not to the languages. For example, when Ofelia speaks in her bilingual home, she uses words such as amigo, casa, room, dinner, comida, árbol, plants, building, cielo, earth, table, etc. Now, we might say that these words belong to Spanish or English as nationally or culturally defined, but for Ofelia these are simply Ofelia's words. In speaking to her grandparents, Tatyana also uses words like TV, stroll, гулять, eat, ужин, home or дома. However, outside of her home Tatyana differentiates between those that are English and those that are Russian because she knows that not everyone shares all the elements of her linguistic repertoire. So Tatyana knows how to select the features that are socially named English from those features that are socially named Russian.

It is important to understand the major difference of our theory of translanguaging from all the other models provided in Figure 1.1. In all the other models besides the translanguaging one, language is considered from the external viewpoint of the political state and imbued with a linguistic reality that is illusory, since named languages have been socially constructed (Heller, 1999). In the translanguaging model, named languages like English, Spanish, and Russian are recognized as having material and *social reality*, but *not linguistic reality* (Otheguy, García & Reid, 2015). That is, there are no linguistic features in "casa" and "table" that make one Spanish and the other English. This gives legitimacy to the practices of multilingual speakers and encourages us as educators to leverage their full language repertoire to support their understanding of content, develop their language performances, and buttress their socioemotional development. By recognizing bilingual students' full language repertoire and their translanguaging capacities, we then not only improve the education of bilingual students, but, in so doing, we build a better and more just world. Thus, translanguaging is also important to build a more equitable society.

The epistemological shift that is needed to go from the notion of language used in traditional studies of bilingualism, in Cummins's transfer theories, and in code-switching studies (the external social view) to that of language as seen in translanguaging theory (the internal linguistic view) is difficult for many, and also for educators. After all, educators work in schools that exist precisely to uphold the notion of political-state languages that translanguaging theory questions as having been socially constructed. And yet, when we first introduce translanguaging, educators who have a child-centered educational philosophy get it. Many say they have been doing it for years but have not had a name for it nor had been given permission to do so.

Most often, the language used in teaching and assessment only permits certain lexical and structural linguistic features, leaving out many other features that are used by people, and especially by those positioned as powerless minorities—the poor, the non-White, the speakers of minoritized languages. In this way, powerful speakers are given undue advantage, whereas language minoritized speakers are taxed unfairly, and sometimes excluded. This has resulted in much social and educational inequality.

Taking up a theory of translanguaging, in which named languages are seen as having social, although not linguistic, reality, means that we start to teach bilingual children from a different place. It means that we start from a place that leverages all the features of the children's repertoire, while also showing them when, with whom, where, and why to use some features of their repertoire and not others, enabling them to also perform according to the social norms of named languages as used in schools.

Extending Translanguaging

Williams's original translanguaging pedagogy (1994) acknowledged the bilingual child's full language repertoire, but used the social markings of the named languages—Welsh and English—to bolster their bilingualism. Notice that Williams did not prescribe the social situation or the social space in which one language or the other was to be used; that is, both languages, and not just one, were accepted in *all* social and communicative situations. It is also not the case that the use of one language would indicate one identity, and the use of another language, the other identity. For Williams there was a *single* bilingual Welsh identity made up of linguistic features that socially, from an external perspective, were seen as Welsh or English. For Williams and other Welsh bilingual educators (see, for example, Lewis, Jones & Baker, 2012a, 2012b), one could not be educated unless both languages were used. Williams's pedagogical strategy consisted of giving students practice in selecting features from their language repertoire to perform a task in one language or another precisely to deepen knowledge and bilingual performances. The use of translanguaging for Williams stems from the *internal linguistic view of language* (one language repertoire of features), although it also responds to the *external social view of language* (Welsh and English). In turn, performances with language features that school marks as being in English or

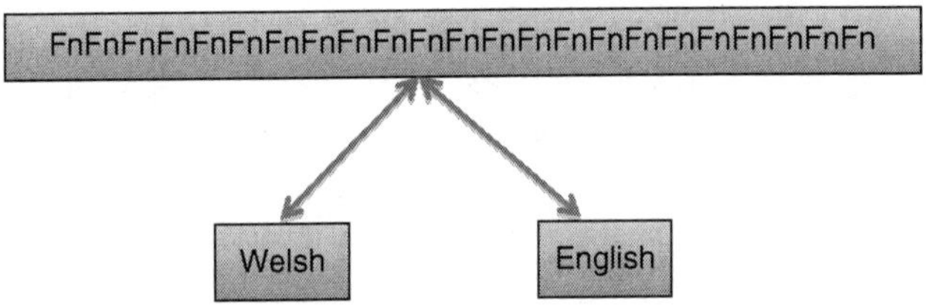

FIGURE 1.2 Williams's Translanguaging Pedagogy

Welsh feed and expand the child's full language repertoire. Williams's translanguaging pedagogy could be diagramed as in Figure 1.2.

Language-education scholars after Williams have been less prescriptive about how translanguaging is used in classrooms, going beyond Williams's one language as input and another as output (see, for example, Blackledge & Creese, 2010; Canagarajah, 2011; Creese & Blackledge, 2010; García, 2009; García & Li Wei, 2014, 2015; García & Sylvan, 2011; Hornberger & Link, 2012; Lewis, Jones & Baker, 2012a, 2012b; Li Wei, 2011). However, the main tenets of Welsh translanguaging remain—

1. bilingual children develop a single complex language repertoire, a unitary language system and a single identity as bilinguals;
2. bilingual children are capable of communicating and acting with only certain features of their repertoire, those that respond to socially named languages;
3. to deepen the bilingual child's performances in socially named languages, it is important to first recognize and leverage their entire language repertoire.

In effect, Figure 1.2 can be applied to the more flexible concept of translanguaging that scholars later developed.

Taking up the Bakhtinian concept of heteroglossic language practices, in which people draw from different voices and discourses that differ greatly from the ways in which named languages, taught in schools, are used, Creese and Blackledge (2010) and García (2009) extended translanguaging from its Welsh origins. In *Bilingual Education in the 21st Century: A Global Perspective*, García introduced the concept of dynamic bilingualism as enacted in translanguaging. *Dynamic bilingualism* goes beyond the notion of additive bilingualism because it does not simply refer to the addition of a separate set of language features, but acknowledges that the linguistic features and practices of bilinguals form a unitary linguistic system that interact in dynamic ways with each other. Working in complementary schools in the United Kingdom, Creese and Blackledge (2010) used translanguaging as the theoretical framework for their extensive ethnographic research in the Bengali, Chinese, Gujarati, and Turkish complementary schools (see also Blackledge & Creese, 2010).

Around the same time, Canagarajah (2011) used the term translanguaging to describe the strategies of a Saudi student in her essay writing. Li Wei (2011) proposed the idea of a "translanguaging space," a social space that can bring together the different dimensions of the multilingual speaker's personal history, experience, context, ideologies, and cognitive and physical capacity into "one coordinated and meaningful performance" (p. 1223). Hornberger and Link (2012) connected translanguaging to Hornberger's notion of "continua of biliteracy," because it allows for the use of "all points along the continua of biliterate context, media, content, and development" (p. 268). García & Li Wei published the first comprehensive short book on translanguaging in 2014. In a very short time, the work on translanguaging, and specifically on translanguaging in education, has been deepened by many.

A theory of translanguaging can be transformative for educators. Once educators start looking at language from the point of view of the bilingual learner and not simply at the named language with its prescribed features, everything changes. Educators then teach in order to discover what, in the child's arsenal of language features, can be enhanced through interactions with others and texts that have different language features. They do not tell students to stop using their own language features or to stop drawing on them for learning. Educators become co-learners (Li Wei, 2014), instead of simply identifying as teachers who transmit a canon of linguistic knowledge. Equipped with translanguaging theory, educators leverage the students' full language repertoires to teach and assess, enabling a more socially just and equitable education for bilingual students.

We repeat, educators who take up translanguaging theory do not simply abandon the traditional understanding of language that is external to the child, for they know that in order to succeed academically the bilingual child will have to exclusively use language features of one or another named language at different times. But educators who leverage translanguaging know that the *starting point* to develop bilingualism lies in the features of the linguistic repertoire that the child already has available in his or her evolving linguistic system. This linguistic repertoire can then be extended through interactions with others and texts with multiple language features.

Recent Scholarship on Translanguaging

Although not without controversy, scholars and educators have taken up the term translanguaging swiftly, often using it in ways different from our own conceptualization described above. In 2015, a new journal, *Translation and Translanguaging in Multilingual Contexts*, made its appearance, focusing not only on educational contexts, but also in the workplace and on travel. The Translation and Translanguaging research team involving researchers from Birmingham, Birkbeck, Cardiff, Leeds, and University College London in the U.K. is also investigating how translanguaging is used in business, sports, heritage, and sociolegal domains. The term translanguaging has also been taken up by scholars who study language socialization of bilingual children, and especially those who study the use of language by bilingual children who serve as translators in what is called "language brokering" (see Alvarez, 2014; also see dialogue between Orellana & García, 2014).

It is in education, however, that the term translanguaging has had the most impact. In Falun, Sweden, there was a conference on translanguaging practices and pedagogies in April 2015, with many contributions from all over the world. Cenoz and Gorter's recent book is titled *Multilingual Education: Between Language Learning and Translanguaging* (2015) and contains contributions that support a translanguaging approach, arguing for the inclusion of the child's full and unique language repertoire in instruction.

The TESOL (Teachers of English to Speakers of Other Languages) profession has also been impacted by translanguaging theory, as shown by the contributions in a 2013 issue of *TESOL Quarterly* edited by Shelley Taylor and Kristen Snoddon. Some of the studies carried out by García and her colleagues (see, for example, Flores & García, 2013; García, Flores & Woodley, 2012; Velasco & García, 2014) have shown how translanguaging is transformative for the child, the teacher, and education itself, as the full language repertoire is used to organize and mediate processes of understanding, speaking, literacy, and learning.

In the United States, many scholars are using the concept of translanguaging to explore the education of bilingual children, especially in bilingual programs. Sayer (2013) describes its use in a 2nd-grade transitional bilingual education classroom in San Antonio, Texas, to mediate not only academic content, but also the standard languages used in the classroom. Palmer et al. (2014) explore the instruction of two experienced bilingual teachers in dual language bilingual classrooms and give evidence of the translanguaging practices used by the students, as well as some translanguaging instructional strategies used by the teachers. All of these scholars document how despite the policy of linguistic compartmentalization in some bilingual programs, teachers and students are crossing these artificial boundaries precisely to ensure that children are educated bilingually. The recent issue of the *International Multilingual Research Journal*, edited by Mileidis Gort (2015), is indicative of the growing appeal of translanguaging for purposes of supporting bilingualism, while making the structures and practices in bilingual education classrooms more flexible.

Material to educate U.S. teachers of all types in the pedagogy of translanguaging is also beginning to appear. García, Johnson, and Seltzer (2016) is but one example of a book that assists teachers in designing instruction and assessment that leverages the students' full use of their language and semiotic repertoire.

There are two educational areas where the take-up of translanguaging theory is providing different conceptualizations of the field itself. One is early childhood education; the other is deaf education. An example of the first is the study of an Arabic–Hebrew bilingual kindergarten in Israel conducted by Schwartz and Asli (2014). Gort and Sembiante (2015) also explore how translanguaging pedagogies support young emergent bilingual children in a preschool Spanish–English dual language bilingual program. Another example is the study by Garrity, Aquino-Sterling, and Day (2015) of infants aged 6 to 15 months that engage in what the authors call "simultaneous translanguaging practice" of Spanish, English, and Baby Sign Language. The bimodal-bilingual translanguaging of deaf children is also well documented in the work of Swanwick (2016), who uses translanguaging to conceptualize the ways in which deaf people use their language repertoires in the different spaces through which they move.

And yet, translanguaging has not been without opponents. Some critics say that it is merely another word for code-switching (see Otheguy, García & Reid, 2015). As we explained in the above sections, for us translanguaging is different epistemologically from code-switching (see Figure 1.1). However, we adhere to what we call a strong version of translanguaging (García & Lin, in press), a theory that poses, as we have said above, that bilingual people do not speak languages, but rather use their repertoire of linguistic features selectively. On the other hand, there is also a weak version of translanguaging circulating, even among some of the scholars cited above. This weak version supports named language boundaries, and yet calls for softening these boundaries (see Cummins 2007; García & Lin, in press).

As we have said before, because named languages of political states have had real and material consequences for students and educators in schools, it is important to acquire them and use them. But again, as we have said before, we start epistemologically from a different position than those who merely see translanguaging as the softening of language boundaries. We argue that advocating for fairer and more just instruction and assessment of bilingual students requires that we understand that named languages, imposed and regulated by schools, have nothing to do with speakers and the linguistic repertoire they use. As García and Lin (in press) say: "From the bilingual child's perspective, the language they have belongs to them, and not to the nation or the state."

There are other critics who allege that translanguaging can be used to disarm bilingual education programs. As we diagrammed in Figure 1.2, translanguaging starts with bilingualism and extends the complex language practices of bilingual children into named languages as defined in schools and society. Socially defined minoritized languages must be protected, but they cannot be totally isolated from other named languages and language practices used by bilingual children, since the entire language repertoire forms their linguistic competence. The language practices of minoritized people must be sustained and developed within the communicative context in which they are used by bilingual speakers and not as isolated museum pieces.

Despite the growing number of scholars who are taking up the term translanguaging, it is difficult for teachers, steeped in the monoglossic language ideologies that schools often promote, to accept it fully. Martínez, Hikida, and Durán (2015) explore how teachers in two Spanish–English bilingual elementary classrooms fluidly use their entire language repertoire, and yet express ideologies of linguistic purism about language separation. Bilingual students have also been schooled to think that only one language can be used at one time and thereby have developed monoglossic language ideologies, even though their practices depart from what they say they do or what they would want to do. We see this tension when we work with teachers and students. The case studies included in Part II of this book reveal some of these conflicts.

We now turn to how three dimensions of educating bilingual children—instructional pedagogies, assessment, and program types—can be transformed through translanguaging. The first two can be changed when educators take up translanguaging theory, and we offer ample examples in the case studies in chapters 3 through 8. For program models to change, however, more support from educational authorities is needed, since schools usually respond to how educational authorities define educational options.

Instruction and Translanguaging

Translanguaging in instruction is not random or haphazard but *strategic*, ensuring that bilingual children are educated deeply by leveraging their full language repertoire and their bilingual ways of knowing. García, Johnson, and Seltzer (2016) identify three dimensions in instruction that takes up translanguaging:

- The teacher's stance
- The teacher's design
- The teacher's shifts

Stance

To adopt translanguaging theory means that teachers develop a philosophical *stance* that often goes against what many think should happen in schools. Ideologies are at the root of what educators do in schools. Schools in the United States have traditionally functioned as English-medium schools, with little interest in bilingualism or in teaching languages other than English. No one questions the idea that education should be monolingual; on the contrary, policies are enacted to abolish bilingual programs. Students are expected to develop English literacy and numeracy and have scientific and historical understandings; but beyond this, almost every other subject is contested—whether it is physical education, art, music, technology, or an additional language. Berliner (2011) has documented how as a result of the focus on high-stakes testing, instructional time for elementary school English Language Arts and math has increased, whereas time for social studies, science, physical education, art and music, and even recess has decreased.

In other words, the ideology in elementary schools is that American children should be taught well in English and about English, and then they should learn to do math. Period.

Many teachers of emergent bilinguals understand, however, that their students cannot meet the high standards that they face in U.S. schools (discussed in more detail in chapter 2) using the limited and monolingual pedagogical approaches they have been taught to use. Some have become disillusioned and have left the profession. Others have developed a stance of resistance to higher standards, wanting to continue the simplified instruction that kept emergent bilinguals behind. Yet others have met the challenge that Walqui (2006) so elegantly set up for teachers of emergent bilinguals: Amplify, don't simplify. How then to amplify?

Teachers who take up translanguaging must first develop a stance that bilingualism is a resource at all times to learn, think, imagine, and develop commanding performances in two or more languages. Second, their stance must position language in the lips and minds of the children, and not in external standards or regulations. Third, teachers must deeply believe that translanguaging transforms subject positionalities, enabling children to perform with their own internal norm that will make them more creative and critical (Li Wei, 2011). Only then can translanguaging become a possibility for teachers.

Teachers hold two different stances on translanguaging. Some develop what we might call a *scaffolding stance*, a belief that the inclusion of the child's full language repertoire is only temporary—a scaffold for comprehension of the new language. Others, however, develop what we might call a *transformative stance*. These teachers' stance is that using the child's full repertoire will transform the language hierarchies in schools—in the U.S. English has the superior role, and Spanish, Russian, Chinese, and the other languages a subservient role that requires protection. These teachers see translanguaging for what it is, a way not only to invert the power positions of the named school languages, but also a way to disrupt the hegemony of the named national languages and of the power of the political state. Thus, they see translanguaging as capable of developing bilingual subjects able to perform in ways that go beyond how monolinguals perform, and that transform their own subjectivities. This transformative stance restores the power of language to the communities and to the bilingual students they teach.

Design

It is not enough, however, to simply have a stance that supports translanguaging theory; it is also important for teachers to *design* and plan translanguaging instruction. Designing instruction based on translanguaging theory requires three elements: 1) constructing collaborative/cooperative structures, 2) collecting varied multilingual and multimodal instructional resources, and 3) using translanguaging pedagogical practices (García, Johnson & Seltzer, 2016).

Instruction that is supported by translanguaging theory is always collaborative and student-centered. Teachers design their instruction in ways that capitalize on social interaction, especially among peers. Recall that translanguaging refers to the deployment of a speaker's full linguistic repertoire that is constantly evolving in social interaction with others. A speaker's linguistic repertoire is not set or static, nor innate, but emerges and is dynamically altered through social interaction. Thus, the translanguaging design of the classroom must capitalize on collaboration among speakers. To maximize discussion and collaboration on tasks, teachers often group students according to home language backgrounds. This allows students to appropriate new language features as they are given opportunities to interact with others who share a common language. García, Johnson, and Seltzer (2016) have referred to this as the *together/juntos* instructional design.

The collaboration among students and the use of the students' full language repertoire promotes what Moll (2014) has called the Bilingual Zone of Proximal Development. Coupling a classroom structure that capitalizes on discussion among peers with the use of students' full language repertoire means that instruction is always mediated by other voices—some external to the students, those of peers and teachers, but others internal to the students, the inner speech that drives all sense-making. For teachers who have a transformative stance, this together/juntos instructional design does much more than simply mediate. It transforms social relations of power.

Teachers who design instruction based on translanguaging theory have to make available appropriate multilingual and multimodal resources. This means that teachers have to go out of their way to find printed multilingual texts, but also multimodal texts such as videos, movies, and other Internet resources. This ensures that different perspectives are included and that students learn to critically analyze authors' viewpoints. Multilingual texts include not only those in different languages, but also those by bilingual authors who use translanguaging for literary effect. To design translanguaging instruction also means bringing the family and community into the school and inviting them to share their readings, stories, teachings, experiences, and funds of knowledge (Moll et al., 1992).

Both classroom groupings and multilingual/multimodal resources are ways of facilitating the use of children's full language repertoire. But teachers also need pedagogical strategies. One of the first tasks of the project that we describe in chapter 2, CUNY-NYSIEB, was to publish a guide of translanguaging strategies authored by two of our team members (Celic & Seltzer, 2012). Pedagogical strategies that build on translanguaging theory are unlike any other. More translanguaging strategies can also be found in Part II of García and Li Wei (2014) and in García, Johnson, and Seltzer (2016). You will also find descriptions of those strategies in the case studies in this book and in chapter 10. Translanguaging strategies ensure that students learn to use language in the ways prescribed by schools, while at the same time drawing this capacity from students' use of their full linguistic repertoire "without regard for watchful adherence to the socially and politically defined boundaries of named (and usually national and state) languages" (Otheguy, García & Reid, 2015, p. 281). Translanguaging simultaneously develops in bilingual students the capacity to bring their own language practices into the classroom, filling these practices with potential for academic and intellectual engagement rather than keeping them in their heads or in their homes.

It is important to understand that the child's linguistic repertoire is present in all classrooms. García, Johnson, and Seltzer (2016) have referred to this translanguaging undercurrent that is always present in classrooms with multilingual students as *la corriente.* Translanguaging pedagogical strategies give permission to bilingual students to bring their language practices to the surface and into the open, so that they can be refracted in an image of language that fits in with state and school definitions. If the lens used in instruction is not one of translanguaging, the light of children's voice simply does not come in or go out. Although the light of their voice may be present, it is not always visible. Unless the teacher has filtered the children's voice through a translanguaging instructional lens, an image of voice appropriate for school will not emerge. Thus, the potential of bilingual children to deeply engage academically is simply silenced.

Translanguaging is, as García (2009) has said, about sense-making. But translanguaging pedagogical strategies also help multilingual children show and build their linguistic virtuosity. In using their full linguistic repertoire, bilingual children become creative language users, going beyond the linguistic capacity that has been set by a political state. In analyzing the features of their repertoire, bilingual children become critical language users, understanding when, where, with whom, and especially why some features are accepted in some situations and not in others. As Li Wei (2011) has said, translanguaging pedagogical strategies help build bilingual children's creativity, as well as criticality.

Shifts

Although teachers design and plan translanguaging instruction, it is also important for teachers to be aware of the force of the translanguaging corriente that bilingual children's language practices promote. This means that teachers that take up translanguaging theory must also be prepared to change the course of instruction in order to respond to individual children's language repertoires. Translanguaging theory, as we have said, stems from an understanding of language from the speaker up, and not from the named language down. From the insider's view of the speaker, there is only his or her full repertoire, what linguists call "idiolects" (see Otheguy, García & Reid, 2015). Each person's idiolect is unique and personal, because it emerges in interaction with different speakers. Thus, no amount of planning can absolutely set the course of a lesson, for even when we teach by grouping students into what educators call "levels" or "stages," there will be differences in the ways in which students use their repertoire. Teachers then must also respond to these differences by being prepared to shift their instructional design.

Assessment and Translanguaging

If every assessment is an assessment of language (American Educational Research Association, American Psychological Association, and National Council on Measurement in Education, 2014), then the ways in which we conceive of language is extremely important. Language in assessment, and especially in summative assessment, usually responds to the definition of language as handed down by state authorities. This approach to language usually persists whether we are assessing the language of children or the content that they are learning. Many scholars have called for a more accurate assessment of the understandings of bilingual children (see especially Menken, 2008; Shohamy, 2011; Solano-Flores, Backhoff & Contreras-Niño, 2009; Valdés & Figueroa, 1994).

Translanguaging theory offers a way of separating two ways of understanding language in assessment. On the one hand, there are the lexical and structural features that schools have helped standardize and that make up what is then accepted as English, Spanish, Russian, Arabic, Yoruba, and so on. On the other, there are the bilingual speakers' own language features that go beyond the bounded designation of what is considered one or the other language, but that speakers can use to carry out linguistic tasks. Translanguaging theory helps teachers separate *language-specific performances* in the named language—English, Spanish, Russian, Chinese or others—from *general linguistic performances*, that is, the students' ability, for example, to argue a point, express inferences, communicate complex thoughts, use text-based evidence, tell a story, identify main ideas and relationships in complex texts, tell jokes, and so forth. We all know students who know English only, and yet cannot effectively use English to argue a point. And we know emergent bilingual students who are developing English, but yet can argue complex thoughts very effectively. Using translanguaging theory would mean that we would be able to separate the two types of performances. We would be able to assess if a bilingual student uses the lexicon and linguistic structures of a specific-named language in socially and academic appropriate ways—the named language-specific performance. And we would be able to assess if he or she is able to perform linguistically to engage in academic and social tasks regardless of the language features used—the general linguistic performance.

Furthermore, translanguaging in assessment levels the playing field between bilingual and monolingual children. Whereas monolingual children are allowed to use most of the features of their language repertoire (with few exceptions) in expressing what they know, bilingual children are asked to suppress more than half of the features in their repertoire in one or the other language. Thus, a translanguaging theory in assessment also promotes equal educational opportunity and social justice. It offers a more accurate assessment of what bilingual students know and can do with language.

It is important to understand that translanguaging in assessment goes beyond simply measuring students' language performances in the other language—Spanish, Russian, etc. The same reasons that make it unfair to assess bilingual children only in English apply to testing them only in their home languages as well. Bilingual children have a more extended repertoire than monolingual children do. Asking them to perform with less than half of their repertoire, regardless of the half that is being excluded, strikes us as unfair.

Teachers whose instruction follows translanguaging theory design formative and summative assessments in which students are given opportunity to show what they know by using their full language repertoire (see García & Ascenzi-Moreno, forthcoming). However, this is rare in standardized assessment. An exception is Alexis López and his associates in Educational Testing Service (ETS), who are developing a middle school math translanguaging assessment (López, Guzmán-Orth & Turkan, forthcoming). On this computer-based platform, students have the opportunity to see or hear an item in both English and/or Spanish, and to then write or say responses regardless of the language in which they are rendered. To create the space for translanguaging, students are asked to select a bilingual avatar, a virtual friend or assistant. This bilingual avatar can then use his or her entire language repertoire, providing students with a model of how to translanguage.

We turn next to considering how translanguaging has the potential to transform program types for bilingual students.

Program Types and Translanguaging

It is easier to help teachers take up translanguaging in instruction and assessment than to transform what are seen as program "models," such as dual language bilingual education, transitional bilingual education, or English as a second language, etc. Although models are "artificial constructs" (García, 2009, p. 114), policymakers and educators continue to use them to shape the ways in which educational programs are organized. These models are then generally used in various combinations by different U.S. states to fulfill the federal government obligation of educating and supporting emergent bilinguals. This section considers how translanguaging works differently in the three types of programs that are more frequently used to educate emergent bilinguals.

Often educators interpret state regulations more rigidly than they were intended. Translanguaging applies a lens to the regulations in order to elucidate ways in which they can work for children. Again, the starting point of translanguaging is the children themselves and the communities from which they come. Those understandings of the children, their families, and their language and cultural practices are then put alongside the state regulations, discovering spaces of practice where translanguaging can work internally for the children, as well as externally to meet requirements. Translanguaging has the potential to transform the models to work for the children. We discuss below the main types of programs in which emergent bilingual students are educated in the United States—ESL and bilingual programs—and the transformations that translanguaging enables, making all of them multilingual programs.

English as a Second/New Language as Multilingual

Instruction in programs of English as a second/new language can take on a variety of forms:

- *Pull out*, where a specialized "English as a Second Language" (ESL) teacher "pulls out" a small group of students, usually from the similar grade level(s) and/or English proficiency, to provide them with the required English-focused instruction. Students miss a part of their regular class instruction while receiving ESL support.
- *Push in*, where a specialized teacher co-teaches or supports a group of students alongside the classroom teacher, providing them with explicit English language instruction and scaffolds needed to engage in the lessons for all students in the class.
- *Self-standing*, also referred to as *structured immersion* or *sheltered English*, refers to programs in which the specially trained educator teaches a self-contained class with scaffolds for literacy and content instruction.

Since the advent of the Common Core State Standards and of the corresponding assessment instruments that have been developed (more on this in chapter 2), English as a second language teachers have been struggling with how to help their emergent bilinguals. One effect of translanguaging theory in English-medium programs has been that teachers have been leveraging the students' home languages in ways that enhance comprehension (García, 2014; Lin, 2013b). For some teachers, leveraging translanguaging has been much more than a simple scaffold. Some use it to raise the critical multilingual awareness among students, turning ESL classrooms into multilingual ones.

In effect, translanguaging theory has had the effect of disrupting the hegemony of English in English-medium classrooms, disrupting the fixed borders in which it had been originally conceived. Figure 1.3 displays how translanguaging has potentialized and extended the ESL/ENL (English as a New Language) program beyond its single square box in which the students' home languages are absent, by uptaking the multilingual practices of the students in those classrooms.

Translanguaging thus offers opportunities to transform these English-medium programs into *multilingual* programs by including linguistic practices that are associated with Languages Other Than English (LOTEs).

FIGURE 1.3 Translanguaging in ESL Classrooms

Bilingual Education as Multilingual

Bilingual education is usually divided into two categories within the U.S.:

- *Transitional bilingual education (TBE),* in which the child's home language is used only until the student is assessed as being fluent in English.
- *Dual language bilingual education (DLBE*), in which two languages are used throughout the child's schooling, usually only through elementary education (5th grade), although sometimes also through middle school (8th grade). Dual language bilingual education is often comprised of two different types:
  - *Two-way DLBE,* also called *two-way immersion* or *dual immersion,* initially consists of a balanced number of students who are officially classified as "English language learners," as well as language majority students who are fluent in English. It is two-way because students are learning each other's language.
  - *One-way DLBE,* also called *developmental maintenance bilingual education,* consists of students of the same home language group who are at different points of the bilingual spectrum. Some are emergent bilinguals developing English; others are bilingual with different levels of expertise in English and the language other than English.

ESL/ENL teachers use translanguaging mostly as a scaffold towards English. However, bilingual teachers, whether in transitional or dual language bilingual classrooms, have always been under attack for their use of a language other than English in instruction. As part of an embattled field, bilingual teachers have developed an armor of protection, a ring of fire around the minoritized language, to protect it from the encroachment of the more powerful language, English. At the same time, bilingual teachers, often members of language-minoritized groups themselves, understand translanguaging practices and theory more than others. They know that translanguaging theory reflects the ways in which they use language, although many times, as victims of the symbolic violence (Bourdieu, 1991) that schools have exerted on them, they stigmatize their own language practices. Bilingual teachers of color have also encountered linguicism and racism much more than White majority teachers. As such, they have a more developed sense of outrage and a deeper recognition of the need for social justice.

Bilingual teachers are then caught in the tension between two views on language. On the one hand, they understand that minoritized languages are in need of nurture and protection—the external view. On the other hand, they know that their own language practices go well beyond what is understood as Spanish, Chinese, Haitian Creole, Russian, and so on—the internal view.

Bilingual programs have been set up to support the sense of language that sees national languages as important and in need of development. Thus, bilingual education programs usually have very strict boundaries between the two languages, responding to the traditional understandings of bilingualism that we displayed in Figure 1.1. But translanguaging theory demands that bilingual education programs also leverage and develop the translanguaging practices of bilingual children, their ability to use their entire language repertoire. To accommodate translanguaging theory, bilingual education programs have to undergo some transformations in structure, transformations that are being increasingly called for by scholars of bilingual education, including Jim Cummins himself (Cummins, 2007; see also García, 2009; Gort, 2015; Gort & Sembiante, 2015; Martínez et al., 2015; Palmer et al., 2014; Weber, 2014; among others).

Instead of two spaces with thick borders, the borders of the two named languages in bilingual education need to be somewhat porous. Of course, one needs to have a space to perform named languages; thus, a language allocation policy is still important. But it is crucial to ensure that the bilingual children's full language repertoire is given a rightful place in the *process* of learning. Even when the *product* of learning is in one or another language, the process must leverage the students' full repertoire. This means different things depending on the task at hand. Sometimes students may be told that they can discuss orally using their entire language repertoire, even when the written product is in one language or the other. Sometimes students are told that they can listen to and research sources in different languages, although their oral performance has to be in a prescribed language. Sometimes students are told that they can conduct research on the Internet and read texts in any language they choose, although they then have to write an argumentative text in one language. But this in itself is not enough.

Beyond the more porous nature of the borders between the two named languages, translanguaging calls for bilingual education programs to also construct a space that ties together all the students' language practices, transforming bilingual students into much more than just two languages in one (see also García & Hesson, 2015; García & Lin, in press). We call this instructional space a *translanguaging space* (see also Li Wei, 2011). This is a space that teachers build over time, to ensure that students "do" language using their full repertoire. The potential of this translanguaging space is related to the greater power and respect given to students who can now express themselves without having to suppress any features of their repertoire. At the same time, it validates the language practices of bilingual communities, with bilingualism enacted not as two monolingualisms in one, but as one bilingualism. Sometimes this translanguaging space is used to compare and contrast features of the two named languages. By putting the two named languages alongside each other, bilingual students develop the capacity to analyze their own language practices, to foster their metalinguistic awareness. The translanguaging space also enables the construction of translanguaged texts, orally and in writing, not only portraying the language practices of the children, but also helping students become critical discourse analysts, reflecting on which features to use when and where in order to maximize legitimate communication among different communities of practice. Figure 1.4 displays the change in bilingual education programs that a translanguaging theory would bring:

FIGURE 1.4 Translanguaging in Bilingual Programs

Notice that the translanguaging space is not between two square boxes with fixed borders. Translanguaging theory always expands bilingual education to become *multilingual education* and beyond. That is, in bilingual education classrooms that take up translanguaging, the English and LOTE spaces include all the language features of the students, regardless of how they are named. Whether named African-American English or Indian English or Portuguese or Mandinka doesn't matter. All the language features of the students' linguistic repertoires are acknowledged, valued, and deployed in learning.

Conclusion

In this chapter, we have begun to explore the dimensions and meanings of translanguaging, as well as how it is capable of transforming teaching, assessing, and learning for bilingual students. In disrupting traditional ways in which language in education has been conceptualized, translanguaging theory has the potential to transform not only the education landscape, but also our social landscape that is increasingly becoming more inequitable. Translanguaging emerges as a linguistic and social theory capable of transforming education, but also containing the elements to disrupt hierarchies and inequities and build a better and more just world. As Flores (2014) has said, "Let us not forget that translanguaging is a political act " (n.p.).

References

Alvarez, S. (2014). Translanguaging tareas: Emergent bilingual youth as language brokers for homework in immigrant families. *Language Arts*, 91(5), 326–339.

American Educational Research Association, American Psychological Association, & National Council on Measurement in Education. (2014). *The standards for educational and psychological testing.* Washington, DC: AERA.

Arthur, J., & Martin, P. (2006). Accomplishing lessons in postcolonial classrooms: Comparative perspectives from Botswana and Brunei Darussalam. *Comparative Education*, 42, 177–202.

Auer, P. (1999). *Code-switching in conversation: Language interactions and identity.* London: Routledge.

Auer, P. (2005). A postscript: Code-switching and social identity. *Journal of Pragmatics*, 37(3), 403–410.

Baker, C. (2001). *Foundations of bilingual education and bilingualism*, 3rd edn. Clevedon, UK: Multilingual Matters.

Berliner, D. (2011). Rational response to high stakes testing: The case of curriculum narrowing and the harm that follows. *Cambridge Journal of Education*, 41(3), 287–302.

Blackledge, A., & Creese, A. (2010). *Multilingualism: A critical perspective.* London: Continuum Press.

Blommaert, J. (2010). *The sociolinguistics of globalization.* Cambridge: Cambridge University Press.

Bourdieu, P. (1991). *Language and symbolic power* (ed. J. B. Thompson). Cambridge: Harvard University Press.

Canagarajah, S. (2011). Translanguaging in the classroom: Emerging issues for research and pedagogy. *Applied Linguistics Review*, 2, 1–27.

Celic, C., & Seltzer, K. (2012). *Translanguaging: A CUNY-NYSIEB guide for educators.* New York: CUNY-NYSIEB, The Graduate Center, The City University of New York. Retrieved on March 16, 2016, from: http://www.cuny-nysieb.org

Cenoz, J., & Gorter, D. (2015). *Multilingual education: Between language learning and translanguaging.* Cambridge: Cambridge University Press.

Conteh, J., & Meier, G. (Eds.). (2014). *The multilingual turn in languages education: Opportunities and challenges for individuals and societies* (pp. 258–277). Clevedon, UK: Multilingual Matters.

Creese, A., & Blackledge, A. (2010). Translanguaging in the bilingual classroom: A pedagogy for learning and teaching? *Modern Language Journal*, 94, 103–115.

Cummins, J. (1979). Linguistic interdependence and the educational development of bilingual children. *Review of Educational Research*, 49, 222–251.

Cummins, J. (2007). Rethinking monolingual instructional strategies in multilingual classrooms. *The Canadian Journal of Applied Linguistics*, 10(2), 221–240.

Del Valle, J. (2000). Monoglossic policies for a heteroglossic culture: Misinterpreted multilingualism in modern Galicia. *Language and Communication*, 20, 105–132.

Flores, N. (2014). Let's not forget that translanguaging is a political act. Retrieved on March 16, 2016, from: https://educationallinguist.Wordpress.com/2014/07/19/lets-not-forget-that-translanguaging-is-a-political-act/

Flores, N., & García, O. (2013). Linguistic third spaces in education: Teachers' translanguaging across the bilingual continuum. In D. Little, C. Leung, & P. Van Avermaet (Eds.), *Managing diversity in education: Key issues and some responses* (pp. 243–256). Clevedon, UK: Multilingual Matters.

García, O. (2009). *Bilingual education in the 21st century: A global perspective.* Malden, MA and Oxford, UK: Wiley/Blackwell.

García, O. (2014). What is translanguaging? Expanded questions and answers for US educators. In *Translanguaging in curriculum and instruction: A CUNY-NYSIEB guide for educators.* New York: The Graduate Center, The City University of New York.

García, O., & Ascenzi-Moreno, L. (forthcoming). Assessment in school from a translanguaging angle. In R. Bekcert, J. Luth, S. Ptashnyk, P. Wolf Farré, & M. Wolny (Eds.), *Gegenwärtige Sprachkontakte im Kontext der Migration.* Heildelberg: Winter Verlag.

García, O., Flores, N., & Spotti, M. (Eds.) (forthcoming). *Handbook of language and society.* Oxford: Oxford University Press.

García, O., Flores, N., & Woodley, H. H. (2012). Transgressing monolingualism and bilingual dualities: Translanguaging pedagogies. In A. Yiakoumetti (Ed.), *Harnessing linguistic variation for better education* (pp. 45–76). Bern: Peter Lang.

García, O., & Hesson, S. (2015). Translanguaging frameworks for teachers: Macro and micro perspectives. In A. Yiacoumetti (Ed.), *Multilingualism and language in education: Current sociolinguistic and pedagogical perspectives from Commonwealth countries* (pp. 221–242). Cambridge: Cambridge University Press.

García, O., Johnson, J., & Seltzer, K. (2016). *The translanguaging classroom: Leveraging student bilingualism for learning.* Philadelphia, PA: Caslon.

García, O., & Li Wei. (2014). *Translanguaging: Language, bilingualism and education.* London, UK: Palgrave Macmillan Pivot.

García, O., & Li Wei. (2015). Translanguaging, bilingualism and bilingual education. In W. Wright, S. Boun, & O. García (Eds.), *Handbook of bilingual education* (pp. 223–240). Malden, MA: John Wiley.

García, O., & Lin, A. (in press). Translanguaging and bilingual education. In O. García & A. Lin (Eds.), *Bilingual education* (Vol. 5): *Encyclopedia of language and education.* Springer.

García, O., & Sylvan, C. (2011). Pedagogies and practices in multilingual classrooms: Singularities in pluralities. *Modern Language Journal,* 95(3), 385–400.

Garrity, S., Aquino-Sterling, C., & Day, A. (2015). Translanguaging in an infant classroom: Using multiple languages to make meaning. *International Multilingual Research Journal,* 9(3): 177–196. DOI: 10.1080/19313152.2015.1048542

Gort, M. (2015). Transforming literacy learning and teaching through translanguaging and other typical practices associated with "Doing Being Bilingual." *International Multilingual Research Journal,* 9(1), 1–6. DOI: 10.1080/19313152.2014.988030

Gort, M., & Sembiante, S. F. (2015). Navigating hybridized language learning spaces through translanguaging pedagogy: Dual language preschool teachers' languaging practices in support of emergent bilingual children's performance of academic discourse. *International Multilingual Research Journal,* 9(1), 7–25. DOI: 10.1080/19313152.2014.981775

Grosjean, F. (1982). *Life with two languages.* Cambridge, MA: Harvard University Press.

Gumperz, J. (1976). The sociolinguistic significance of conversational code-switching. *Working Papers of the Language Behavior Research Laboratory* 46. Berkeley: University of California.

Heller, M. (1999). *Linguistic minorities and modernity: A Sociolinguistic ethnography.* London: Longman.

Heller, M. (2007). Bilingualism as ideology and practice. In M. Heller (Ed.), *Bilingualism: A social approach* (pp. 1–22). Basingstoke, Hampshire: Palgrave Macmillan.

Hornberger, N. H., & Link, H. (2012). Translanguaging and transnational literacies in multilingual classrooms: A Bilingual lens'. *International Journal of Bilingual Education and Bilingualism*, 15(3), 261–278.

Jacobson, R. (1990). Allocating two languages as a key feature of a bilingual methodology. In R. Jacobson & C. Faltis (Eds.), *Language distribution issues in bilingual schooling* (pp. 3–17). Clevedon, UK: Multilingual Matters.

Lambert, W. E. (1974). Culture and language as factors in learning and education. In F. E. Aboud & R. D. Meade (Eds.), *Cultural factors in learning and education* (pp. 91–122). Bellingham, Washington: 5th Western Washington Symposium on Learning.

Lambert, W. E., & Tucker, G. R. (1972). *The bilingual education of children.* Rowley, MA: Newbury House.

Lewis, G., Jones, B., & Baker, C. (2012a). Translanguaging: Developing its conceptualisation and contextualisation. *Educational Research and Evaluation*, 18(7), 655–670.

Lewis, G., Jones, B., & Baker, C. (2012b). Translanguaging: Origins and development from school to street and beyond. *Educational Research and Evaluation*, 18(7), 641–654.

Li Wei. (2011). Moment analysis and translanguaging space: Discursive construction of identities by multilingual Chinese youth in Britain. *Journal of Pragmatics*, 43, 1222–1235.

Li Wei. (2014). Who's teaching whom? Co-learning in multilingual classrooms. In S. May (Ed.), *The multilingual turn: Implications for SLA, TESOL and bilingual education* (pp. 167–190). New York and London: Routledge.

Lin, A. M. Y. (2013a). Classroom code-switching: Three decades of research. *Applied Linguistic Review*, 4(1), 195–218.

Lin, A. M. Y. (2013b). Towards paradigmatic change in TESOL methodologies: Building plurilingual pedagogies from the ground up. *TESOL Quarterly*, 47(3), 521–545.

Lin, A. M. Y., & Martin, P. W. (Eds.). (2005). *Decolonisation, globalization: Language-in-education policy and practice.* Clevedon, UK: Multilingual Matters.

López, A., Guzmán-Orth, D., & Turkan, S. (forthcoming). *The use of translanguaging to assess the content knowledge of emergent bilingual students.* Princeton, NJ: Educational Testing Service.

Makoni, S., & Pennycook, A. (2007). *Disinventing and reconstituting languages.* Clevedon, UK: Multilingual Matters.

Martínez, R., Hikida, M., & Durán, L. (2015). Unpacking ideologies of linguistic purism: How dual language teachers make sense of everyday translanguaging. *International Multilingual Research Journal*, 9(1), 26–42.

May, S. (2015). *Addressing the multilingual turn: Implications for SLA, TESOL and bilingual education.* New York: Routledge.

Menken, K. (2008). *English learners left behind: Standardized testing as language policy.* Bristol, UK: Multilingual Matters.

Moll, L. (2014). *L.S. Vygotsky and education.* New York: Routledge.

Moll, L., Amanti, C., Neff, D., & Gonzalez, N. (1992). Funds of knowledge for teaching: Using a qualitative approach to connect homes and classrooms. *Theory into Practice*, 31(2), 132–141.

Myers-Scotton, C. (2005). *Multiple voices: An introduction to bilingualism.* Malden, MA: Wiley.

Orellana, M. F., & García, O. (2014, May). Language brokering and translanguaging in school. *Language Arts*, 91(5), 386–392.

Otheguy, R., García, O., & Reid, W. (2015). Clarifying translanguaging and deconstructing named languages: A perspective from linguistics. *Applied Linguistics Review*, 6(3), 281–307.

Palmer, D. K., Martínez, R. A., Mateus, S. G., & Henderson, K. (2014). Reframing the debate on language separation: Toward a vision for translanguaging pedagogies in the dual language classroom. *The Modern Language Journal*, 98(3), 757–772. DOI: 10.1111/modl.12121

Pennycook, A. (2010). *Language as a local practice*. London and New York: Routledge.

Sayer, P. (2013). Translanguaging, TexMex, and bilingual pedagogy: Emergent bilinguals learning through the vernacular. *TESOL Quarterly*, 47(1), 63–88.

Schwartz, M., & Asli, A. (2014). Bilingual teachers' language strategies: The case of an Arabic-Hebrew kindergarten in Israel. *Teaching and Teacher Education*, 38, 22–32.

Shohamy, E. (2011). Assessing multilingual competencies: Adopting construct valid assessment policies. *The Modern Language Journal*, 95(3), 418–429.

Solano-Flores, G., Backhoff, E., & Contreras-Niño, L. (2009). Theory of test translation error. *International Journal of Testing*, 9(2), 78–91.

Swanwick, R. (2016). Scaffolding learning through classroom talk: The role of translanguaging. In M. Marschark & P. Spencer (Eds.), *The Oxford handbook of deaf studies: Language and language development* (pp. 420–430). New York: Oxford University Press.

Taylor, S., & Snoddon, K. (Eds.). (2013). *TESOL Quarterly*, 47(3), entire issue.

Valdés, G., & Figueroa, R. (1994). *Bilingualism and testing: A special case of bias. Second language learning*. Westport, CT, US: Ablex Publishing.

Velasco, P., & García, O. (2014). Translanguaging and the writing of bilingual learners. *The Bilingual Research Journal*, 37(1), 6–23.

Walqui, A. (2006). Scaffolding instruction for English learners: A conceptual framework. *International Journal of Bilingual Education and Bilingualism*, 9(2), 159–180.

Weber, J. J. (2014). *Flexible multilingual education: Putting children's needs first*. Bristol, UK: Multilingual Matters.

Williams, C. (1994). Arfarniad o Ddulliau Dysgu ac Addysgu yng Nghyd-destun Addysg Uwchradd Ddwyieithog [An evaluation of teaching and learning methods in the context of bilingual secondary education]. Unpublished Doctoral Thesis (University of Wales, Bangor).

2

A TRANSLANGUAGING EDUCATIONAL PROJECT

Ofelia García and Tatyana Kleyn

Introduction

This chapter describes the CUNY-New York State Initiative on Emergent Bilinguals (CUNY-NYSIEB), an education project that has shaped our understandings of how translanguaging theory interacts with practice. The aim of the project was to improve the education of emergent bilinguals. To build new understandings about the students, their bilingualism, and the ways in which they were educated, the project drew on translanguaging theory. The case studies that we include in Part II of the book (chapters 3 to 8) make evident not only the ways in which theory has been able to transform practice, and vice versa, but also the tensions that continue to exist as translanguaging is taken up in educational circles (see also chapter 9).

This chapter also describes how we carried out the research on translanguaging in practice. Our purpose in conducting this research was in keeping with the collaborative approach of our project. The researchers took up positions as teachers, sometimes co-teaching lessons and always co-designing them with classroom teachers. The teachers took up positions as researchers, interpreting their own performances and those of the students through their own lenses. This collaborative approach also corresponded with another goal of our research: to keep a tight relationship between theory, research, and educational practice. In working out the lessons with the classroom teachers, we learned more about the workings of teaching and learning with translanguaging on the ground. At the same time, the teachers deepened their understanding of translanguaging theory and research. In our project, theory, practice, and research mutually transformed each other. They were not separate entities, but rather formed a continuum. We will discuss this relationship at the end of the chapter.

Before we describe in detail the vision of CUNY-NYSIEB and the ways in which it has been carried out, it is important to contextualize the project in relationship to the existing language education policies of the United States and New York State, focusing on those that are specifically aimed at bilingual learners. The political economy of a society, that is, the interrelationship between economic and political processes, always shapes ideologies and has deep implications for educational and language policy. We start by reviewing the past before we focus on the present policies of our neoliberal era.

U.S. Language Education Policies

Past

Teaching bilingual learners in the United States is not new. The U.S. has been using languages other than English to educate immigrants from its very beginnings to ensure that the newcomers contribute to its economy. Starting in 1839 and continuing throughout most of the 19th century, public schools in Ohio (especially in Cincinnati) and in St. Louis, Missouri, taught bilingually in English/German (see Crawford, 2004; García, 2009; Wiley, 1996). But the languages of enslaved and conquered minorities were suppressed forcefully. Enslaved people from Africa were silenced and kept illiterate. Native Americans were sent to boarding schools at the end of the 19th century to ensure that they would shift to English (Reyhner & Eder, 1989). And after Mexico ceded nearly half of its territory to the United States in the Treaty of Guadalupe Hildago (1848), Spanish was eradicated from schools by the end of the 19th century. Thus, language policies had the effect of differentiating workers—enslaved Africans, Native Americans, and Mexican Americans at the lowest rungs; other White immigrant workers at higher rungs.

During the 20th century, between 1890 and 1930, 16 million immigrants entered the United States, a growing number of them Italian and Jewish (García, 2009). As the U.S. entered the First World War, with Germany as its enemy, education for immigrants became increasingly focused on Americanization and English. Assimilation was also a goal of public education during this time. By 1923, 34 states had passed laws to restrict the use of languages other than English in education. Despite the Supreme Court's ruling in Meyer v. Nebraska in 1923, which overturned the Nebraska statute forbidding the teaching of languages other than English, the emphasis of education remained the teaching of English.

The civil rights era brought about an emphasis on equal educational opportunities. The Chicano community in the Southwest and the Puerto Rican community in the Northeast established developmental maintenance bilingual education programs in the 1960s. In Dade County/Miami, the Ford Foundation supported the development of the Coral Way bilingual program in 1961 to educate Cuban-American children. By 1968, the Bilingual Education Act

(Title VII of the Elementary and Secondary Education Act) was passed, opening up funding opportunities for schools with large numbers of students who did not speak English. Bilingual education expanded. At around the same time, the Immigration and Naturalization Services Act of 1965 abolished the quotas that had limited immigrants to 2% of people from that country already living in the U.S. in 1890. An unprecedented number of non-White immigrant workers from Asia, Latin America, and Africa entered the United States. Workers were again needed and the emphasis on Americanization and English of the former era was no longer viable in an increasingly global world (for more on this history, see Castellanos, 1983; Crawford, 1991, 2004; Wiley, 1996).

However, the opening up of bilingual spaces during the civil rights era never changed the ideology that American education should take place in English only. And, as soon as society moved away from civil rights during the Reagan era, bilingual education programs became contested yet again.

The Present Neoliberal Era

We are living in an age of neoliberal globalization driven by what Harvey (2004) has called "accumulation by dispossession." Through privatization, free markets, and free trade, the individual is said to enjoy entrepreneurial freedoms, which are supposed to lead to human well-being. The purpose of education then becomes to service the economy through the production of "human capital" (see Block, Gray & Holborow, 2012).

Neoliberalism relies on networks of relationships supported by new forms of communication advanced by technology. Power is thus not imposed through explicit language policies, but is dispersed through these networks of relationships. This neoliberal ideology meshes well with the U.S. stance on language policy, which has seldom been explicit (especially at the federal level), and has supported the right of individuals to languages, over the rights of groups to languages (for more on the difference between group language rights and individual language rights in the U.S. see Kloss, 1977).

Over the last several decades, changes in the U.S. language education policy have been subtle and implicit, but have had a major impact on the education of bilingual students. Spaces for bilingualism in education have shrunk and bilingual children and their teachers are punished for not performing at what are deemed to be appropriate levels in English only. In January 2002, No Child Left Behind (NCLB) was passed, bringing to an end Title VII of the Elementary and Secondary Education Act, the Bilingual Education Act. Title III of No Child Left Behind (Public Law 107–110) was entitled "Language Instruction for Limited English Proficient and Immigrant Students," shifting the goal of education to merely "attain English proficiency" (cited in García, 2009, p. 185).

No Child Left Behind also ushered in a new stage of accountability for all students based on high-stakes tests. NCLB requires states to test students in grades 3 to 8 each year and to judge the school and the teachers' performance based on these test scores. For students classified as "English language learners," NCLB requires that states assess their English language proficiency annually, and these students are obliged to make "adequate yearly progress" (AYP), that is, growth over time in English reading and English Language Arts, as well as math. The federal government holds states, school districts, and individual schools accountable for student growth in these areas. Schools failing to make required performance-gains face sanctions over time such as reallocation of funding, closure, or restructuring.

As NCLB took shape, and under the leadership of the National Governors Association Center for Best Practices and the Council of Chief State School Officers, Common Core State Standards (CCSS) were developed in English Language Arts and math, to ensure that high school graduates were adequately prepared for college and careers. The development of the CCSS was motivated by the poor performance of the U.S. in the Program for International Student Assessment (PISA), a worldwide survey of 15-year-olds in mathematics, science, and reading, conducted every three years by the Organization for Economic Cooperation and Development (OECD). The link between the CCSS and a neoliberal ideology is clear. In the words of Dane Linn, Director of the Education Division for the National Governors Association Center for Best Practices: "Governors recognize the irrefutable links between a quality education, a productive workforce, and a sound economy" (cited in National Governors Association, 2009, n.p.).

The CCSS document only devotes two-and-a-half pages to "English language learners." It acknowledges that, "these students may require additional time, appropriate instructional support, and aligned assessments as they acquire both English language proficiency and content area knowledge" (www.corestandards.org, n.p.). But there is no further attention given to the bilingualism of these students, silencing and erasing the growing multilingualism of our country (for more on bilingualism and the CCSS, see García & Flores, 2013).

At the time of this writing, 42 states and the District of Columbia have adopted the Common Core State Standards.[1] Two different Common Core–aligned assessment consortia (Partnership for Assessment of Readiness for College and Careers, PARCC, and Smarter Balanced Assessment Consortium) have been formed. Although initially 26 states joined PARCC, only six and the District of Columbia remained in 2016. States joining Smarter Balanced have shrunk from 31 to 17 in 2016. Race to the Top, a U.S. Department of Education competitive grant, distributed $4.35 billion to states that adopted educational policies that embraced Common Core standards, expanded charter schools, adopted performance-based evaluation of teachers and principals, and developed large data systems of accountability scores. Thus, the federal government promoted adoption of the Common Core State Standards and of aligned assessment consortia by states. But as objections grew—from students, parents, teachers, and local educational authorities—the federal government assumed a different position vis-à-vis states. On December 10, 2015, President Barack Obama signed the Every Student Succeeds Act to replace No Child Left Behind. Besides giving states more flexibility in how to test students, how to support failing schools, and whether to adopt the Common Core State Standards, competition, testing, and accountability continue to dominate an education policy that responds to a neoliberal agenda.

The emphasis across the nation is to get students to perform at proficient levels in English and to show what they can do in other subject areas—usually also in English, without regard to the increasing language diversity of the nation. And yet, it is precisely the raising of the bar to educate all students that has shifted some understandings for teachers of emergent bilinguals. Teachers have started to realize that teaching only in English will only leave them behind, as Menken has shown (2008). Other ways have to be found to enable emergent bilingual students to participate equitably not only in education, but also in U.S. society. And this is precisely what a translanguaging theory has offered many educators.

New York State Language Education Policies

To respond to the federal government requirements of No Child Left Behind, states developed proficiency standards and assessments for emergent bilingual students. One consortia of 37 states is known as WIDA (originally World Class Instructional Design and Assessment); another is ELPA21 (English Language Proficiency Assessment for the 21st Century). California and New York have developed their own language standards for emergent bilinguals and assessments. All four sets of standards (WIDA, ELPA21, California's, and New York's) use performance indicators to demonstrate how emergent bilingual students would process or produce language at various progression levels (for example, emerging, expanding, transitioning, commanding). All of the systems view the home languages of the students differently. WIDA considers the student's home language as a kind of interactive support or scaffold. ELPA21 specifically states: "ELLs' primary languages and other social, cultural, and linguistic background knowledge and resources . . . are useful tools to help them navigate back and forth among their schools and their communities' valuable resources" (Council of Chief State School Officers, 2014, p. 1). New York State has also supported the use of the students' home languages in meeting the standards through the Bilingual Common Core Initiative (Velasco & Johnson, 2014).

New York State policies to educate emergent bilinguals are encoded explicitly in Commissioner's Regulations (CR Part 154). CR Part 154 requires that bilingual students who are new to a school have a family member complete a home language survey, and, if students speak a language other than English, they are given a screening test. Emergent bilinguals in New York State are designated "English language learners" through this initial screening test (the New York State Identification Test for English Language Learners [NYSITELL]). To be declassified as an "English language learner," students have to pass the New York State English as a Second Language Assessment Test (NYSESLAT), which is administered every spring. Emergent bilinguals are divided into three categories that reflect the time they have spent in the program:

- Newcomers (0–3 years)
- Developing (4–6 years)
- Long-Term ELLs (more than 6 years)

There are two types of educational support provided to these children:

- English as a New Language, in which instruction is mostly in English.
- Bilingual Education, in which English and another language are used as media of instruction.

Although traditionally instruction for emergent bilinguals is in English only, New York State supports the use of home language as scaffold when core content is taught.

Like the overwhelming majority of states, New York has adopted the Common Core State Standards, as of this writing. But beyond other states, New York State has attempted to pay attention to the bilingualism of its students, developing and adopting what is known as the Bilingual Common Core Initiative (Velasco & Johnson, 2014). Despite these moves to recognize bilingualism, New York State schools and educators have also fallen prey to policies that seem to reduce opportunities for bilingual students. As we will see, the work of CUNY-NYSIEB with translanguaging theory and practices has had the effect of opening up spaces of possibility within existing policies and practices.

New York State: Common Core Standards, the Bilingual Common Core Initiative and Curricula

New York State adopted the Common Core State Standards in 2011, with a phased-in implementation. These standards dictate what preschool to 12th-grade students should know and be able to do by the end of each grade, from age four until their final year of high school. The Common Core Learning Standards (CCLS), the term used in New York State, are divided into English Language Arts and literacy on the one hand, and mathematics on the other. For grades 6–12, there are also literacy standards connected to history/social studies, science, and technical subjects. The standards do not mandate a specific curriculum, pedagogical approach, or required materials. They apply to all students, regardless of English development, disability, or any other difference, although there is very little about how to support these groups of students in the actual standards documents.

The English Language Arts standards are organized into four overlapping strands: (1) reading, (2) writing, (3) speaking and listening, and (4) language. The reading strand is subdivided into literature, informational text, and foundational skills. The language strand is the only one that is specifically about the English language, whereas the others are broader literacy concepts and skills that can be interpreted as being taught or met through any language. The mathematics standards are also not specific to a particular named language (http://www.p12.nysed.gov/ciai/common_core_standards/faq.html).

The implementation of the Common Core Learning Standards has been controversial in New York for a number of reasons. Students were initially tested on the standards before they were a part of their instruction. Additionally, the curricula that were initially developed to align to the standards were provided only in English, creating a challenge for emergent bilingual students and their teachers. During the school year 2014–2015, more than 20% of students in New York State declined to take the test, more than four times the opt-out rate in the prior year (Harris, 2015). That same year, the passing rates for emergent bilinguals was 2.6% on the English Language Arts exam and 11% in math, compared to 31% and 36% for all students, respectively (New York State Education Department, August 2014). In spite of all these challenges, the Common Core Learning Standards drive curriculum and pedagogy in New York State.

As we stated before, very little was included in the CCSS to specifically address emergent bilingual students, who were held to these new standards. To fill this gap, New York State developed a Bilingual Common Core Initiative to support teachers in adapting their instruction. Under the leadership of Angélica Infante-Green, Lissette Colón-Collins, and Arlen Benjamin-Gómez from the New York State Department of Education, Patricia Velasco, professor at Queens College, CUNY, developed the New York State Progressions in the New Language (English) and the Home Language (the language other than English) (https://www.engageny.org/resource/new-york-state-bilingual-common-core-initiative; see also Velasco & Johnson, 2014). More than the other progression systems of WIDA and ELPA21, New York State progressions guide teachers to use their students' home language in scaffolding the standards in English, or to use English to help develop the students' home languages in bilingual and heritage language classes.

The Bilingual Common Core Initiative takes each standard, for each grade level, and presents receptive and productive performance indicators for each of five levels of language progression (entering, emerging, transitioning, expanding, and commanding). It also presents the related linguistic demands. In general, for emergent bilinguals in the entering and emerging stages, the tasks to meet the standards specifically indicate they can be reached "in the new and/or the home language." For the transitioning level, the task specifies completion "in the new language, and occasionally in the home language." But in order to be moved to the expanding or commanding levels, the student must perform the task in the language of the specific standard. The New York State New Language and Home Language progressions affirm the value of translanguaging, although only as a scaffold.

Although a curriculum is not mandated, the New York State Education Department has developed modules, or units, in the areas of English Language Arts and math that align with the CCSS. The curriculum for English Language Arts is Expeditionary Learning, whereas for math it is the NYS Common Core Math Curriculum, which are both accessible through the state's Engage NY website (https://www.engageny.org/common-core-curriculum). Whereas Expeditionary Learning is all in English, some math modules have been translated into Spanish and simplified Chinese. Both of these curricula, as well as others that are being used by schools across New York State, are developed for students who are proficient in English (and only English) in mind, with little to no accommodations for emergent bilinguals. In order to find support for emergent bilinguals, teachers are referred to optional curricular material for these modules. At the elementary level, this means going through modules that can be hundreds of pages long to identify options for emergent bilinguals, since the curriculum is somewhat prescriptive. On the other hand, the secondary-level modules seem less scripted and are significantly shorter, thus making it easier for teachers of emergent bilinguals to use.

Some lesson plans are highly scripted, giving teachers specific directions in not only how they should be teaching, but also the exact language to use with their students, as well as possible student responses. However, the State claims, "Some lessons provide detailed instructions or recommendations but it is important to note that the lessons are not scripts and rather they should be viewed as vignettes so that the reader can imagine how the class could look" (https://www.engageny.org/common-core-curriculum). How these lesson plans are being interpreted and enacted by teachers and administrators, however, may not align with the State's caveat, as teachers may stay close to the outlined plan given the density of the lessons or pressured to adhere to the curriculum by administrators. This high level of specificity leaves little space for integrating different elements of students' language and cultural practices to support content learning and language development.

Not all schools across New York State have adopted these modules. But most use some type of scripted curriculum in an effort to ensure their students' success in high-stakes tests (Menken, 2010) that are aligned to the Common Core. In preschool through 2nd grade, many New York schools have adopted Core Knowledge Language Arts. Many elementary schools have adopted ReadyGen, another scripted curriculum developed by Pearson, an educational publishing and assessment corporation with a stronghold on education across the United States.

As we will see in the case studies of Part II of this book, teachers of emergent bilinguals are often constrained by these scripted curricula. Translanguaging practices have enabled teachers to open up spaces of possibilities within the constraints of the mechanized routines of these curricula.

The CUNY-NYSIEB Project

The City University of New York (CUNY) is a system of 24 higher education institutions located throughout the five boroughs of New York City. As we said in the Introduction, the City University of New York's State Initiative for Emergent Bilinguals is a project funded by the New York State Education Department to support schools across the state in the education of their emergent bilingual students. Founding faculty members Ricardo Otheguy, Ofelia García, and Kate Menken developed the vision for CUNY-NYSIEB, starting in the summer of 2011. CUNY-NYSIEB is a collaborative project of two units at The Graduate Center, the doctoral granting institution of CUNY—the Research Institute for the Study of Language in Society (RISLUS) and the Ph.D. Program in Urban Education. We describe below the vision of the project, and also the way in which it operates. We do so to offer a blueprint as to how a state education department, a university, and schools can work collaboratively to change practices to educate bilingual students.

Foundations: Vision and Principles

The CUNY-NYSIEB vision emanates from students, their lives, and their language and cultural practices, specifically viewing and referring to them as *emergent bilinguals* (EBL). We use this term in place of others that only focus on the learning or absence of English (i.e., English language learner or limited English proficient). By using this term, we emphasize the potential of these students to become bilingual and biliterate and our vision of how bilingualism emerges. The *vision* of CUNY-NYSIEB is centered on three principles or tenets:

1. the creative emergence of individual language practices;
2. the dynamics of bilingualism; and
3. the dynamic processes of teaching and learning of emergent bilinguals (for the entire vision statement, see www.cuny-nysieb.org/our-vision).

The tenet of *creative emergence of language practices* asserts that "bilingual development is not linear, static, or able to reach an ultimate endpoint of completion; rather, it is always emergent, continuous, never-ending, and shaped by relationships with people, texts, and situations" (www.cuny-nysieb.org/our-vision). It responds to the contexts in which bilinguals perform with language. In this view, a speaker never has a language, but simply uses or performs a language. Through interactions at home and in their community, school, and other institutions, bilinguals add linguistic features to their language repertoire, and these features work together in functional interrelationship to shape the bilingual's unitary linguistic system (http://www.nysieb.ws.gc.cuny.edu/our-vision/).

The second tenet takes the stance that *bilingualism is dynamic*, not simply additive (García, 2009). The vision statement continues:

> In our global world, bilingual practices reflect the language user's adaptation to specific communicative situations and to the communicative resources provided by others. Rarely do bilingual individuals learn one language completely and then begin to acquire another. A bilingual speaker is thus never a fully balanced bilingual. Rather, what bilingual speakers do is to language bilingually, or translanguage, in order to make meaning from the complex interactions that are enacted by different human beings and texts.
>
> *(http://www.nysieb.ws.gc.cuny.edu/our-vision/)*

The final tenet—*the dynamic processes of teaching and learning*—urges educators to encourage emergent bilinguals to use their language repertoire in fluid and dynamic ways. When the language practices of bilingual individuals are viewed holistically, rather than as double (or multiple) monolingualism, the pedagogical approach to supporting them also changes. Educators must provide the affordances and opportunities that are needed for new language practices and understandings to emerge. It is when the right affordances are provided that students can construct new knowledge and understandings of, and with, language. This requires breaking down the rigidity of language separation within the classroom so that bilingual individuals can have the freedom to express themselves fully and to access content completely. In action, teachers honor this tenet when they engage bilingual children by leveraging their entire range of language practices, including those associated with English for academic purposes, as their very own. As the vision statement maintains:

> For bilingual children to successfully perform academically in English, schools support a multilingual context that recognizes the language and cultural practices of bilingual children as an important part of the school's learning community.
>
> *(http://www.nysieb.ws.gc.cuny.edu/our-vision/)*

The three tenets of the CUNY-NYSIEB vision were shaped by translanguaging theory as posed by García (2009), as well as understandings of the importance of bilingualism in education that the three founding faculty members held and that were shared by the CUNY-NYSIEB team. The vision statement informs the work that we have done with schools over the last three years, as well the resources we have produced. The vision has also shaped the two non-negotiable principles, which all participating schools have been required to observe.

Non-negotiable Principles

CUNY-NYSIEB has worked with a wide range of schools. In the beginning of the project, we worked only with schools deemed "failing" because of their emergent bilingual students' standardized test scores. Over time, CUNY-NYSIEB was also able to work with schools that are partially successful, although their emergent bilinguals continue to lag behind. Because all schools are very different, we have agreed to work with any school that signs on to the following two non-negotiable principles:

1. *Bilingualism as a resource in education*: Regardless of program structure (i.e., whether the program is called ESL or bilingual), all home language practices of emergent bilingual students are not only recognized, but also leveraged as a crucial instructional tool and, to the greatest extent possible, nurtured and developed. The entire linguistic repertoire of bilingual children is used flexibly and strategically in instruction.
2. *Support of a multilingual ecology for the whole school*: The entire range of language practices of all children and families are evident in the school's textual landscape (e.g., in signs throughout the school, in texts in the library and classrooms), as well as in the interactions of all members of the school community. That is, even in bilingual schools, attention is paid to *all* the language practices of all the students, and not just to those languages that are used as a medium of instruction, and includes all vernacular practices.

CUNY-NYSIEB's vision and principles are different from those to which many schools with bilingual students have been exposed. And yet, as we describe in the following section, we have been able to help a broad range of schools revamp the education of their emergent bilinguals.

Participating Schools

For the last four years, CUNY-NYSIEB has served 67 schools across the state. To be eligible to participate in the initiative, schools across the state have to apply and meet two criteria: (1) have an above average number of emergent bilingual students and (2) not have had emergent bilingual students meet New York State standards in English Language Arts and/or math. In addition, school leaders have to show their commitment to the multifaceted work with the CUNY-NYSIEB team.

Schools admitted to the project have been diverse in myriad ways. Some have been elementary, middle, or high schools. Some of these schools have had only English as a second/new language programs, whereas others have had different types of bilingual programs. In some schools, the majority of students have spoken Spanish, whereas other schools have been highly linguistically heterogeneous. In spite of their differences, all schools have come together to enact the CUNY-NYSIEB vision in a way that works best for their school-based context, their students, and their communities.

Collaboration and Faculty Development

The CUNY-NYSIEB team (their names appear in the Introduction, note 2) has a unique composition in that it brings together teacher education faculty in programs to prepare ESL/ENL and bilingual teachers from different campuses. Although most of the faculty is from the City University of New York (CUNY), two faculty members from the State University of New York (SUNY) have joined the team in an effort to serve the northwestern parts of the state, specifically Buffalo, Rochester, and Syracuse (for more on the structure of CUNY-NYSIEB, see García & Menken, 2015).

Prior to the inception of the project, most of the faculty members worked independently at their campuses. By engaging teacher education faculty, CUNY-NYSIEB has been able to support faculty who are often isolated in their colleges, as they collaboratively transform ideologies and practices. This has meant that the project has also had an impact on the teacher education programs in the CUNY and SUNY systems and the ways in which teacher candidates who will teach emergent bilingual students are being educated (see chapter 10). To promote dialogue among faculty members, we have met consistently every two to three weeks.

These regularly scheduled team meetings, however, do not take place among faculty in isolation, but with doctoral students in the Ph.D. program in Urban Education, who also make up the CUNY-NYSIEB team. Doctoral candidates in education become the teacher educators of the future. Involving them with teacher education faculty has meant that we are all transformed together, charting a different future for a language education field that incorporates translanguaging theory as essential for practice.

During our team meetings, we consider the best ways to support the different schools, share successes and challenges, and plan for the multilayered support that educators and students need. We have also developed materials, strategies, and ideas, as we together imagine what the education of emergent bilinguals would be like if we started from the language practices with which the students performed, instead of starting with the language legitimated in school. That is, we imagine what it would be like to educate and develop students' language performances if we started with the students' own internal language repertoire, rather than from the external definition of the language of school.

A Multilevel Approach to Working with Schools

When schools are accepted to CUNY-NYSIEB, their participation is expected on a variety of levels. First, principals and other school leaders must take part in leadership seminars at the university where the vision and non-negotiable principles are presented and deepened. Although the timing of the seminars have changed—the first year we offered the five seminars over a four-month period, and now seminars occur over the school year, with some online-blended instructional opportunities to encompass schools in upstate New York—the seminars remain the cornerstone of our project.

Engaging school principals has been a critical tenet of the project from the very beginning. Too many times, we had been in schools where we had overheard a principal tell an assistant principal in charge of "English language learners" to do something because "those are not the kids I know about." We wanted to make sure emergent bilinguals were the responsibility of everyone, starting from the school administration. Menken and Solorza (2014) have pointed out that many administrators are not formally prepared with theoretical and practical underpinnings about bilingualism, yet are required to make decisions about programming and practices for emergent bilinguals. We understood the vital role that principals play in schools, and we knew that unless we involved them from the outset, schools and practices could not be transformed.

Because we recognized the importance of distributive leadership (Hunt, 2011), we expected the principals to attend the first two seminars, and then to form an emergent bilingual leadership team in their schools made up of administrators and teachers from different programs and/or subject areas. Some schools also included family members and high school students on their leadership teams. Members of the emergent bilingual leadership team for the school and other school personnel are invited to participate in the seminars.

The topics of the leadership seminars evolve from the vision and theoretical foundations of dynamic bilingualism and translanguaging and the non-negotiable principles. From there, we move into translanguaging practices and the strategies that can be used to support a translanguaging theory in different contexts. We discuss current topics—Common Core State Standards (CCSS), assessment, and immigration—and how translanguaging theory impacts the ways in which we understand the issues and improves the education of bilingual students.

The all-day seminars are divided into two parts. In the morning, the large group is engaged in lectures that include dialogue and activities. In the afternoon, we break up into small groups and engage participants in a process of *collaborative descriptive inquiry*. Collaborative descriptive inquiry is a disciplined process of inquiry derived from the work of Patricia Carini in the Prospect Center for Education and Research in the 1990s and continued by many educators, especially Cecilia Traugh (see Carini, 2000; García & Traugh, 2002). The core of the process is, as García and Ascenzi-Moreno say (2012), the "valuing of human capacity to teach and to learn. Through disciplined description of the process of teaching and learning, a group can collaboratively make the complexity of the classroom reality more visible, and enlarge understandings that can generate ideas for collective action" (p. 7). Educators come together in small groups by grade levels, geographical area, or with their school-based CUNY-NYSIEB teams to reflect and learn from one another. They describe their practices, identify areas in which they are grappling with issues of translanguaging, and together come up with recommendations for each other, based on their own experiences.

Building off the seminars, work at each school takes place in a variety of ways. Each faculty–doctoral student team is given responsibility to work on-site with three to four schools throughout a year and a half. The CUNY-NYSIEB team supports the formation and functioning of the school-based emergent bilingual leadership teams. These teams meet regularly to plan on how to enact the non-negotiable principles of CUNY-NYSIEB and implement their school improvement plan. The CUNY-NYSIEB team provides professional development on translanguaging to teachers, especially on how to integrate translanguaging into other practices taking place in the school. For example, one school has been working to develop the ability of their emergent bilingual students to write argumentative essays. To build on this work, the CUNY-NYSIEB team in that school offered professional development on how to use translanguaging to leverage the students' linguistic resources in the writing of the essays.

The teams also work intensively with a small number of teachers, usually selected or recommended by the principal, to fine-tune their practice and eventually lead the translanguaging work with other teachers in the school. These teachers are selected because they show interest in translanguaging—regardless of their program or content area—and have been leaders, or have the potential to become leaders. They are open to taking risks and trying out different approaches to better serve their emergent bilinguals. The CUNY-NYSIEB team then coaches, models for, and co-teaches with these educators throughout the year.

Following the seminars and school-based visits of the first year, schools in the second year of the project and beyond have continued to work with CUNY-NYSIEB, although in a less intensive manner. They have been invited to attend circle of care seminars at the university that expand on topics addressed in the leadership seminars. These sessions have also allowed schools to come together in small groups, deepening the work through collaborative descriptive inquiry so they may consider ways of moving forward. The goal is for schools to take ownership of this work. Some educators and principals from earlier cohorts also return to share their successes and struggles with the newer schools.

Publications and Resources

To provide the schools an additional layer of support, materials and resources have been published by the CUNY-NYSIEB team. These publications are the result of our belief that we cannot wait for commercial publishers to come up with resources that are urgently needed. Such resources may not be attractive to commercial publishers because they will not generate substantial commercial profits. We have not only authored these publications ourselves, but we have made them available on the CUNY-NYSIEB website to be downloaded for free by anyone, anywhere in the world (www.cuny-nysieb.org). We know, for example, that beyond the U.S., our materials, and most especially our *Translanguaging Guide* (Celic & Seltzer, 2012) are being used in Canada, France, Hong Kong, India, Italy, Germany, Spain, South Africa, Sweden, and many other countries.

Our publications have grown from the needs expressed by the participants in the project. When our schools told us that they were not familiar with the languages their students spoke, we published a guide to the top languages of New York State, authored by Alex Funk (2012). We also published short and simple guides to help educators who clamored for ways to help the growing population of students with low literacy in their home languages (students with incomplete/interrupted formal education, SIFE) (García et al., 2013) and students who had been classified as English language learners for over six years ("long-term English learners, LTELs") (Ascenzi-Moreno, Kleyn & Menken, 2013).

As our project has grown, our materials have had to adjust to the educational context in which schools exist. For example, when we developed the translanguaging strategy guide (Celic & Seltzer, 2012), the Common Core State Standards had not yet been adopted by New York State. But within the year, educators were concerned that all pedagogical programs needed to be aligned with the Common Core. CUNY-NYSIEB listened, and within a year, we published a *Translanguaging in Curriculum and Instruction Guide* (Seltzer, Hesson & Woodley, 2014). This new guide took one of the curricula that New York State was supporting (Expeditionary Learning), and created a parallel curriculum to show teachers how to adapt it to the needs of their emergent bilinguals by using translanguaging strategies.

Because most of the emergent bilingual students whom our schools serve are Latinos, one of our team members, Vanessa Pérez Rosario (2014), developed and published a guide to translanguaging in Latino/a literature. Teachers need models of how translanguaging is being used in literature, and this publication filled an important void. Furthermore, it is critical for educators and students to understand that prize-winning fiction writers also translanguage (Pandey, 2015). We have also published a guide to a translanguaging pedagogy for writing (Espinosa, Ascenzi-Moreno & Vogel, 2016).

Our Transformative Action Research

The nature of CUNY-NYSIEB's work applying translanguaging theory has been transformative for professional development, educational structures, and practices in the teaching of emergent bilinguals. As researchers, we have also been interested in learning more about how translanguaging was being used and resisted by both teachers and students. Specifically, we were interested in researching the following questions:

a. What does it mean for teachers and students to take up translanguaging?
b. How, when and why is translanguaging taken up or resisted by students and teachers?
c. What does using translanguaging mean for students and teachers?

Because of the close relationship between the teachers in the schools and the CUNY-NYSIEB teams, traditional research methodologies were not appropriate for us. It made sense to do research *with* the teachers, as opposed to *on* them. We call the research approach we have taken *Transformative Action Research.*

Transformative Action Research is action research that is collaborative and participatory, taking on some of the features of Collaborative Action Research and of Participatory Action Research. As action research, it involves self-reflection to improve participants' understandings of practice (Carr & Kemmis, 1986), but it goes beyond the collaboration of teams of practitioners, as in traditional Collaborative Action Research (Burns, 1999), in that it also includes researchers as practitioners, and practitioners as researchers. Through Transformative Action Research, we have been able to share the ownership and direction of the research, as this has mirrored the type of collaboration that was already taking place between the university teams and the school teams. Furthermore, we have been able to shift the identities of the teachers and researchers. Researchers collaborated with the teachers in designing instruction (becoming teacher-researchers), and the teachers collaborated with the researchers in designing the study itself (becoming researcher-teachers). Transformative Action Research inverts the power position of researchers and teachers, as each brings their own expertise into the process, becoming co-learners. In the process, both research and teaching is transformed in ways that improve understandings and educational conditions. Thus, Transformative Action Research creates space for educators to value research on teaching and learning, and space for researchers to value the work of those involved in the act of teaching. In this way, Transformative Action Research generates knowledge as a launching pad for action in pursuit of improving socioeducational conditions and, in our case, the education of bilingual students.

Transformative Action Research also shares many of the features of Participatory Action Research (Whyte, 1991), which according to Kemmis & McTaggart (2005) is grounded in six core principles—(1) a social process, (2) participatory, (3) practical and collaborative, (4) emancipatory, (5) critical, and (6) reflective. Kemmis & McTaggart go on to explain that:

> Participatory action research aims to help people recover, and release themselves from the constraints of irrational, unproductive, unjust, and unsatisfying

> social structures that limit their self-development and self-determination. It is a process in which people explore the ways in which their practices are shaped and constrained by wider social (cultural, economic, and political) structures and consider whether they can intervene to release themselves from these constraints—or, if they cannot, how best to work within and around them to minimize the extent to which they contribute to irrationality, lack of productivity (inefficiency), injustice, and dissatisfactions (alienation) as people whose work and lives contribute to the structuring of a shared social life.
>
> *(p. 567)*

Our Transformative Action Research modifies Participatory Action Research (PAR) in ways that make it applicable to the work of teachers in schools. As PAR does, it releases teachers from traditional educational structures and practices and engages them in reflecting how those have been constrained by economic and political structures. But it goes one step further in the action itself, for it transforms how teachers within classrooms use and view language, by taking up translanguaging theory. Our research approach then was not as open as that of Participatory Action Research, for we went in with specific research questions about translanguaging, and we did not involve the practitioners in the research process from the initial design. And yet, Transformative Action Research is more dynamic and transformative than what usually is done through PAR, since it transforms teaching itself, and not just describes how it is constrained by the political economy in which it operates. We thus view our research as being liberating, uncovering the workings of the political economy in which schools operate, while also providing schools with another alternative, a different lens through which to view language education—a translanguaging lens. Although Transformative Action Research is steeped in critical theory, it *accompanies* practitioners, as practitioners accompany researchers, in a symbiotic process of teaching/learning/researching.

Transformative Action Research also mirrors some of the principles of the collaborative descriptive inquiry process used in our conversations with school staff. The voices of the teacher and researcher are put alongside each other, as expert knowledge is called into question. Through the collaboration there is a deep sense that, as Pat Carini has said, "human capacity is widely distributed" and that teachers have much to contribute to scholarly and theoretical understandings of language and education, as well as researchers have much to contribute to practice. Since expert knowledge of research or teaching is called into question, Transformative Action Research allows for grappling with the "rough edges of work" that characterize all human work. It also values long-looking and long-listening to each other. And it understands that collaborative teams can make the complexity of reality more visible and enlarge understandings that can generate ideas for collective action. Transformative Action Research became an important way to investigate how translanguaging could push back against educational and societal structures that have silenced bilingual students.

The lessons featured in Part II of this book give a glimpse of our Transformative Action Research in practice. In the case studies that follow, a single lesson or series of lessons are portrayed, although the teams made up of researcher and teacher had worked intensively over a period of six months to a year on embedding translanguaging as a normative practice in classrooms. The lessons shared in each chapter were planned collaboratively with the classroom teacher and CUNY-NYSIEB team member(s). Together they worked on opening up spaces for translanguaging within the regular curriculum, often mandated by the district. These were not artificial settings, but rather the actual classroom settings of real teachers and students working within the constraints of educational policies developed in our neoliberal era, negotiating them, and at times resisting them.

All the lessons were audio recorded, and in some cases video recorded, and transcribed to analyze the teacher's pedagogical practices, the student learning actions, and the actual language use of educators and students. The data analysis was not done by the researcher in isolation, but collaboratively as the teacher/researcher team watched or listened to the classroom discourse. The reflective dialogue that ensued became part of the data. Student work that resulted from the lessons was also collected and analyzed. Finally, students who had participated in the lessons were given a voice in the interpretation of the findings, as their own views became part of the data. In some cases, this was done as focus groups of students watched or heard parts of the lessons and discussed how using their full linguistic repertoire influenced their learning, as well as their perceptions of the language used in instruction. In other cases, the students were engaged in reflecting on the lesson they had just experienced.

An additional layer of the research process has included meetings of CUNY-NYSIEB team members at various stages of the planning and data collection process to discuss the development of the lessons, share and reflect upon each other's data, and provide feedback to one another. This collective work has deepened the collaborative approach of our research study, which is now reflected in this book.

The writing of the case studies was also a collaborative process between the CUNY-NYSIEB team member(s), who wrote the body of the chapter with the input of the teachers, and the teachers. As we will see, most of the chapters conclude with a reflective piece by the teacher, ensuring that her/his own voice is not lost in the academic writing. Our Transformative Action Research has not ended with the writing of these case studies, but is a continuous and dynamic process.

Conclusion

This chapter sets the stage for the case studies that follow. It does so by contextualizing the work that we have done within the U.S. political economy that shapes how educational structures and practices to educate bilingual students are construed. It then discusses the vision of the educational project that we have carried out and the practices that we have developed to transform the educators' theories about language and education, as well as their pedagogical practices. We end this chapter by outlining the Transformative Action Research methodology that we have followed to produce the case studies that are included in chapters 3 through 8.

Readers of Part II of this book should remember that we have been mindful to *accompany* the teachers and their students as we have worked alongside them to transform their theoretical understandings of language and bilingualism, as well as their pedagogical practices. We have not left educators of bilingual students or bilingual students behind, but have brought them forward to the important place they must occupy in the diverse world in which we live, in the superdiversity that Vertovec (2007) has taught us to recognize. This has meant that we have insisted on working with the real constraints that educators and their students face, as the policies described in this chapter take effect. Thus, as we will see, the case studies show both the potential of translanguaging to open spaces within the stark reality of the present, as well as the missed opportunities to leverage the full potential of translanguaging within those realities.

Note

1. Some states that joined the CCSS have since dropped out, including Indiana and Oklahoma. At the time of this writing, four more states are reviewing whether to continue with the adoption. In addition, more than half the states that initially signed up to the two testing consortia have abandoned them, including Massachusetts, which has the nation's best results on standardized exams.

References

Ascenzi-Moreno, L., Kleyn, T., & Menken, K. (2013). *A CUNY-NYSIEB framework for the education of 'Long Term English Learners': 6–12 grades.* New York: CUNY-NYSIEB, The Graduate Center, The City University of New York. Retrieved on March 16, 2016, from: http://www.nysieb.ws.gc.cuny.edu/files/2013/06/CUNY-NYSIEB-Framework-for-LTELs-Spring-2013-FINAL.pdf

Block, D., Gray, J., & Holborow, M. (2012). *Neoliberalism and applied linguistics.* London and New York: Routledge.

Burns, A. (1999). *Collaborative action research for English teachers.* Cambridge: Cambridge University Press.

Carini, P. (2000). Prospect's descriptive processes. In M. Himley & P. Carini (Eds.), *From another angle: Children's strengths and school standards: The Prospect Center's descriptive review of the child* (pp. 8–20). New York: Teachers College Press.

Carr, W., & Kemmis, S. (1986). *Becoming critical: Knowing through action research.* Geelong, VIC, Australia: Deakin University.

Castellanos, D. (1983). *The best of two worlds: Bilingual–bicultural education in the US.* Trenton, NJ: New Jersey State Department of Education.

Celic, C., & Seltzer, K. (2012). *Translanguaging: A CUNY-NYSIEB guide for educators.* New York: CUNY-NYSIEB, The Graduate Center, The City University of New York. Retrieved on March 16, 2016, from: http://www.nysieb.ws.gc.cuny.edu/files/2013/03/Translanguaging-Guide-March-2013.pdf

Council of Chief State School Officers (CCSSO). (2014). *English Language Proficiency Standards with correspondences to K–12 English Language Arts (ELA), mathematics and science practices, K–12 ELA Standards, & 6–12 Literacy Standards.* Retrieved on March 16, 2016, from: http://www.elpa21.org/sites/default/files/Final%204_30%20ELPA21%20Standards_1.pdf

Crawford, J. (1991). *Bilingual education: History, politics, theory, and practice.* Trenton, NJ: Crane.

Crawford, J. (2004). *Educating English learners: Language diversity in the classroom,* 5th edn. (formerly *Bilingual education: History, politics, theory, and practice*). Los Angeles: Bilingual Educational Services.

CUNY-NYSIEB. (n.d.). Our vision. Retrieved on March 16, 2016, from: http://www.nysieb.ws.gc.cuny.edu/our-vision/

Espinosa, E., Ascenzi-Moreno, L., & Vogel, S. (2016). *A translanguaging pedagogy for writing: A CUNY-NYSIEB guide for educators.* Retrieved on May 7, 2016, from: http://www.nysieb.ws.gc.cuny.edu/files/2016/04/TLG-Pedagogy-Writing-04-15-16.pdf

Funk, A. (2012). *The languages of New York State: A CUNY-NYSIEB guide for educators.* New York: CUNY-NYSIEB. Retrieved on March 16, 2016, from: www.nysieb.ws.gc.cuny.edu/files/2012/07/NYSLanguageProfiles.pdf

García, O. (2009). *Bilingual education in the 21st century: A global perspective.* Malden, MA and Oxford, UK: Wiley/Blackwell.

García, O., & Ascenzi-Moreno, L. (2012). How to use this translanguaging guide: The collaborative descriptive inquiry process. In C. Celic & K. Seltzer (Eds.), *Translanguaging: A CUNY-NYSIEB guide for educators* (pp. 7–10). New York: CUNY-NYSIEB, The Graduate Center, The City University of New York. Retrieved on March 16, 2016, from: http://www.nysieb.ws.gc.cuny.edu/files/2013/03/Translanguaging-Guide-March-2013.pdf

García, O., & Flores, N. (2013). Multilingualism and common core state standards in the US. In S. May (Ed.), *Addressing the multilingual turn: Implications for SLA, TESOL and bilingual education* (pp. 147–166). New York: Routledge.

García, O., Herrera, L., Hesson, S., & Kleyn, T. (2013). *A CUNY-NYSIEB framework for the education of emergent bilinguals with low home language literacy: 4–12 grades.* New York: CUNY-NYSIEB, The Graduate Center, The City University of New York. Retrieved on March 16, 2016, from: http://www.nysieb.ws.gc.cuny.edu/files/2013/05/CUNY-NYSIEB-Framework-for-EB-with-Low-Home-Literacy-Spring-2013-Final-Version-05-08-13.pdf

García, O., & Menken, K. (2015). Cultivating an ecology of multilingualism in schools. In B. Spolsky, O. Inbar-Lourie, & M. Tannenbaum (Eds.), *Challenges for language education and policy: Making space for people* (pp. 95–108). New York: Routledge.

García, O., & Traugh, C. (2002). Using descriptive inquiry to transform the education of linguistically diverse U.S. teachers and students. In Li Wei, J. Dewaele, & A. Housen (Eds.), *Opportunities and challenges of (societal) bilingualism* (pp. 311–328). Berlin: Walter de Gruyter.

Harris, E. (2015). 20% of New York State students opted out of standardized tests this year. *The New York Times,* August 12, 2015. Retrieved on March 16, 2016, from http://www.nytimes.com/2015/08/13/nyregion/new-york-state-students-standardized-tests.html

Harvey, D. (2004). The 'new' imperialism: Accumulation by dispossession. *Socialist Register*, 40, 63–87.
Hunt, V. (2011). Learning from success stories: Leadership structures that support dual language programs over time in New York City. *International Journal of Bilingual Education and Bilingualism*, 14(2), 187–206.
Kemmis, S., & McTaggart, R. (2005). Participatory action research: Communicative action and the public sphere. In N. K. Denzin & Y. S. Lincoln (Eds.), *The Sage handbook of qualitative research* (pp. 559–604). Thousand Oaks, CA: Sage Publications.
Kloss, H. (1977). *The American bilingual tradition*. Rowley, MA: Newbury House.
Menken, K. (2008). *English learners left behind: Standardized testing as language policy*. Bristol: Multilingual Matters.
Menken, K. (2010). No Child Left Behind and English language learners: The challenges and consequences of high-stakes testing. *Theory into Practice*, 49(2), 121–128.
Menken, K., & Solorza, C. (2014). No child left bilingual: Accountability and the elimination of bilingual education in New York City schools. *Educational Policy*, 8(1), 96–125.
National Governors Association. (2009). NGA, NCSL, CCSSO and NASBE release Accelerating the agenda: Actions to improve America's high schools. Retrieved January 13, 2009, from: http://www.nga.org/cms/home/news-room/news-releases/page_2009/col2-content/main-content-list/nga-ncsl-ccsso-and-nasbe-release.default.html
New York State Education Department. (August 2014). Measuring student progress in grades 3–8 English Language Arts and mathematics. New York: NYSED. Retrieved March 16, 2016, from: http://www.p12.nysed.gov/irs/ela-math/2014/2014Grades3-8ELAMath-final8-13-14.pdf
Pandey, A. (2015). *Monolingualism and linguistic exhibitionism in fiction*. Basingstoke: Palgrave Macmillan.
Pérez Rosario, V. (2014). *The CUNY-NYSIEB guide to translanguaging in Latino literature*. New York: CUNY-NYSIEB, The Graduate Center, The City University of New York. Retrieved on March 16, 2016, from: www.nysieb.ws.gc.cuny.edu/files/2015/02/CUNY-NYSIEB-Latino-Literature-Guide-Final-January-2015.pdf
Reyhner, J., & Eder, J. (1989). *A history of Indian education*. Billings, MT: Eastern Montana College.
Seltzer, K., Hesson, S., & Woodley, H. H. (2014). *Translanguaging in curriculum and instruction: A CUNY-NYSIEB guide for educators*. New York: CUNY-NYSIEB, The Graduate Center, The City University of New York. Retrieved on March 16, 2016, from: http://www.nysieb.ws.gc.cuny.edu/files/2014/12/Translanguaging-Guide-Curr-Inst-Final-December-2014.pdf
Velasco, P., & Johnson, H. (2014). New York State bilingual common core initiative: Creating scaffolds for the successful education of language learners. In L. Minaya-Rowe (Ed.), *Effective educational programs, practices, and policies for English learners* (pp. 29–62). Information Age Publishing (IAP).
Vertovec, S. (2007). Super-diversity and its implications. *Ethnic and Racial Studies*, 30(6), 1024–1054.
Whyte, W. F. (Ed.) (1991). *Participatory action research*. Thousand Oaks, CA: Sage Publications.
Wiley, T. G. (1996). *Literacy and language diversity in the United States*, 2nd edn. Washington, DC: Center for Applied Linguistics.

PART II

The Case Studies

3

STUDENT VOICES SHINING THROUGH

Exploring Translanguaging as a Literary Device

Ann E. Ebe with Charene Chapman-Santiago

Introduction

The students in Ms. Chapman-Santiago's 8th-grade English Language Arts class file into the room and read the Do Now questions on the board, questions about the class novel they are currently reading, *Inside Out and Back Again* (Lai, 2011). It's a story, written in verse, about a young girl who leaves Vietnam after the fall of Saigon and comes to the United States, a story to which many of the immigrant students in Ms. Chapman-Santiago's class could relate.

The class settles into their table groups made up of students speaking the same languages—Arabic, Bengali, French, Fulani, Haitian Creole, and Spanish. On their tables, they find a sheet with the same questions that are on the board translated into their home languages. The Do Now reads: *The author uses a lot of vocabulary words in Vietnamese in this book. Explain your thoughts as to why she didn't use all English words. How are you able to infer the meaning of the Vietnamese words?* The students talk to their same language peers about these questions for just a few minutes. Some groups talk in their home language, while others discuss the questions in English. Ms. Chapman-Santiago then directs students to write a response to these questions in their journals. Most students write their responses in English.

The fluid movement between English and students' home languages described above is what García (2009) describes as translanguaging. Translanguaging is the communicative norm for the multilingual students in this classroom. This chapter examines how Ms. Chapman-Santiago engaged her students in a study of translanguaging as a literary device using a culturally relevant class novel.

School and Community Context

The 8th-grade English Language Arts lesson described in this chapter took place in a diverse middle school in New York City. The school is home to just over

300 students from 21 countries. The school is a microcosm of the community whose residents are predominantly African and Caribbean. Close to one-fourth of the student body have been formally identified as "English language learners" (ELLs). The students in the school speak nine different languages. The largest single language group is Spanish; Haitian Creole and Fulani follow closely. Students in the school also speak French, Arabic, Bengali, Mandinka, Soninke, and Twi.

Due to rezoning, the school's student population has changed dramatically over the past few years, from predominantly Spanish-speaking to the current diversity of languages. In the past, the school was able to provide Spanish/English bilingual education. The school's programming for emergent bilinguals (EBL) has now shifted to an English as a second language (ESL) push-in model of support. In this model, ESL teachers work with content area teachers in their classrooms to support emergent bilingual students who speak a variety of languages.

Many of the students come to this school with challenges. A number of the emergent bilinguals have been classified as students with incomplete or interrupted formal education (SIFE). Several of these students come from war-torn regions of West Africa. The school's principal reported that many of the students are undocumented. In addition, close to 30 of the students are homeless and live in shelters (Interview with Principal, 2014). While many of the students have come to the school from challenging situations, teachers like Ms. Chapman-Santiago have gotten to know their students well in order to tailor the curriculum to build on the backgrounds, knowledge, and strengths they bring to the classroom.

Classroom Context

The lesson explored in this chapter took place in Ms. Chapman-Santiago's 8th-grade English Language Arts (ELA) class. Twenty-one students participated in the lesson, 18 of whom were designated as English language learners. The class runs as a double period so students are together for an hour and a half. The walls of the classroom provide a colorful, print-rich environment for the students. Lesson objectives are neatly written on chart paper along with the Common Core State Standards (CCSS) to which they align. Student work, primarily illustrated essays and responses to literature, fills up most available wall space. Teacher-made anchor charts are also displayed around the room. These charts provide students a record of key strategies and processes for reading and writing that have been reviewed in previous lessons. A multilingual word wall covers a large bulletin board in the back of the room. This word wall includes key vocabulary for the current unit of study. The vocabulary words are written by students on sentence strips in English and in the home languages represented in the class. There is an interactive whiteboard at the front of the room that is used for each lesson. Desks are clustered together forming six groups. These groups create a "U" shape around the perimeter of the classroom.

In addition to English, six languages are spoken by the students in this class. Table 1 lists the student names (pseudonyms) and their self-reported home languages.

TABLE 3.1 Students in Chapman-Santiago's Class and Home Languages

*Students**	*Home Language*
Yushua	Arabic
Haseeb	Arabic
Rajesh	Bengali
Kemar	English
Daniel	English
Dante	English
Laura	French
Ciel	French
Boubacar	Fulani
Mamadou	Fulani and French
Lisette	Haitian Creole
Staisy	Haitian Creole
Joseph	Haitian Creole and French
Amaury	Haitian Creole and French
Abella	Haitian Creole and French
Jasmin	Spanish
Benjamin	Spanish
Ronaldo	Spanish
Mark	Spanish
Carla	Spanish
Christian	Spanish

*Names are pseudonyms.

As outlined in Table 3.1, in addition to speaking English, two students speak Arabic, one student speaks Bengali, three students speak English only, two students speak French, one student speaks Fulani, one student speaks both Fulani and French, two students speak Haitian Creole, three students speak both French and Haitian Creole, and six students speak Spanish. Ms. Chapman-Santiago, a Jamaican American, is an experienced educator who has been teaching at the school for the past 11 years. She has made an effort to learn at least a few words in each of her student's home languages. The lesson described below came from the all-English curriculum adopted by the school. However, Ms. Chapman-Santiago provides multiple opportunities for students to use their home languages as they work. To help facilitate this, students sit in home language groups for this lesson.

The Lesson and Background

As briefly described in the introduction, the 8th-grade class had been reading the novel *Inside Out and Back Again* (Lai, 2011). Ms. Chapman-Santiago had been following and adapting lessons for teaching this required text from the

Common Core aligned Expeditionary Learning curriculum used by the school (EngageNY, 2014). This novel was of particular interest and culturally relevant for her class of 8th graders. While the students in the class were not Vietnamese, like the main character, most were immigrants or had immediate family who had recently moved to the United States.

Research supports the importance of providing students, especially emergent bilinguals, with culturally relevant texts (Faggella-Luby, Ware & Capozzoli, 2009; Freeman, Freeman, Soto & Ebe, 2016; Herrera, Perez & Escamilla, 2015; Larrotta & Yamamura, 2011; Ma'ayan, 2010). Defined as books to which readers can connect (Freeman, Freeman & Freeman, 2003), culturally relevant books draw on students' background knowledge and experiences. Studies show that students demonstrate greater engagement, comprehension, and proficiency when reading culturally relevant texts (Ebe, 2010, 2012, 2015; Goldenberg, 2013; Rodríguez, 2014).

Ms. Chapman-Santiago understands the importance of using culturally relevant texts to support her students' literacy development as well as to engage them. She also knows that her students are more engaged when the lessons she prepares around these texts include opportunities for them to make connections to what they are reading. Ms. Chapman-Santiago worked with CUNY-NYSIEB team members Ivana Espinet and the author of this chapter, Ann Ebe, to develop a lesson that would explore how the author of the poem used translanguaging in her writing as a literary device while, at the same time, facilitating the students' own use of translanguaging during their study of the novel and in their writing.

When writing in one language, bilingual writers often include words from what others consider their other language as a way to express their creativity (Albakry & Hancock, 2008). In the scholarly literature, this explicit use of the other language for literary purposes is referred to as code-switching. In his article on bilingual code-switching in English poetry, Barnes (2011) points out that very few studies examine code-switching in written texts but that "code-switching has played a limited but significant role as a literary device throughout the long tradition of English literature, from the days of Chaucer and Wyatt to those of Eliot and Pound" (p. 23). Barnes argues that English poetry has been greatly enriched by the inclusion of other languages and that there should be further study of code-switching as a literary device.

In the 21st century, writers have increasingly released features from their entire language repertoire to express themselves, as readers have become more accustomed to the dynamics and complexity of bilingualism. No longer constrained by choice of a national language, bilingual literary writers have started contributing to the translanguaging epistemological shift, treating their entire language repertoire as a whole. Fu (2009), for example, writes about bilingual expression. She explains that writers may choose to mix languages "for convenience, for accuracy, or for cultural expressions" (p. 52). Recently, Dumitrescu

(2014) has written about the bilingual writing of Dominican-American author Junot Díaz:

> Díaz does not limit himself to the use of a sustained alternation between Spanish and English, but rather, through congruent lexicalization, he produces a sort of code-fusion which is reflective of the heteroglossic practices of postcolonial bi- and multilingual societies, known as *translanguaging.*
>
> *(p. 399, emphasis in original)*

Hélot (2014) has also explored translanguaging in the literary works of bilingual authors. In her work with student teachers, this exploration has helped challenge the notion of keeping the languages of bilinguals separate. After examining how select bilingual authors creatively translanguage in their writing, Hélot encouraged her trainee teachers to also encourage their students to do the same:

> I wanted to make bilingual trainee teachers aware of new ways of understanding bilinguals' experiences and engagement with the world. Because translingual authors break with the traditional ideological barriers that separate languages, new bilingual literary voices emerge, thus I hoped trainee teachers would understand the creative dimension of translanguaging and reflect upon new possibilites in bilingual pedagogy.
>
> *(p. 30)*

The lesson described in this chapter further explores bilingual ways of writing, focusing not on the change of national languages as codes, but as the creative use of all the language features of the bilingual writers' repertoire. We use the term translanguaging to refer to the creative writing act from the perspective of the bilingual writer.

The English Language Arts lesson detailed below involved reading and analyzing a poem from the class novel. Students learned about the form of poetry used and analyzed the use of Vietnamese and English as the author, Thanhha Lai, translanguaged in her writing. Following this study of the author's craft, students wrote their own poems using translanguaging as a literary device. The lesson was video recorded. Following the lesson, Ms. Chapman-Santiago watched the recording with Ebe and reflected on the lesson. A focus group of students also reflected on the lesson and discussed their experiences with the homework, which involved sharing and editing their poems with their families.

Lesson Design and Moves

In prior lessons, Ms. Chapman-Santiago's students had already begun reading and discussing the novel and understanding the historical context around the story. For this lesson, the students would be focused on a poem from the novel, *1975: Year of the Cat*, about New Year's Day in Vietnam. The summary of the lesson from the curriculum guide, which was designed for the study of this poem, is as follows:

> In this lesson, students will read *1975: Year of the Cat* by Thanhha Lai and use text-based inferences to support analysis of the poem. Students will then complete a short writing task asking them to show evidence of themes from the poem and make predictions as to what will happen next. Finally, students will work in groups to decipher unknown words and phrases in the poem.
>
> *(EngageNY, 2014, p. 1)*

The "Do Now": Exploring Translanguaging in Writing

With our focus on translanguaging, we were immediately drawn to the idea of deciphering unknown words and phrases in the poem. However, rather than analyzing words in English, as suggested in the original plan, we decided to have the students think about why the author included some words in Vietnamese. By considering the author's use of translanguaging as a literary device, students could reflect on why Lai chose to use Vietnamese words in certain places in her novel. The students could also explore what she did to make the Vietnamese words comprehensible in her writing.

We began the lesson with a Do Now (see Figure 3.1) to explore these questions. As the name suggests, a Do Now is typically a short activity, given at the beginning of a class session, designed to get students to interact with the content immediately. We thought it would be helpful to provide translations of the questions in the student's home languages on a handout so that all students would have immediate access to what they were to do at the start of class. Ms. Chapman does not read and write her student's home languages, so she used an online translator website to produce this handout and others for the lesson. While translations using this website are far from perfect, they provide the students with at least a rough translation to start and guide their discussions.

Most students settled into the Do Now activity right away. Students made use of the home language translations of the questions to get their discussions going. While the group conversations occurred in the student's home languages and English, all but two of the individual responses written in the journals were in English. Jasmin, who had joined the class from El Salvador only six months earlier, wrote in Spanish, and Rajesh, who had been in the United States for only four months, wrote notes in Bengali and English. Following the writing time, students were invited to share their responses orally with the class. Three students volunteered to read their journal entries. Abella stood to read: "I think the author didn't use all English words because maybe she wanted to show off her native language. I was able to determine the Vietnamese words because the sentences after showed the meaning." Christian then stood and read from his journal: "The author used not all English words because she wanted to express

Name: ____________________ January 15, 2014
EFMS – 352 Classes 812

DO NOW: In your journal –
The author uses a lot of vocabulary words in Vietnamese in this book.

1. ***Explain your thoughts as to why she didn't use all English words.***
2. ***How are you able to infer the meaning of the Vietnamese words?***

SPANISH

HACER AHORA: En su diario -
El autor utiliza una gran cantidad de vocabulario nativo de Vietnam.
1. Explique sus pensamientos sobre por qué ella no escribió todas las palabras en inglés.
2. ¿Cómo eres capaz de inferir el significado de las palabras vietnamitas?

FRENCH

FAIRE MAINTENANT: Dans votre journal -
L'auteur utilise beaucoup de vocabulaire indigène au Vietnam.
1. Expliquez vos pensées pour expliquer pourquoi elle n'a pas écrit tous les mots en anglais.
2. Comment êtes-vous en mesure de déduire le sens des mots vietnamiens?

ARABIC

DO الآن: في دفتر يومياتك -
يستخدم الكاتب الكثير من المفردات الأصلي إلى فيتنام.
1. اشرح أفكارك ل ماذا لم أكتب كل من الكلمات في اللغة الإنجليزية.
2. كيف حالك قادرة على استنتاج المعنى من الكلمات الفيتنامية؟

HAITIAN CREOLE

Fè kounye a: Nan jounal ou, -
Otè a sèvi ak yon anpil nan vokabilè natif natal nan Vyetnam.
1. Eksplike panse ou kòm poukisa li pa t ' ekri tout nan mo sa yo nan lang angle.
2. Ki jan ou kapab fè dégager siyifikasyon an nan mo sa yo Vyetnamyen?

BENGALI

এখন না: আপনার জার্নাল ইন -
লেখক ভিয়েতনাম নেটিভ শব্দভান্ডার অনেক ব্যবহার করে.
1. তিনি ইংরেজি শব্দের সমস্ত লিখুন না কেন আপনার চিন্তা ব্যাখ্যা করুন.
2. আপনি কিভাবে ভিয়েতনামিজ শব্দের অর্থ আবিষ্কার করতে পারবেন?

FIGURE 3.1 "Do Now" Handout

her feelings. I can determine the Vietnamese words by reading before and after the words it shows the meaning." Haseeb shared last. While he had discussed the questions in Arabic with a partner, he wanted to share his thoughts on the first question in English. Ms. Chapman-Santiago encouraged him and assisted some during his response: "She wanted to use Vietnamese to explain her culture."

These students provided three different reasons for translanguaging in literature: to *show off* the home language, to *express feelings*, and to *explain or share about an author's culture.* Abella and Christian both had similar responses about being able to make sense of the words written in Vietnamese by drawing on context clues provided in the sentences around the word.

Understanding Free Verse Narrative Poetry

In addition to analyzing the use of translanguaging in the poem, we also thought it would be important for the students to understand the type of poetry used in the book. With this in mind, we developed the following ELA content objective: *Students will build knowledge and understanding about the elements or components of a narrative free verse poem.* Because Ms. Chapman-Santiago is required by the school administration to post the content objectives for her lessons, she displays them on the interactive whiteboard in her students' multiple home languages for each class session.

Following the sharing of the Do Now, a volunteer was invited to read the lesson objective aloud from the interactive whiteboard. Rajesh stood and, without prompting, read the objective aloud first in Bengali and then in English. Ms. Chapman-Santiago then explained that they would read a definition of this type of poetry and asked for a volunteer to read from the interactive whiteboard. The definition was also provided in multiple languages through the assistance of online translators. Laura stood and read the definition in French first. Before reading the English translation she explained to the class that "In English it means that . . ." and then continued on to read through the definition in English.

To ensure that students were making sense of the definition, Ms. Chapman-Santiago called on Dante to share his interpretation of the definition. Dante, a monolingual English speaker, explained that with free verse, "basically you don't have to rhyme, you can just say what you feel." Mamadou, who had come from Guinea, then asked what a rhyme was and a brief discussion including examples of rhyming words ensued.

Shared Reading

After reading and briefly discussing the definition of free verse poetry, students further developed their understanding of this form by engaging in a shared reading of the poem led by Ms. Chapman-Santiago. Allen (2002), who writes extensively about using shared reading with middle school students, describes this instructional structure as "eyes past print" with a fluent reader's voice support. Having students listen to the poem being read by Ms. Chapman-Santiago as they follow along in their copies of the novel allows them to focus on the flow of the language in the poem. The scaffolding provided through shared reading also allows students to focus on comprehending the poem rather than having to decode the text during this first read through.

Analyzing and Connecting to the Text

Following the shared reading, students were given three minutes in groups to discuss the elements that made the poem a free verse narrative. Following the group discussions in English and home languages, students were asked to share their thoughts with the class. Yushua shared that "a narrative is a story and that the author was telling about her life." Christian shared that the story was "like a diary where the author told about her life using free verse."

Students were also asked to think about why the author used free verse rather than other forms of poetry for this book. Daniel shared:

> Author Lai used a free verse poem because she wanted to explain her cultural and her countries' feelings because you cannot rhyme with Tết [Vietnamese New Year] or any of the other words she used in her own language. She used names in Vietnamese and if she was trying to rhyme, it would stop the flow of what she was writing.

Abella then shared:

> I think that the author uses a free verse poem rather than other forms of poetry because with free verse she doesn't have to worry about rhyming all her Japanese words. Oh sorry! Her Vietnamese words, and also like to put more feeling in it and just making it different from other novels.

After this analysis of the poetry form, students were invited to make connections to the content of the poem by sharing their own New Year's traditions—a central aspect of the poem they read—with their groups. Students were invited to do this using their entire language repertoire. As Ms. Chapman-Santiago explained these instructions, she shared that her family comes from Jamaica where one New Year's tradition is to set off fireworks.

As soon as Ms. Chapman-Santiago finished giving instructions, the room was abuzz with sharing. The students were eager to talk about their New Year's traditions. Students shared in English and in their home languages. When it was time to share out with the class, several eager hands went up. Staisy shared that in her country, Haiti, "I call my friends and family to eat. Like the food that we do is chicken, poisson [fish]. And after midnight we just throw fireworks." Mamadou shared with the class next. "I'm from Guinea and when the holiday come, we buy a cow and we give to people who don't have something to eat, we give to them." When Jasmin was called to share, she consulted with Christian who told Ms. Chapman-Santiago that she wanted to "say it in Spanish." Ms. Chapman-Santiago encouraged this, so Jasmin stood and shared:

> En mi país de El Salvador, nosotros nos reunimos cada año con familia y entre amigos. Hacemos diferentes tipos de comida. Hay música, música

> navideña y cualquier tipo de música. Las personas o familiares que quieren bailar, pues bailan y los demás solo se quedan platicando, contando cosas. Y allá se hace la tradición de levantar también cohetes, para hacer más bonita la noche. Y al igual que, como estaba comentando a mi compañero, que se quedan hasta la medianoche o algunos se quedan hasta el siguiente día.

Once Jasmin finished sharing, Christian was asked to translate what she had said for the class. Christian stood and explained,

> She gets together with her family members and she sits around with them and they talk about stuff and sometimes they put music and they usually stay up until midnight or they just wait until the sunrise. And at midnight when it's New Year's time, to make the night more beautiful, they throw fireworks.

Haseeb was the last to share, as Ms. Chapman-Santiago wanted to keep the lesson moving along. Haseeb shared, "Well I come from Yemen and back home we eat, we cut the cows, and after that the kids play and the big kids go play soccer and stuff like this. In the night we get together and dance and after that everyone goes to sleep."

Independent Writing Following the Model

Once students had finished sharing their New Year's traditions, Ms. Chapman-Santiago reviewed the writing assignment. The students were to create their own New Year's poem using *The Year of the Cat* as a model. Like the author, the students were to use both English and their home languages in the poem. They were encouraged to think carefully about which words they might want to write in their home language, keeping in mind the author's translanguaging choices as well as the ways she had made the Vietnamese words understandable. The students were encouraged to use some of the same strategies the author used in their own writing. Through this reading/writing connection, students were working toward the following two translanguaging objectives: (1) Students will discuss how the author uses translanguaging in her poem and will use the poem as a model for creating their own poems using translanguaging as a literary device, and (2) Students will be able to identify key words and phrases to write in their home language to enhance their poems.

Ms. Chapman-Santiago provided each student a handout (see Figure 3.2) that had two levels of writing scaffolds on it. Students could select which scaffold to use. Students who were less proficient in English (Tier III) were encouraged to use the more detailed sentence frames where students could basically fill in the blanks to form the first draft of their poem. More advanced students (Tier II) could use the simple descriptions of what each stanza of their poem could include.

Name: ____________________

EFMS – 352

January 15, 2014

Classes 812

Free verse is an open form of poetry. It does not use consistent meter patterns, rhyme, or any other musical pattern. It thus tends to follow the rhythm of natural speech.

Emergent Bilinguals Tier 3 - This is just a template to get you started. Use "1975: Year of the Cat" as a model for your personal poem. Also, you may use as much of your home language as desired. You may use Google Translate where necessary.

Title_________

Stanza 1

Today is __________

The first day

Of___________

Stanza 2

Every _________

We eat ____

We wear_____

Stanza 3

In our family

(insert traditions)

(insert traditions)

Stanza 4

Everyone in my country

(insert traditions)

(insert traditions)

Stanza 5

Things we can do

(insert traditions)

Things we cannot do

(insert traditions)

Stanzas 6 - 10

Discuss the best or the worst experience you have had on this holiday

(Continued)

FIGURE 3.2 Writing Scaffolds for New Year's Poem

Name: ____________________ January 15, 2014
EFMS – 352 Classes 812

Free verse is an open form of poetry. It does not use consistent meter patterns, rhyme, or any other musical pattern. It thus tends to follow the rhythm of natural speech.

Emergent Bilinguals Tier 2 - This is just a template to get you started. Use "1975: Year of the Cat" as a model for your personal free verse poem. Also, you may use as much of your home language as desired. You may use Google Translate where necessary.

Title ____________________

Stanza 1	Describe your holiday using your home language
Stanza 2	Discuss what you eat and whether you dress in special clothes
Stanza 3	Discuss your traditions
Stanza 4	Discuss what people do and say
Stanza 5	Describe things you can and cannot do
Stanzas 6 -10	Discuss the best or the worst experience you have had on this holiday

FIGURE 3.2 (Continued)

In addition to this writing scaffold, students had English/home language dictionaries at their tables. With the exception of Rajesh, the only Bengali speaker in the class, students had home language partners to talk with, as they worked on their poems. At the beginning of the writing period, Ms. Chapman-Santiago helped Rajesh get set up with a laptop he could use for translation. A second laptop was also set up for translation work and was made available for all students to use. In addition, students had their novels opened to the poem and out on their desks as a model to refer to as they began writing.

After going over the instructions for writing their poems, students were asked to take a moment to discuss the instructions in their groups so that they could ask any questions they might have about the assignment. Students then talked in their groups using English and their home languages. Throughout the writing time, Ms. Chapman-Santiago circulated among the groups to answer questions, listen to students' ideas for writing or initial drafts, and provide feedback.

Group Share and Review of the Homework

After 20 minutes of writing time, Ms. Chapman-Santiago brought the class back together so that students could share some of their initial New Year's poem drafts. Laura volunteered to share her poem first. She stood and read:

Today is trente et un
The first day of
Bonne Année.

Every Bonne Année
we eat chicken, poisson,
frite poulet, igname etc. . . .

We wear nice clothes like
robe, pantalon, habit.

In our family we
pray and we eat.
After eat we dancing,
and have fun.

Next Yushua shared his first draft with the class. He had used the more structured sentence frames to start his writing. In Figure 3.3, the original version is on the left. In the right column, I provide a typed version.

While Laura included many words in French in her poem, Yushua described New Year in Yemen primarily using English. However, in his first draft, he did include one word in Arabic, the traditional dish aseed, or "eseyd," as he spelled it. It is interesting to note that he provided a transliteration of this word rather than writing using Arabic script.

Abella, Joseph, Mamadou, and Christian all shared their poems as well. After each student shared, the class clapped to celebrate and encourage their efforts. Once each of these drafts was shared with the class, Ms. Chapman-Santiago reviewed the homework. Students were asked to continue writing and editing the poems using a dictionary and/or thesaurus as needed to prepare their poems for publication. Ms. Chapman-Santiago asked students to bring a second draft of their poems back to school the next day. She encouraged the class to share their poems with their families, to check the vocabulary they used in their home languages, and to see if their families had additional ideas to add. An excerpt from Yushua's second draft of his poem, which was completed as homework, is shown in Figure 3.4. This version includes some writing in Arabic script, possibly as a result of the home language support he received from his family.

Exit Slip

To reflect on the lesson, students were given two questions to answer before dismissal:

1. For today's lesson you read, talked, and wrote in your two languages. How did that affect your participation and learning?
2. How does using both languages in class make you feel?

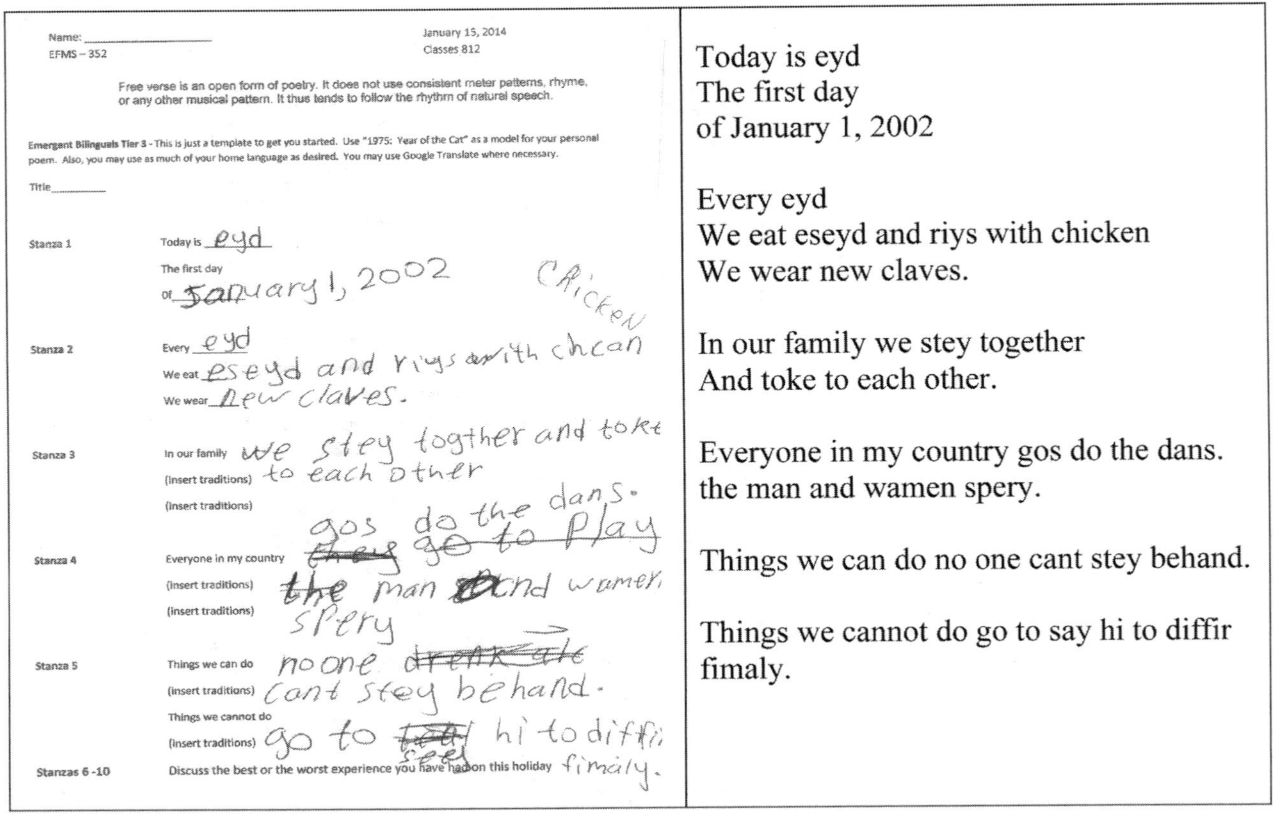

Name: ____________
EFMS – 352

January 15, 2014
Classes 812

Free verse is an open form of poetry. It does not use consistent meter patterns, rhyme, or any other musical pattern. It thus tends to follow the rhythm of natural speech.

Emergent Bilinguals Tier 3 - This is just a template to get you started. Use "1975: Year of the Cat" as a model for your personal poem. Also, you may use as much of your home language as desired. You may use Google Translate where necessary.

Title______

Stanza 1 — Today is eyd
The first day
of January 1, 2002 Chicken

Stanza 2 — Every eyd
We eat eseyd and riys ~~an~~ with chcan
We wear new claves.

Stanza 3 — In our family we stey togther and toke
(insert traditions) to each other
(insert traditions)

Stanza 4 — Everyone in my country gos ~~they~~ do the ~~go to Play~~ dans.
(insert traditions) ~~the~~ man ~~a~~ and wamen
(insert traditions) spery

Stanza 5 — Things we can do no one ~~drenk ate~~
(insert traditions) cant stey behand.
Things we cannot do
(insert traditions) go to ~~tell~~ seel hi to diffi
Stanzas 6 -10 — Discuss the best or the worst experience you have had on this holiday fimaly.

Today is eyd
The first day
of January 1, 2002

Every eyd
We eat eseyd and riys with chicken
We wear new claves.

In our family we stey together
And toke to each other.

Everyone in my country gos do the dans.
the man and wamen spery.

Things we can do no one cant stey behand.

Things we cannot do go to say hi to diffir
fimaly.

FIGURE 3.3 First Draft of Yushua's Poem

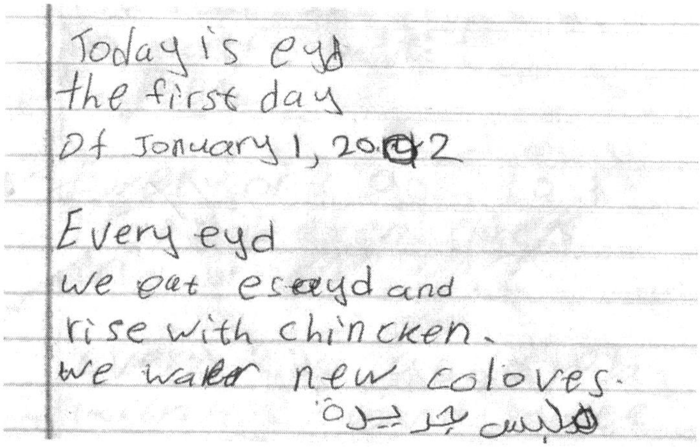

FIGURE 3.4 Second Draft Excerpt from Yushua's Poem

After a brief time for writing, students were invited to share their responses orally. The researchers also led the class in a short discussion to reflect on the lesson.

Taking Up Translanguaging

The layers of translanguaging that occurred in this lesson allow us to examine translanguaging both as a scaffold for learning *and* as transformative practice. On one level, translanguaging is used as a scaffold. The school-adopted curriculum was adapted to include translanguaging. This helped students access what was originally an all-English curriculum. For example, at the beginning of the lesson students were provided translations of the Do Now questions in order to jump right into the content. While this scaffold was provided by the teacher, students then engaged in discussions that flowed between English and their home languages as multilinguals do naturally, further building a linguistically inclusive classroom environment. In both cases, translanguaging engaged students in the content and enhanced their learning. As García, Johnson, and Seltzer (2016) point out:

> The translanguaging design is not a simple scaffold for the kinds of languaging and understandings that the school deems valuable. Instead, students' language practices and ways of knowing are seen as both informing *and* informed by the classroom.
>
> *(p. 28, emphasis in original)*

While translanguaging can certainly be leveraged strategically as a tool, it also must be recognized as the communicative norm for these multilingual students and their communities. Below I further explore moments in the lesson in which translanguaging was used as a scaffold and moments where translanguaging was evident as the students' discursive norm. I conclude with a discussion of how

Ms. Chapman-Santiago's strategic planning for translanguaging as a scaffold, over time, has contributed toward creating a classroom environment in which translanguaging has now become the comfortable, communicative norm for this multilingual group of students.

Translanguaging as a Scaffold and as the Communicative Classroom Norm

In our initial planning of this lesson, a major focus was translanguaging as a scaffold. We were thinking about translanguaging as a strategy to help make the all-English curriculum accessible for this multilingual group of 8th graders with a variety of language and literacy proficiencies. In other words, translanguaging was a way for us to differentiate the instruction. This type of differentiation was not new to Ms. Chapman-Santiago, who purposefully organized students into language groups for many of her lessons. The multilingual word wall displayed in the classroom, which she created and updated with her students throughout the year, is another strategic support Ms. Chapman-Santiago put into place when the year began.

As our research team reflected together on our lesson plan, as well as on the video of the lesson, we identified several moments that involved strategically planned scaffolds for engaging students in translanguaging in order to access the curriculum. We found that translanguaging happened across a variety of literacy modes—reading, writing, listening, and speaking—and that it involved the class members in various ways (Figure 3.5).

When we began our work supporting emergent bilinguals in schools, an early concern teachers had about translanguaging was that it would be a great deal of work for the teacher. There was the misconception that in schools, translanguaging primarily involved teachers providing their students with translations of class materials. While this can be one way to facilitate translanguaging, we see that translanguaging can occur in a variety of ways.

Providing students the Do Now questions in multiple languages involved a *teacher-to-student* translanguaging action that engaged students in reading. Next, giving students time to talk about these questions in groups, where translanguaging was welcomed and encouraged, involved listening and speaking and

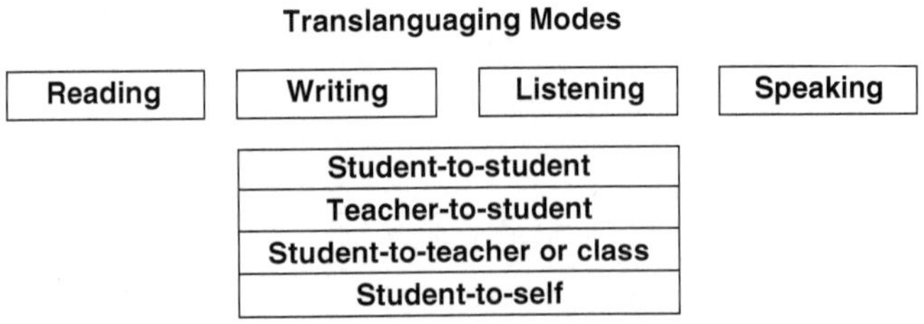

FIGURE 3.5 Translanguaging Modes

was a *student-to-student* interaction. Once language grouping is established, this type of translanguaging takes little effort for teachers to facilitate. In the case of this lesson, having this time for students to talk in English and their home languages ensured that all students engaged with the content. While Ms. Chapman-Santiago encouraged students to use their language of choice, students did not just stick with one language as they worked in their groups. Their language use varied according to the discussion question and the interactions with classmates at their tables. Finally, the students wrote their responses to the questions in their journals, and most wrote in English. Creating the journal entries involved *student-to-self* translanguaging interaction as students took ideas they had discussed bilingually and wrote them in English.

Students engaged in four literacy modes—reading, writing, listening, and speaking. In addition, the translanguaging interactions involved a variety of modes—teacher-to-student, student-to-student, and student-to-self. Recognizing the various translanguaging modes in the lesson helps us further understand that translanguaging in the classroom goes beyond being a scaffold for learning provided solely by teachers.

The Do Now plan began with strategic translanguaging scaffolds for accessing the content. Students were provided translations of the discussion questions and Ms. Chapman-Santiago planned for student groups to discuss the questions in their home languages. However, this strategic planning for translanguaging evolved into translanguaging as the discursive norm of the students in the class. This was evident as groups did not use only their home languages to discuss the questions, but rather engaged in translanguaging in what García (2009) refers to as a dynamic process of performing bilingually and drawing on their entire linguistic repertoire. The bilingual students in the class moved fluidly between English and their home languages as it made sense for engaging in this group work with their classmates. For some students, their linguistic repertoire enabled them to move from their home-language conversations into writing in English. Others, with emerging English proficiency, wrote their responses in their home languages or bilingually.

Translanguaging as a Literary Device

Layers of translanguaging occurred in this lesson. Students analyzed translanguaging in order to explore the author's use of multiple languages in her novel. Through the analysis of translanguaging as a literary device in this work of literature, Ms. Chapman-Santiago was helping to position translanguaging as a legitimate form of communication for her multilingual students. This lesson, therefore, provided further validation for translanguaging as the discursive norm in the classroom.

An analysis of the students' written responses to the Do Now questions revealed three major reasons for the author's use of Vietnamese in her writing. The first reason identified by the students was to *show off* the home language, the second was to *express her feelings,* and the third was to *explain or share about her culture.* The students were able to provide thoughtful responses to this question that align to what Pérez Rosario (2014) has identified as some of the key reasons Latino authors use translanguaging in their work.

Using these reasons for translanguaging as a starting point, along with the model of the New Year's poem provided in the novel, the students were able to write their own poems that incorporated translanguaging as a literary device. Seventeen of the 21 students used English and an additional language in their poems. Jasmin wrote her first draft completely in Spanish and three students wrote their poems only using English. Of the students who wrote their poems bilingually, many used their home language for writing "New Year" following the author's model of using the word Tết. Students also wrote words for food and clothing in their home languages.

As seen in in the first draft of Yushua's poem (Figure 3.3), which was written in class, Yushua wrote the name of the traditional dish eseyd (his spelling) in Arabic. However, he did not include any Arabic script in his poem. In contrast, his second draft, which was written as homework, did include ملابس جديدة [new clothes] written in Arabic script under the words in English (see Figure 3.4). This was the only poem from the class that included a writing system other than the Roman script. Haseeb did not use Arabic script in his poem, and Rajesh did not use Bengali script. While students were not asked about this specifically during the study, perhaps these students perceived that the use of English transliterations of Arabic or Bengali words, rather than using a different script, would make it easier for their teacher and classmates to read their poetry.

The three students in the class who identified themselves as being English monolinguals did not use translanguaging in their writing. However, they were able to make their poems unique by writing about their cultural traditions. Writing about New Year, a universal theme, facilitated making cultural connections. Dante, for example, wrote about always watching the ball drop in Times Square, a famous New York tradition for his family. Daniel wrote about playing Ludi, a game from his family's home country of Jamaica.

Translanguaging to Support Home-School Connections

Students were given time to work on their poems in class and their homework assignment was to continue writing and editing their poems at home. Ms. Chapman-Santiago encouraged students to share their poems with their families. This was an assignment where the immigrant class parents, many with beginning English proficiency, could help their children with their English Language Arts homework. Students could draw on their families' funds of knowledge (González, Moll & Amanti, 2005) to learn more about traditions from their home countries. As families discuss these traditions using the home language, students could select key words or phrases from the home language to incorporate into their poems.

A few days after the lesson, the research team called together a group of six emergent bilingual students who had participated in the lesson to discuss their experiences with the homework. Our focus question for the group was "Did you talk about your poem with anyone at home?" We used the online translator to have the questions available in writing in the student's home languages as well. Rajesh was quick to correct the Bengali translation, which indicated to us that he was able to use both the English and Bengali versions of the question to make sense of what we were asking.

Students talked about enjoying the writing of the poem and sharing their cultural traditions, but only half of the students in this focus group had shared their poems at home. Perhaps it should not be surprising that these middle-school-aged students preferred to work independently rather than with their families. The three students who did share their work at home confirmed that they had bilingual conversations where they translanguaged as they talked about their poems with their parents. Rajesh, whose father is an English teacher, spoke about having his father correct the English part of his poem. He was particularly concerned about practicing his English and the importance of developing English, especially as this was an assignment for an English Language Arts class. However, Rajesh also talked about his father being interested in the content of the poem as well.

Mamadou and Jasmin also talked about sharing their poems with their parents. Jasmin stated that she just read hers to her mother, who liked it. Jasmin had written her first draft all in Spanish. Because she was given the flexibility in class to do this, her mother, a monolingual Spanish speaker, was able to participate in Jasmin's learning by hearing and proving positive feedback on her schoolwork. Mamadou said he asked his parents for more information about New Year's traditions in Guinea. He wanted to learn more about his family's traditions in order to incorporate that information into his poem. His first draft written in class included information about buying a cow, but after speaking to his parents, Mamadou added the tradition of going to pray on New Year's morning.

There were three aspects of this homework assignment that made it conducive to building home–school connections. The first was that the poem was on a universal topic with which all students and families could engage and make culturally relevant connections. The second was that the poem included translanguaging as a literary device. Words and ideas that students identified as being of cultural significance were written in the students' home languages. Finally, Ms. Chapman-Santiago worked toward strengthening the home–school connection, as well as the student work produced, by encouraging students to share their drafts at home. Because the poems were bilingual, family members who were not proficient in English could play a larger role than usual in editing the home language vocabulary used. Also, they could discuss additional New Year's traditions that could be incorporated into the poems in either English or their home language. This homework assignment, which included opportunities for both oral and written translanguaging, opened the door to greater family involvement in their child's English Language Arts schoolwork.

Participant Responses to the Translanguaging Classroom

When our research team began working together, we quickly realized that we were exploring translanguaging in a unique setting. Much of our previous work in schools had involved bilingual teachers or classes where the students only spoke two or three different home languages. This lesson involved a monolingual English-speaking teacher and students who spoke six different home languages. Documenting teacher and student responses to translanguaging in this classroom context was an important aspect of our work.

During our research team's reflection on the lesson, Ms. Chapman-Santiago stressed that "any teacher can do this . . . Teachers do not need to know their students' home languages in order to engage the class in translanguaging." García, Johnson, and Seltzer (2016) echo this in their book. A teacher in a translanguaging classroom need not be bilingual. However, all teachers in translanguaging classrooms must be co-learners, discovering and learning from their students. One of the consequences of having a teacher who is a co-learner is that bilingual students are empowered. Being a co-learner also means that the teacher will become more effective with the growing population of bilingual students. As Ms. Chapman-Santiago watched the video of the lesson, she also pointed out: "This type of instruction may seem like more work, and it is, but it actually helps me in the classroom. There is more student participation and engagement."

An analysis of the students' exit slips, their written reflections on the use of translanguaging once the lesson was complete, revealed that all but one student felt positive about the use of multiple languages in the classroom. Students repeatedly used the words "good," "happy," "comfortable," and even "proud" as they reflected on using their home languages in class. Two students wrote about feeling at home. Carla, for example, wrote: "Using both Spanish and English made me feel like I was at home because I speak both languages at home." Abella wrote:

> It feels good. You get to express yourself. This is the main class where we get to write in our own language and express ourselves in our own language, showing people that we know how to speak in our languages and write in it and say certain things in it.

This comfortable use of home languages was clearly evident in the lesson when Rajesh volunteered to read the learning objective to the class. When Rajesh stood to read, he first read the objective aloud to the class in Bengali. This indicates that he was focused on reading for meaning, not reading as a performance for the group. Laura did the same thing when the next slide was displayed and she volunteered to read the definition of free verse poetry. Laura chose to read the definition in French first. By starting with their home languages, Rajesh and Laura were able to make sense of the text. There was no reaction by the class to this home language reading, which suggests that the class is comfortable with hearing a variety of languages during class sessions, thus becoming more linguistically accepting toward others.

Later in the lesson, when students were encouraged to share their New Year's traditions orally, Jasmin stood and talked about New Year in El Salvador, all in Spanish. Christian was happy to translate for her. Having the opportunity to speak in her home language enabled Jasmin to participate fully in the lesson, to engage with the content, and to practice speaking in public. The students in the class listened attentively and patiently to both her Spanish and Christian's English translation. Translanguaging—the fluid movement between languages as defined socially and externally, and the deployment of the bilingual's full language repertoire as defined from the bilingual's internal point of view—had become the discursive norm in this classroom.

In addition to feeling positive and comfortable about translanguaging, students also wrote about translanguaging being a benefit to learning. Jasmin wrote "no me costó entender" [it wasn't an effort to understand]. Joseph wrote that it helps him "concentrate in the work more." And as Ciel wrote: "it save more from my mind," perhaps meaning that it took less mental energy to work in her home language. The monolingual English-speaking students also wrote about the benefits of translanguaging. Dante wrote that he appreciates that with the use of translanguaging in the classroom, "everyone knows what to do. It makes me feel comfortable even though I don't understand most of my classmates that don't speak English." Daniel wrote that he only speaks one language and does not always understand his classmates but he "feels comfortable" and is "expanding my education and what I know about culture and religions and new things."

Benjamin, a student who is developing Spanish, was the only student who was not as positive in his reflection on translanguaging in the classroom. Benjamin wrote: "I really don't know how to speak Spanish that much or write in Spanish. I didn't understand what to write or say." While he incorporated Spanish into his poem, it was clear from his response that he felt uncomfortable and frustrated by not knowing as much Spanish as the students in his group. The task of using translanguaging as a literary device, where Benjamin was expected to incorporate some Spanish in his poem, was a challenge. Benjamin's response is a reminder of the importance of being aware of all students' linguistic abilities in the translanguaging classroom, whether students are monolingual or at various stages of bilingualism and biliteracy.

Larger Meanings and Implications

The study of translanguaging as a literary device, using a culturally relevant text, provided all of the students in Ms. Chapman-Santiago's multilingual class opportunities to fully engage with a challenging middle school ELA curriculum. By exploring how Lai (2011) used Vietnamese in her novel, translanguaging was brought to the attention of students as a literary device used by real authors in published work. Students studied this literary device and then used it in their writing.

Studying and using translanguaging as a literary device can be done with students from a variety of language backgrounds and grade levels. This exploration can begin from an early age. Many children's authors use translanguaging as a literary device in their writing of picture books. For example, Gary Soto's (1996) *Too Many Tamales*, Grace Lin's (2003) *Dim Sum for Everyone*, and Alma Flor Ada's (2004) *I Love Saturdays y domingos* are picture books that include translanguaging as a literary device, even in their titles. Pérez Rosario (2014), a member of the CUNY-NYSIEB team, has developed a *Guide to Translanguaging in Latino Literature* that includes books for a variety of age ranges. Teachers and students can work together to find instances of translanguaging as a literary device in books from their school or classroom libraries. After studying this aspect of the author's craft, students can work to create their own writing that incorporates translanguaging as a literary device.

The study of translanguaging as a literary device can also strengthen home–school connections. Family members, who might not be proficient in English, can help with homework by serving as language and culture experts. This type of literacy assignment can help students and their families see that their language and culture are important and valued by the school.

As noted in the analysis of the lesson, it is important to consider how to include monolingual students, or students who are at the early stages of bilingual development, when engaging in bilingual writing. As illustrated in Benjamin's reflection on the lesson, students with no or limited bilingualism may feel uncomfortable during a lesson that includes translanguaging. In Benjamin's case, he felt uncomfortable using Spanish. Reflecting on this as a class could help students develop empathy for their classmates. For example, they may come to better understand students like Jasmin, who have to write in their new language on a daily basis. Encouraging students to work with partners who can help provide language support can be helpful. Students could also co-author bilingual writing in pairs. In this way, all students, including monolingual students, would be able to produce bilingual writing in order to explore translanguaging as a literary device. Engaging in culturally relevant reading and writing, where students can draw on their backgrounds and experiences, in addition to their languages, can also help facilitate greater student engagement and class participation. Many students, including the monolingual English-speaking students in Ms. Chapman-Santiago's class, shared that they enjoyed sharing their culture as well as learning about the cultural traditions of others.

Conclusion

Ms. Chapman-Santiago's skillfully crafted shared reading lesson provided opportunities for her 8th-grade students to use their home languages as a resource for literacy learning. In their review of the literature, Creese and Blackledge (2010) found that "moving between languages has traditionally been frowned upon in educational settings, with teachers and students often feeling guilty about its practice" (p. 105). Clearly, this was not the case in Ms. Chapman-Santiago's classroom where students felt positive about translanguaging, which had become the discursive norm of the classroom. Starting with the study of translanguaging as a literary device can be one way that teachers can begin to open the doors to further oral and written translanguaging in their classrooms.

In the section that follows, Ms. Chapman-Santiago reflects on her emergent bilingual students and the role translanguaging has played in her classroom. In this reflection, Ms. Chapman-Santiago describes the variety of translanguaging opportunities she has afforded her students and what it means for them.

TEACHER'S VOICE BY CHARENE CHAPMAN-SANTIAGO

The day I started teaching back in 2002, I was thrust into a class with students from Tibet, Haiti, Guinea, Sierra Leone, Nigeria, Senegal, Yemen, and the Dominican Republic. I looked at these students and didn't know where to begin. I felt way out of my comfort zone; nothing in my training and education had prepared me for the sheer diversity of my classroom. It was overwhelming to think of the vast distance there was between my students' cultures and languages and English that I, as their teacher, was somehow supposed to bridge. It dawned on me that I had to meet these children at their comfort level. I was sympathetic to these emergent bilingual learners because as a teenager, I too had moved to a new country, Jamaica. Even though I knew the language, the cultural shock was daunting. My personal experience guided my steps and helped me figure out where to begin. It was imperative that I create a classroom culture where all the students felt included and a part of the class. I wanted to preserve the students' culture and not sacrifice it in their process of learning English. I paired students with same-language partners, or had the emergent bilinguals in a guided group. I also invested in electronic dictionaries to help with translations.

As years went by, and the face and the demographics of the neighborhood changed, I admittedly became overwhelmed. The language diversity in my classroom had seemingly become more and more daunting with new languages and cultures appearing. I was at a loss for how to incorporate all these children's cultural identities and backgrounds. Unfortunately, as time went by some students were left by the wayside and I'm sure they felt marginalized in a class where their needs were not being met.

(Continued)

(Continued)

In 2011, when the CUNY-NYSIEB researchers came to our school and made a presentation about translanguaging and what it means for students and teachers, I was intrigued, renewed, and revitalized. I started making plans about how to incorporate translanguaging strategies into my daily practice. I came up with my "Multilingual Translanguaging Word Wall" where each word is translated into all the home languages of my students. Also, I started providing students and/or groups with laptops that have access to Google Translate. But most importantly, I translated my lesson, tasks, and assignments for each lesson. I remembered having a colleague say to me that I was doing too much and I began to think that maybe that person was right. But then came Hussein. I can still remember his face when I handed him a translated lesson. He looked up at me and said, "Thank you Ms. Chapman" with an air of relief and gratitude. He was clearly struggling, but having the side-by-side (English and Arabic) translation allowed him to finally feel a level of success. The feeling of seeing Hussein, who had struggled so much, solidified in me the necessity of continuing and expanding upon the practice of translanguaging. It's the kind of moment that reminds us why we are in this profession. I was firmly committed to translanguaging; and knew that regardless of how much more work I had to do, I had to do it for the sake of my students.

One thing that I must say is that incorporating translanguaging into a typical lesson is actually much easier and more natural than you would think. It is something that happens organically. In order to facilitate this, I've created and established an environment in my class in which my students respect all cultures and backgrounds. The students in my class do not feel "different" or feel like they are being put on the spot. My students understand that we live in the biggest melting pot in the world and we are a global society where all cultures and languages are welcomed. The monolingual English-speaking students understand that as they become closer to becoming college and career ready, they will have many encounters with people from all walks of life. Therefore, they are one step ahead of the game. In addition, my emergent bilingual students understand that not everything will be translated and that it is a gradual release process where eventually, they may not need translations to access the curriculum. However, my bilingual students should always feel comfortable using whatever mode of communication is necessary to learn.

I argued with my supervisor a few years ago because she always gave me classes that were heavily populated with speakers of languages other than English. Her response was, "You have a way with them." With tears in my eyes, I argued that I never have a feeling of success because of the test scores and the statistics. However, translanguaging has given me another feeling of success. My numbers and stats [in standardized tests] may not be as high as my counterparts, but I am making a huge impact on the lives of my students in my small pocket of the world.

Discussion Questions and Activities

1. Look through the books in a classroom library. What percentage of the books represents the students' languages and cultures? How many books use translanguaging as a literary device? Explain what changes, if any, you would recommend. Identify additional books that include translanguaging that could be added to the library. Work with a group to create an annotated bibliography of texts. Refer to the stories listed in the chapter, along with Pérez Rosario's (2014) *The CUNY-NYSIEB Guide to Translanguaging in Latino Literature* as a starting point.
2. Throughout the lesson described in this chapter, translanguaging occurred across a variety of literacy modes and involved the class members in various ways. The multiplicity of ways in which translanguaging occurred was described in detail for the Do Now. Select another part of the lesson and analyze the various translanguaging modes and which class members each mode involved. Discuss your analysis with a group.
3. The translanguaging aspect of the lesson described in this chapter provided an opportunity for families to be involved and helpful with their child's homework. Consider where a translanguaging opportunity could be added to a lesson you have written and/or taught to help integrate the school and students' families and communities.

References

Ada, A. F. (2004). *I love Saturdays and domingos*. New York: Atheneum Books.

Albakry, M., & Hancock, P. (2008). Code switching in AhdafSoueif's 'The Map of Love'. *Language and Literature*, 17(3), 221–234.

Allen, J. (2002). *On the same page*. Portland, ME: Stenhouse.

Barnes, L. (2011). The function and significance of bilingual code-switching in English poetry with a special focus on the work of Eliot and Pound. *English Academy Review: Southern African Journal of English Studies*, 28(1), 23–38.

Creese, A., & Blackledge, A. (2010). Translanguaging in the bilingual classroom: A pedagogy for learning and teaching. *Modern Language Journal*, 94, 103–115.

Dumitrescu, D. (2014). 'Dude was figureando hard': El cambio y la fusión de códigos en la obra de Junot Díaz. In A. Enrique-Arias, M. Gutiérrez, A. Landa, & F. Ocampo (Eds.), *Perspectives in the study of Spanish language variation* (pp. 399–434). A Coruña, Spain: Universidade de Santiago de Compostela.

Ebe, A. (2010). Culturally relevant texts and assessment for English language learners. *Reading Horizons*, 50(3), 193–210.

Ebe, A. (2012). Supporting the reading development of middle school English language learners through culturally relevant texts. *Reading & Writing Quarterly*, 28(2), 179–198.

Ebe, A. (2015). The power of culturally relevant texts: What teachers learn about their emergent bilingual students. In Y. S. Freeman & D. E. Freeman (Eds.), *Research on preparing inservice teachers to work effectively with emergent bilinguals* (pp. 33–53). Bingley, West Yorkshire, UK: EmeraldBooks LTD.

EngageNY. (2014). Grade 8 English Language Arts—inside out and back again—unit 1 lesson 2. Retrieved February 6, 2015, from: http://www.engageny.org/file/7756/

download/grade_8_english_language_arts_inside_out_and_back_again_unit_1_lesson_2.docx

Faggella-Luby, M. N., Ware, S. M., & Capozzoli, A. (2009). Adolescent literacy-reviewing adolescent literacy reports: Key components and critical questions. *Journal of Literacy Research*, 41(4), 453–475.

Freeman, Y., Freeman, A., & Freeman, D. (2003). Home run books: Connecting students to culturally relevant texts. *NABE News*, 26(3), 5–12, 28.

Freeman, Y., Freeman, D., Soto, M., & Ebe, A. (2016). *ESL teaching: Principles for success.* Portsmouth, NH: Heinemann.

Fu, D. (2009). *Writing between languages: How English language learners make the transition to fluency.* Portsmouth, NH: Heinemann.

García, O. (2009). *Bilingual education in the 21st century: A global perspective.* Malden, MA and Oxford, UK: Wiley/Blackwell.

García, O., Johnson, J., & Seltzer, K. (2016). *The translanguaging classroom: Leveraging student bilingualism for learning.* Philadelphia, PA: Caslon.

Goldenberg, C. (2013, Summer). Unlocking the research on English learners: What we know-and don't yet know—about effective instruction. *American Educator*, 4–38.

González, N., Moll, L., & Amanti, C. (2005). *Funds of knowledge: Theorizing practices in households, communities and classrooms.* Mahwah, NJ: Erlbaum.

Hélot, C. (2014). Rethinking bilingual pedagogy in Alsace: Translingual writers and translanguaging. In A. Blackledge & A. Creese (Eds.), *Heteroglossia as practice and pedagogy* (pp. 217–238). New York: Springer.

Herrera, S., Perez, D., & Escamilla, K. (2015). *Teaching reading to English language learners: Differentiated literacies.* Boston, MA: Pearson Education, Inc.

Lai, T. (2011). *Inside out and back again.* New York: Harper Collins.

Larrotta, C., & Yamamura, E. K. (2011). A community cultural wealth approach to Latina/Latino parent involvement: The promise of family literacy. *Adult Basic Education and Literacy Journal*, 5(2), 74–83.

Lin, G. (2003). *Dim sum for everyone!* Decorah, IA: Dragonfly Books.

Ma'ayan, H. (2010). Erika's stories: Literacy solutions for a failing middle school student. *Journal of Adolescent & Adult Literacy*, 53(8), 646–654.

Pérez Rosario, V. (2014) *The CUNY-NYSIEB guide to translanguaging in Latino literature.* New York: CUNY-NYSIEB, The Graduate Center, The City University of New York. Retrieved on March 16, 2016, from: www.nysieb.ws.gc.cuny.edu/files/2015/02/CUNY-NYSIEB-Latino-Literature-Guide-Final-January-2015.pdf

Rodríguez, A. (2014). Culturally relevant books: Culturally responsive teaching in bilingual classrooms. *NABE Journal of Research and Practice*, 5, 1–24.

Soto, G. (1996). *Too many tamales.* New York: Putnam.

4

BALANCING WINDOWS AND MIRRORS

Translanguaging in a Linguistically Diverse Classroom

Heather H. Woodley with Andrew Brown

Introduction

Eight home languages. Twenty-seven students. Twenty-seven levels of English language development, home language literacy, and content knowledge. One room. One teacher. This is the reality of Andrew Brown's 5th-grade class. Sitting at these desks are young voices reflecting the linguistic and cultural diversity of the city. A teacher such as Mr. Brown is faced with many questions: How can I differentiate for emergent bilinguals in my class? What is the starting point to ensure that Carmen, who arrived in September from Bolivia, is engaged, challenged, and held to the same high expectations as Owen, a monolingual English-speaking student struggling with his reading? How do I balance what students know and what is new? These questions are the driving forces for a dynamic approach to multilingual literacy instruction in this classroom.

Mr. Brown's class includes all the students labeled English language learners (ELL) in the 5th grade, along with some monolingual English-speaking students who are considered "struggling readers" through the school's assessment and teacher observations. The approach taken in this classroom is immersion into language—*all* languages—the language practices of every student in the classroom. These languages are vividly displayed in the classroom's multilingual ecology on walls, signs, labels, on the interactive whiteboard, and in notebooks of students. Different languages are used to varying extents in the room, depending on the needs, desires, and abilities of individual students. English, Spanish, Arabic, and Polish are visible in the room to reflect the most common home languages of the students, while Ukrainian is also heard. This multilingual ecology is created with the support of translation technology, students, families, and teachers and school staff, all providing written support to display the different languages. In the classroom, four written languages—English, Spanish, Polish, and Arabic—are visible in the linguistic landscape. Figure 4.1 displays the multilingual Word Wall. Cognate lists, labels, and signs for classroom routines are also rendered in multiple languages.

Students are immersed in speaking, as well as seeing, languages. Turning to partners for brief conversations at strategic moments of a lesson, working in small groups, participating in question-and-answer-style lessons, students produce language in English and home languages throughout their learning. Students are also engaging with multimodal multilingual literacies, reading content-based texts in print and online in multiple languages, as well as listening and seeing multilingual videos. In addition, there are multilingual resources on the students' desks, including dictionaries, glossaries, and classroom computers for online translations.

It is this drawing out of differences, this acknowledgement that the diversity of a class is an attribute to build on, that shapes the translanguaging in this unique classroom. There is a balance to be achieved here in learning with a linguistically diverse group, a balance between connecting personally to students and learning new perspectives. One would be hard-pressed to find a teacher who spoke as many languages as the students in this classroom. And so, the situation is ripe for students to take the lead, to facilitate learning in their home languages, and to use translanguaging to support themselves and others. This is also a valuable opportunity for a teacher to be a co-learner in the classroom. It is the teacher's

FIGURE 4.1 Multilingual Classroom Linguistic Landscape

active role, the way she or he sets the stage for translanguaging and student leading, that enables the space for student voices to lead the learning.

This translanguaging, running through each aspect of a daily lesson, embodies the metaphor of windows and mirrors introduced by Gutiérrez (2007). This balance of teaching new information and language (windows) combined with the consistent and deliberate use of personal and cultural connections (mirrors) through translanguaging enables students to access learning of new worlds, ideas, and languages in meaningful ways. This also provides the space for students to learn more deeply and broadly about diversity and language around them, while building home language literacy and taking on the roles of teacher of languages other than English. Translanguaging then becomes to the key to creating and balancing windows and mirrors and making learning accessible for all in a multilevel, multilingual classroom.

Context

This elementary school sits in Queens, a borough of New York City that is home to some of the most linguistically diverse neighborhoods in the world. Churches display times for masses in Polish, Spanish, and English. Deli signs highlight their Halal foods, Eastern European imports, and Goya products. Social and business multilingual conversations flow against the backdrops of multilingual radios, televisions, and mobile devices. This neighborhood's multilingualism is reflected in its public schools, which bring together immigrant youth from various corners of the world with other multilingual and monolingual children born in New York.

Two blocks away from a high-traffic street full of storefronts and mechanics' garages is the school's neighborhood, comprised of attached brick homes and multifamily dwellings. Based on student, family, and teacher surveys, it is considered an academically high-performing school. The school is home to 1,420 students in grades pre-K through 6 with a student population that is 72% free-lunch eligible and self-identifies as 7% Asian, 1% Black, 48% Hispanic and 43% White.

Upon entering the building, visitors are met with a visual display of 17 different languages expressing "Welcome!" Accompanying each printed word or phrase for "welcome" are flags representing the 28 home countries of students. The welcome mural guides visitors into the school. Hearing, seeing, and speaking languages is a part of the everyday experience for a majority of students and adults in this school and community, so the school as a whole has embraced a multilingual ecology and bilingualism as a resource in many classrooms and common spaces.

The school has an average class size of 32 and is struggling to meet the needs of emergent bilinguals, who account for about 11% of the student population. In recent years, the increased neighborhood immigration from Mexico, Poland,

Central and South America, and the Middle East has become more evident in the student population. Although the majority of students speak languages other than English at home and/or with each other, only a small percentage of the school's bilingual student population is still receiving support services. Mr. Brown's 5th-grade classroom mostly comprises students who still are classified as English language learners, and state mandates are met through the time and support they receive from a certified push-in ESL teacher. However, Mr. Brown's classroom uses every student's bilingualism as a resource in individual and group learning, both with, and without, the presence of an ESL teacher.

It is important to note that the school leadership has been supportive in starting meaningful conversations about multilingualism and translanguaging. Both the principal and assistant principal have been actively engaged in CUNY-NYSIEB seminars, along with many of the school's teachers, including Mr. Brown. The school's multilingual ecology is rich and vibrant, but some classrooms with emergent bilinguals remain English-only in instruction and teachers have not taken up translanguaging. At one point during a school visit, I sat in Mr. Brown's room discussing his lesson and students' learning. A fellow teacher passed by, popped her head in the room, nodded towards the Arabic written on the board and quipped, "What is this shit?" She smiled and walked away before a response could be received. Although this is an isolated incident, it is symbolic of a perspective present in some educational communities—an oppressively xenophobic attitude towards languages other than English. This is not, by any means, the point of view of the majority of the teachers in the school, and certainly not that of leadership. However, it is worth noting that teachers and students using and invested in translanguaging do face challenges of discrimination within—as well as outside of—their school community.

On the surface, Andrew Brown is strikingly similar to many of his colleagues. He is a young, well-educated, native-born New Yorker. He identifies as Irish and German American and spoke only English growing up in his home. Mr. Brown himself is a language learner in both Spanish and American Sign Language. He uses his conversational Spanish in his everyday teaching, while relying on other students, technology, and school community members for more advanced Spanish and other language understandings. However, his teaching is far from the mainstream English-dominated instruction taking place in other classrooms and more closely reflects the diversity of his class. Mr. Brown has taught 7 of his 10 years in this school and shows genuine care for diverse students and commitment to culturally and linguistically sustaining teaching.

With about half of this 5th-grade class (ages 10 and 11) having moved to the United States within the last two years, Mr. Brown's class represents a diverse range of English language practices. There are several newcomer students who immigrated in the past year from Bolivia, Poland, and Yemen, and some of their first introductions to English have been in this classroom. Other emergent bilinguals in the class joined the school within the last few years from Poland, Mexico,

Egypt, Yemen, Morocco, and the Ukraine and have more advanced English language abilities. There are several students in the classroom who were either born in the United States or emigrated at a very young age. Some of these students are considered "former ELLs" or "students in need of academic support." These labels have inspired school leaders to group them with emergent bilinguals so as to provide more scaffolded instruction.

Although English is the main language of the curricula and the teacher, the classroom is rich in multilingual print, including Spanish, Polish, Arabic, and some Ukrainian. Mr. Brown describes how he started to construct the multilingual landscape of the classroom and take up translanguaging in instruction:

> At the beginning of the year, I kind of would just label things in English. Then after a couple of translanguaging professional developments, I started putting things in different languages and the kids would correct me on those. They would help me translate them themselves. Just having the essential question and the actual problem itself in their languages gets them more involved and engaged in the lesson. They see something in a language they know, in their language and they are more into whatever the topic may be.

In this room, translanguaging is the norm. The next section describes Mr. Brown's teaching utilizing this multilingual approach.

Lesson Design and Moves

When Mr. Brown plans a lesson, translanguaging is integrated throughout each step—from the essential question translated into four languages on the interactive whiteboard to multilingual turn-and-talks. The lesson we planned and facilitated together, central in the analysis below, focused on exploring slavery in the U.S. through literature. The literacy units in this school follow a packaged, English-only curriculum called ReadyGen. However, every day Mr. Brown works within the structures of this curriculum, making deliberate spaces for translanguaging. He adds scaffolds, including visuals, role playing, and myriad opportunities for students to engage with home language literacy. The lesson plans created by the publishing company of ReadyGen are not developed with emergent bilinguals in mind. They do integrate literacy with historical content and highlight vocabulary, but from a monolingual perspective for students with very specific cultural knowledge. Therefore, Mr. Brown's lesson design must fill in these gaps for emergent bilinguals.

The text for this particular lesson, entitled "Heart and Soul," attempts to make the atrocity of American slavery approachable and understandable for a young audience. Because many students have been educated outside the United States, they have had limited exposure to the idea of slavery and its role in this new country. It is important then to create a space for students to express their opinions and feelings and ask questions freely about slavery. The lesson is designed as a whole-class experience with an interactive read-aloud and multiple moments for emergent bilinguals to work with classmates who share home languages in a "think-pair-share" (partner discussion) small group work, followed by independent practice. This allows time for students to discuss issues openly and gain new factual information, while being able to draw on classmates' experiences for deeper understanding. The continuous move back and forth between whole-class discussions and small group work provides multiple spaces for translanguaging, specifically home language clarification and discussion to ensure this new content is accessible to all students.

Mr. Brown introduces new concepts by asking students to make connections to their own lives, prior experiences, and knowledge, and to first make meaning in their home languages. He begins this lesson by going over what the class discussed the previous day, starting with the slave trade. He poses the question, "How were slaves acquired?" and allows time for students to generate ideas. Jeremy responds, "They stole people," and goes on to detail how people were stolen from their homes and sold to owners. Mr. Brown appreciates his contributions and asks, "What else?" As is customary in the classroom, now it is Jeremy's job to call on someone else to add more detail to the discussion. He calls on Benjamin who begins to describe the voyage on a slave ship from Africa. He recounts, "chains on their necks and backs." As Mr. Brown takes a moment to recap what Benjamin has described to the whole classroom, Benjamin whispers in Spanish to his classmate and asks him to tell him how to say "escapar" in English. Benjamin then adds that some people tried to escape the boats. Mr. Brown uses this to connect to the last piece the class read, which focused on a slave revolt. Students are eager to share details they remember from their reading and discussion including the whipping tree and the Underground Railroad, "the secret passage and how they escape," as Aldo explains.

The back and forth, the question and answer rapport between Mr. Brown and his students goes on as students make connections between what they read earlier, their own understandings of slavery, injustice, unfairness, and other incidents of discrimination and inequities in other historical and current events. Mr. Brown uses each student's response as a springboard to make a point about the content. When he asks students what they know about slavery, Andrés adds, "It's like child labor, only with adults." Mr. Brown acknowledges the strength of this connection and reminds the class that children were also slaves. He then asks students about the various roles of children on a plantation. Other students share examples of unfairness from current, personal, or historical events, and with each contribution Mr. Brown draws it back to their focus on slavery.

After an extensive class discussion activating prior knowledge about slavery, the reading begins with an illustration of a plantation house on the interactive whiteboard with the word "plantation" in English, Spanish, Arabic, and Polish.

Mr. Brown asks students of various home languages if the word "plantation" in each language is written correctly, and asks them to read it out loud. Several students add that this is the first time they are seeing the word "plantation" in their home language, so they presume it is right, but cannot say for sure considering this is new in both languages. Translanguaging here not only helps students learn a new language, but is also a way to continue developing their home language, even when the teacher does not speak it. Students then share what they know or remember about the crops of plantations, taking cues from the visual resources in the text and the board. Mr. Brown prepares the students to listen and read along.

The read aloud begins. He stops for a moment and asks the students to compare the photographs of plantations to where they live. They laugh with an exaggerated, "Nooo," then the mood changes. The reading continues, bringing to light the dreadfulness of slavery and how the horrific lived experiences of slaves starkly contrast with the beauty of the building. Mr. Brown reads the words sadly and slowly, as students follow along in their own books. At the word "liberty," he asks the class for a synonym, to which they reply in unison, "freedom."

Mr. Brown takes a quick poll to see who has never heard of a swamp before and six hands go up. He goes to the interactive whiteboard and pulls up visuals of cypress swamps in Florida and beaches in Mississippi, two references made in the reading. He also displays multilingual translations for "swamp," although Iman notes, "I don't know what that means," referring to the Arabic word on the slide. Nizar, Mehdi, and Wahiba all chime in using Arabic and English, describing in detail what a swamp would look like, the water and trees and animals. Iman nods and smiles, having just learned the new word in both English and Arabic.

The reading concludes and students share ideas of how the mood in the poem changes from a "nice" description of the house with the line:

> That was until they caught sight of the African men and women slaves whose raggedy clothes, sad faces, and smelly bodies revealed the ugly truth that this was no heaven at all.
>
> *(Nelson, 2011, p. 29)*

This whole line is displayed on the interactive whiteboard, translated into Spanish, Arabic, and Polish. A conversation in English and Spanish ensues about the appropriateness of the translation for "smelly" and "raggedy." The students discuss how there is really no Spanish translation for "raggedy," and offer possibilities such as "andrajosa," "desigual," and "harapiento." Saira offers how an expression, rather than just one word, could capture the meaning better, and Mr. Brown closes the conversation by reminding students how there are many ways to say the same thing in one language, and how one person's ways of saying things in Spanish might be different from that of someone else.

The students then take time in small groups to reflect more deeply on these words with what are called "Shades of Meaning" cards. Using paint swatches displaying several shades of a color on a sample card, students write a new vocabulary word from the lesson in the top color bar. With each new shade comes a synonym or alternate way of saying the focal word. The purpose of this activity is for students to study one word deeply and to understand different "shades" of the word, including direct synonyms and phrases that capture the same meaning. Figure 4.2 displays the completed slide for the word "raggedy," which was filled in one word at a time during a guided discussion and which is then used as a model for students to fill out their own cards.

Students are given additional time to complete their cards with home language partners. When students do not have a home language partner, they work in English with the support of a bilingual dictionary, notes, or online translation. Students discuss the possible translations and synonyms for the words.

The lesson concludes when the class is asked to consider a central concept in slavery as it pertains to their own experiences—unfair. What does it mean if something is unfair? Do synonyms and other words such as "injustice," "unequal," or "not right" capture the same meaning as "unfairness"? How do you say "unfair" in your home language? Next, students are asked for examples to illustrate this concept—"What is something you are familiar with that is unfair?" Using translanguaging, emergent bilinguals discuss examples from current events or their own experiences in language pairs. When volunteers are asked to share their ideas with the whole class, hands shoot up. Sasha shares what she discussed with her partner, "It's like the Ukraine, cause it's unfair that a lot of people have to die because our president is not a good president." In a follow-up question, another student asks Sasha about how she learned this. "We talk about it in my house," she explains, "and I see it on the television there and we listen to it from the station from home on the computer." She pauses and then continues

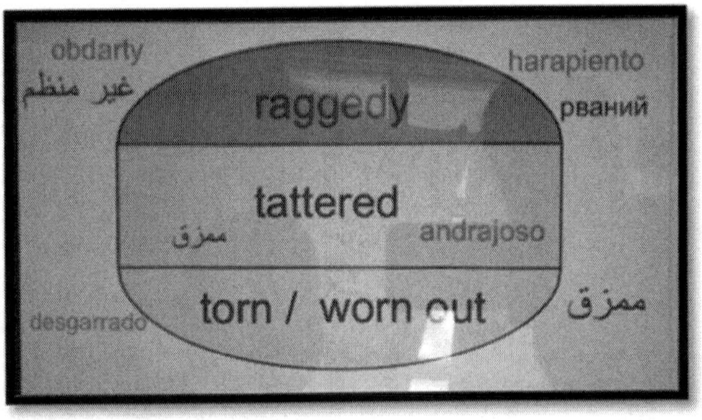

FIGURE 4.2 Shades of Meaning Slide for the Vocabulary Word "Raggedy"

with emphasis, "It is *all* they are talking about in the Ukrainian news right now, so you can hear it a lot."

Nizar, who came from Yemen last year, volunteers what he has talked about in Arabic with Mehdi, an Egyptian student. At first he hesitates. "Philistine?" he questions Mehdi, who reassures him by saying "Palestine." Nizar says a few sentences in Arabic, Mehdi nods his head in agreement, and explains to the class in English, "It's unfair, like how some people cannot vote or have a good job and that is unfair." Nizar adds his agreement in English and references what was brought up by Sasha by adding, "This is *all* Arabic news talk about too." As Mr. Brown wraps up the lesson, he reminds students that they will continue this conversation tomorrow and to "keep bringing in these great examples from all that you already know."

Taking Up Translanguaging

Students' linguistic diversity is a salient characteristic of Mr. Brown's classroom. It shapes how he thinks about his teaching and how he plans for his students. Becoming familiar with translanguaging pedagogies through work with CUNY-NYSIEB spoke in loud, exciting ways to this teacher. It came across as a response to the grand questions of how to both provide linguistically diverse students with personal connections to learning, while also opening doors for all students to new information, languages, and diverse and critical perspectives.

Here we extend Gutiérrez's metaphors of window and mirror (2007, 2012) to conceptualize how and why students and this teacher take up translanguaging in this diverse classroom. Students in Mr. Brown's class are learning in ways that reflect their home languages, cultures, and experiences, while opening their eyes to new ideas and perspectives.

Translanguaging as Mirror

In Mr. Brown's classroom, mirrors of language practices are everywhere for emergent bilinguals and all his students. Students access new content in home languages and engage with home language literacy practice building both metalinguistic awareness and confidence as learners. Using students' home languages in the classroom has roots in liberatory education, culturally relevant and culturally responsive teaching and multicultural education as conceptualized by Paolo Freire (1970), Gloria Ladson-Billings (1995), Sonia Nieto and Patty Bode (2011), and more recently as culturally sustaining pedagogy (Paris, 2012). Teaching for equity and social justice speaks to the need for teachers and schools to integrate students' home languages into learning opportunities and building on students' funds of knowledge (Moll, 2007).

Language is intrinsically linked to students' identities and the ways in which young people perceive the educational value of their home languages. Languaging in the classroom then has a unique impact on students' sense of belonging to their learning environment. Students from traditionally oppressed groups, including racial and linguistic communities, often do not see reflections of themselves in schooling. However, through translanguaging, Mr. Brown brings reflections of all students' language practices and cultural backgrounds into the classroom. He explains, "I want them [students] to know that it's OK for them to hold on to their ties in the world, and to embrace where they're from. We're not an English-only speaking school."

As a teacher, Mr. Brown makes explicit connections between his decisions to incorporate translanguaging and the use of language practices as mirrors of personal and cultural connection for students. To make the historical framing of literacy lessons more accessible to students coming from a variety of knowledge and linguistic backgrounds, Mr. Brown gives them space to grapple with these issues through home language practices. He provides home language translations of central parts of texts and seats students with language partners for multilingual turn-and-talk. And he always allows students, including English monolingual students, to deploy all their language resources, not just those that have been legitimated in school. Mr. Brown creates these language partners as mirrors for his students, reflections of their own language and cultural practices that would, ideally, enable them to participate fully in the lesson no matter where they were on the English-language or content-knowledge spectrum.

For both Sasha and Nizar, their personal reference points, their own mirrors to learning, are shaped by multilingual interactions, including family and news media from the Ukraine or the Arab world. For these students, the recognition of translanguaging outside the classroom enables them to bring reflections of their own lives and history into the classroom. When asked to reflect on the mirrors she brings to her learning, Sasha explains,

> I like to think what I know from my home and take it to what we do in class. It makes me feel like my Ukrainian is a helpful thing for . . . If I don't use my language, I wouldn't know what the news said and it would be hard to understand my parents sometimes. Then in class I write what I heard first in Ukrainian, and then my writing to English.

Sasha shows a clear understanding of her language as a valuable learning tool, as a connection between herself and her education. Her home language allows her to bring knowledge of current events and cultural perspectives into the classroom, and is also a tool in her personal writing process. For Sasha, the space made for translanguaging in and out of the classroom is the mirror where she sees her own language practices as a learning tool.

Nizar has also taken his translanguaging experiences outside the classroom to create a mirror for his learning. When asked to reflect on how this makes him feel in class, he beamed with a smile and shared proudly, "Happy because it's like

I know about the . . . what we doing, even if it is new for me." This ability to feel confident in learning and to find a personal connection to new material is how translanguaging creates mirrors for newcomer emergent bilinguals such as Nizar. In a traditional English-only classroom, it would be difficult for Nizar to share such elaborate ideas without the translanguaging support of his peers, teachers, and technology resources. Sasha and Nizar have engaged in their own independent learning and research about current events and consulted various sources in home languages and English, including their own families and international news outlets. Both these students perceive the use of translanguaging activities as helpful to their own learning in the classroom by enabling them to bring their outside knowledge into the classroom. Therefore, translanguaging creates several different mirrors depending on thc perspective and backgrounds not only of the students, but also of the teacher.

Translanguaging as Windows Into the Unknown

On the other side of Gutiérrez's metaphor are the windows, which are used as framing both the students' and Mr. Brown's meaning-making of translanguaging in their classroom. Integrated into literacy instruction, language is explored deeply and specifically, as students learn new ways of expressing an idea in the same language, or in a new one. This exploration of language pragmatics, critical metalinguistic awareness, and language as a tool for multicultural awareness are all ways in which translanguaging is utilized and conceptualized as a window into newness. The windows created by translanguaging are a unique part of the learning experience for this last group of students. Rather than allow language difference to cause riffs or create cliques among students, translanguaging makes space for all students' language practices, including those of Mr. Brown's English monolingual students. Mr. Brown makes evident to all his students that translanguaging is about deploying all the features of their language repertoire to learn. His monolingual students soon see that they are using most of the features of their repertoire in school, whereas bilingual students are only using less than half. They soon become supporters of translanguaging, for their classmates, but also because it allows them to explore their classmates' diverse worlds. Learning about, and from, others through language is an important aspect of the classroom community that Mr. Brown builds and fosters with translanguaging.

Emergent bilinguals are gaining knowledge about languages other than English and opening new windows into the world through translanguaging. Arabic speakers take part in reading out loud in Spanish as they make connections to their home and new languages. In a previous lesson, Spanish- and Arabic-speaking students engaged in a conversation exploring how the phrase "My name is" in either language did not translate directly to English. Using "me llamo Carmen" and "ismi Mehdi" as their points of reference, students looked closely at their own home language, and were able to learn about and explore languages side by side.

For emergent bilinguals, home language literacy and increased metalinguistic awareness have valuable implications for content and language learning. Students can ask and explore, "How are my linguistic practices different or similar from those of Spanish, Arabic, or Polish speakers? What historical and geographical circumstances might account for those differences?" These questions lead not only to develop performances in English and languages other than English, but also to greater sociopolitical and historical understandings.

As a learner of languages other than English, Mr. Brown's experiences and background most closely align with the monolingual English speakers in the class. It is this connection that he draws on when thinking about the reasons for the use of translanguaging with monolingual English speakers: "For all the students to understand, you know, that there are other languages besides English in the world," and to examine their own language practices. He speaks with pride about students who, because of the translanguaging in his classroom, learn how to be accepting, proud, and interested in other languages, as well as their own. He recalls students discussing different ways to say the same word in Spanish or Arabic depending on which country or region one is from. This often evolves into larger conversations of how languages differ across cultural and geographical borders, as well as generations, and even individuals. English-speaking students share their own ideas of languages, drawing on their knowledge of different ways of speaking varieties of English, and their use of certain lexical items and expressions in different circumstances. Mr. Brown draws on the multiple languages of other students to enhance meaning for English-speaking monolingual students who are also building their English language lexicon.

Translanguaging also opens up windows for cross-cultural learning by giving space for emergent bilingual students to be leaders in their classrooms. These students are often silenced in English-only classrooms. However, in Mr. Brown's classroom, these students lead the class, presenting diverse perspectives and different ways of languaging and making connections to international current events. The use of translanguaging makes it possible for a wider array of student experiences to be shared.

In our lesson, centered on a short read-aloud, students explored the inside of a plantation and analyzed the juxtaposition between a physically beautiful mansion and the injustice inside. As we said before, Mr. Brown draws their attention to the line about the African men and women with "raggedy clothes, sad faces, and smelly bodies" which has been translated into many languages. Students are asked to come to the interactive whiteboard and evaluate the translation that Mr. Brown gives using the online translator. The Arabic-speaking students noticed that the word "ghyrmenezam," that the online translator gives for "raggedy" also means "unorganized." This led to a discussion: "What does this tell us about the word 'raggedy'?" Other students offered insight into the connection between the two concepts. They drew upon inferences of how slaves looked or maybe felt. Translanguaging here is taken up in ways that draw out deeper discussions of new content. It is a catalyst for *all* students to explore connections between languages and express their understanding of a central concept, as well as new vocabulary.

By pulling out this one phrase, and going deeply into what it means in both English and different home languages, the teacher deepens understandings of both content and language. This moment is a mirror for some students, those drawing upon their own home language and content knowledge, as it is simultaneously a window moment for others, providing new ways of seeing the content.

Implications

Framing translanguaging as a series of diverse mirrors and windows has significant and valuable implications for educators, school leaders, and students. Meeting his diverse students' needs is constantly at the forefront of Mr. Brown's lesson planning and instruction. A teacher could have viewed the language diversity of this class as something to be silenced, clinging to English-only as the "great equalizer" with the dangerous rhetoric of remaining "language-blind." But Mr. Brown develops an instructional and learning space that brings the different language practices of his diverse students into full view. Translanguaging is an answer to the question of differentiation, of how to encourage participation of all students from diverse language backgrounds and English abilities. Translanguaging is, for this teacher and his students, both the reflective mirror bringing students' worlds into the classroom and a window into new perspectives and multilingual/multicultural awareness. Whether it is the mirror or the window, translanguaging is what makes the diversity of this classroom its most valuable asset to student learning.

Mr. Brown recalls moments when newcomer students participated with eager excitement, given the space to explain their ideas or responses in Spanish, Polish, or Arabic. He reflected on how his class was impacted by translanguaging:

> I find that the kids who are more shy, when they're new to the country, they'll tend to participate more when there's a problem written in their home language. They feel more involved instead of it just being in English when they speak it and don't even know what they're saying. So I find that they're more interactive and they see themselves in what we are doing.

The meaning of slavery—including its atrocities and role in the U.S. economy and political standing—can be a very difficult concept for some immigrants to grasp. Translanguaging, however, enabled these newcomers to understand the legacies of slavery in U.S. society today.

For English-speaking students, translanguaging opened up windows into new ideas as well. In reflecting on this lesson, several students, both emergent bilingual and monolingual, expressed the value of learning from "how other students bring in things that they know." When asked for examples of this, students referred back to Sasha's connections to Ukrainian current events and Nizar's Palestinian example.

Mr. Brown acknowledges that many of the English-dominant students in his class have not traditionally been successful in literacy instruction, struggling with reading comprehension. Since incorporating translanguaging into his classroom and providing more windows and perspectives about content and language, he has noticed their increased engagement as well. Some of these students were written off by former teachers as disengaged, but as Mr. Brown notices, they simply "were not engaged in the way we were teaching before. Now that they are hearing more from other students, and every class is about many perspectives, they're clearly more involved."

Mr. Brown specifically points to how vocabulary lessons are more vibrant, bringing in multiple languages and translations, and how he finds all individuals more invested in their learning, as students are given the floor to lead the class every day in different ways and using different languages.

Student engagement and investment are central concepts in learning (Norton, 1995). Many teachers, like Mr. Brown, see these as key indicators that they are doing a "good job" or being an "effective teacher." This drives teacher decisions about their own craft. The desire to ensure that students engage and invest in their learning is answered through translanguaging. Mr. Brown takes translanguaging to create the windows and mirrors that facilitate learning. All students need opportunities for translanguaging in order to explore language and its workings and extend their language practices.

All students deserve to hear what their classmates have to say about how they use languages. This can help to dispel stereotypes or negative perspectives about multilingualism and others' translanguaging. It can also open doors for more complex conversations about student relationships and learning together in a multilingual environment. And it can justify the valid deployment of students' entire language repertoire, their translanguaging.

Considering some students are reluctant to use their entire language repertoire in school, unpacking the language prejudice or norms that may be embedded in these ideas is an integral step in building a strong multilingual class (and school) community. These ideologies drive some of today's most oppressive policies of racial-linguistic profiling. Taking up a translanguaging theory where all students are encouraged to deploy their entire language repertoire can spark meaningful conversations and rethinking of language, power, and identity for youth (Alim, 2015). As emergent bilingual students have opportunities to lead the class and act as language experts, their classmates can see firsthand how translanguaging can be used to gain knowledge and access meaningful learning.

Conclusion

Teaching is a consistently challenging and rewarding balancing act. Teachers such as Mr. Brown strive to balance academic rigor with well-being, as well as newness of the English language and American cultural practices with the familiarity of students' home language and cultural practices. Translanguaging is a way for a multilingual, multilevel classroom to become an engaging space for all students. Students learn through both the reflections of themselves and their language practices (mirrors) and the deep interaction with new perspectives and voices (windows). Only by ensuring that the new linguistic features become part of each student's language repertoire, which also encompasses the features associated with their home language, would bilingual children be successful language learners and students.

TEACHER'S VOICE BY ANDREW BROWN

Translanguaging in my class is an everyday practice for all students, no matter what languages they speak. Understanding new vocabulary is an objective for all of my lessons, especially during literacy and specifically for my emergent bilinguals. Whether we act the words out using drama with silly skits, come up with songs to remember their meaning, play a game to find out their part(s) of speech, or identify antonyms or synonyms, I want my students to be able to "own" the words and have them forever. They write these new words in their word-work notebook or write the word and similar words on their paint swatch "shades of meaning" cards, along with their home languages translation or explanation of the word. I see they own it when a student uses a new English word or phrase in the appropriate context after learning it for the first time. They may use it in a follow-up lesson or, even better, during a casual conversation with a classmate or teacher.

In my school, we post our learning objectives daily and display essential questions for every math, English Language Arts, and social studies unit. Many of these objectives and essential questions contain words unfamiliar to my students, especially my emergent bilinguals. Taking the time to have students translanguage when learning content and vocabulary helps create some of the most engaging classroom environments in which I've been. Every student, emergent bilingual or not, sees not only English, but the language they speak at home, or the language their parents speak, or even a language their classmates speak. The amount of student participation and investment in their learning is beyond anything I have experienced in a monolingual class. A Polish student sees the word "tattered" on the interactive whiteboard but is unsure of its meaning. They may then see the Polish words "obdarty" or "obszarpanya" written underneath and then a picture of a torn-up piece of clothing next to a picture of a brand new suit or tuxedo. An arrow is pointing to the tattered clothing. Instantly, the kids shout out in understanding.

(Continued)

(Continued)

This has opened doors for all students to really be a part of class, and for students to learn from each other in new ways using language to start some really important conversations about culture. And in these conversations, the students have led the way. My Arabic-speaking students will often use the purple interactive whiteboard pen to write out the translations for vocabulary words since there are many different Arabic varieties. They compare their words while teaching the class how to say something in Arabic as well. I remember some of my Latina girls getting into a polite debate about what is the correct way to say "barrette" in Spanish—"hebilla," "pasador," "gancho" or "horquilla." They took turns speaking, and it showed my class how different cultures have ways of saying things differently in the same language. I just took a step back and let the kids go, and it was really amazing to watch them lead.

My English speakers are learning through translanguaging as well. They see it as a normal part of our lessons and embrace it. Translanguaging has helped them understand that all the features of their own repertoire are also valid, even though schools might only value some of them. And they also use translanguaging as an opportunity to learn words in other languages as well.

I used to translate words, objectives, and essential questions on my own, but now I let the students do it. They won't let me forget about it. It instantly gets them engaged in the unit or the lesson. Students are given time to correct any mistakes on the interactive whiteboard that I have made (either accidentally or on purpose). Just like I want them to own the new vocabulary, I want them to own the class, to make it theirs. The students feel like a bigger part of the lesson with translanguaging and become leaders in their class.

Discussion Questions and Activities

1. What are ways that translanguaging can be used in a multilingual classroom as both a "mirror" for students to see reflections of themselves and as a "window" into new ideas, language practices, or perspectives?
2. What are ways that families and communities of students can be engaged in creating translanguaging materials for the classroom? Especially consider when home languages are not shared by the teacher, and families and communities are the language experts.
3. Consider a multilingual classroom with emergent bilinguals and monolingual English speakers. What are ways that translanguaging can enhance the learning of this second group of students?

References

Alim, H. S. (2005). Critical language awareness in the United States: Revisiting issues and revising pedagogies in a resegregated society. *Educational Researcher*, 34(7), 24–31.

Freire, P. (1970). *Pedagogy of the oppressed*. New York: Continuum.

Gutiérrez, R. (2007). Context matters: Equity, success, and the future of mathematics education. In T. Lamberg & L. R. Wiest (Eds.), *Proceedings of the 29th annual meeting of the North American Chapter of the International Group for the Psychology of Mathematics Education* (pp. 1–18). Reno: University of Nevada.

Gutiérrez, R. (2012). Embracing Nepantla: Rethinking 'knowledge' and its use in mathematics teaching. *Journal of Research in Mathematics Education*, 1(1), 29–56.

Ladson-Billings, G. (1995). But that's just good teaching! The case for culturally relevant pedagogy. *Theory into Practice*, 34, 159–165.

Moll, L. (2007). Bilingual classroom studies and community analysis: Some recent trends. In O. García & C. Baker (Eds.), *Bilingual education: An introductory reader* (pp. 272–280). Clevedon: Multilingual Matters.

Nelson, K. (2011). *Heart and soul: The story of America and African Americans. ReadyGEN Text Collection: Grade 5.* New York: Balzer and Bray.

Nieto, S., & Bode, P. (2011). *Affirming diversity: The sociopolitical context of multicultural education*, 6th edn. Boston, MA: Pearson Education, Inc.

Norton, B. (1995). Social identity, investment, and language learning. *TESOL Quarterly*, 29(1), 9–31.

Paris, D. (2012). Culturally sustaining pedagogy: A needed change in stance, terminology, and practice. *Educational Researcher*, 41(3), 93–97.

5

THE GRUPITO FLEXES THEIR LISTENING AND LEARNING MUSCLES

Tatyana Kleyn with Hulda Yau

Introduction

With the widespread adoption of the Common Core State Standards (CCSS), New York and many other states across the U.S. have found themselves pressed to align their curricula to these new standards. The federal funding connected to a tight implementation timeline has led to new curricula being developed at a rapid rate and mostly in English only, at least in the early stages. Schools with large numbers of emergent bilinguals (EBLs) and bilingual education programs have had to adapt to these new, challenging monolingual curricula with few home language resources and supports.

This large-scale scenario played out on the ground level in a 2nd-grade bilingual classroom, where the teacher used translanguaging to help her emergent bilingual students access an English-only curriculum. This approach only worked because translanguaging was an inherent part of the classroom culture and instruction. Had it only been used with certain students, it would have been viewed as a remedial tool, rather than a natural communicative practice used by bilinguals. This chapter will illustrate how an English-only scripted curriculum and translanguaging pedagogies came together within one lesson to provide students with in-depth understandings that could have only taken place through the validation and use of their full linguistic repertoire.

Context

Sotomayor Elementary (pseudonym) is located in Western New York, and is a long way from the hustle and bustle of New York City. The kindergarten through 6th-grade school is located in a suburban area and serves a lower socio-economic community, in which over 90% of the students qualify for free or reduced lunch. The school has slightly more than 500 students, half of whom are Latino, 42% Black, 7% White, and 1% Asian. Of these students, 27% have an individualized educational plan (IEP) and receive special education services, while 32% are designated as "English language learners" (mostly Spanish speaking). Of the emergent bilinguals in the school, 40% are also students with disabilities (SWD). Sotomayor Elementary has special programs for students with disabilities, such as self-contained classes for students on the autism spectrum and bilingual integrated co-teaching classes. Students with IEPs from across the district attend Sotomayor Elementary for these programs.

The classroom where this study took place was one of the school's transitional bilingual (Spanish/English) integrated co-teaching (ICT) 2nd-grade settings. In this classroom, there are three teachers who support students with disabilities so they can remain in the same setting as their peers, rather than being isolated from them. As with most transitional bilingual programs, the objective of the instruction is to move students into a general education classroom after they pass the NYSESLAT (New York State English as a Second Language Achievement Test) and show that they are proficient in English, although students are permitted to stay for up to two years after testing out of their English language learner (ELL) status as per New York State guidelines. Out of the 22 emergent bilingual students, six have an identified disability ranging from speech and language impairment to attention deficit hyperactivity disorder (ADHD).

The lesson outlined in this chapter took place within a small group during the English Language Arts period. It was led by Ms. Yau, a bilingual teacher of Puerto Rican descent with 10 years of experience and certification in the areas of childhood education and secondary Spanish and with a bilingual extension credential. Although Ms. Yau has stayed in education longer than most teachers have, she remains open to learning and improving and has fully embraced translanguaging as a new element of her teaching repertoire. Ms. Yau's small group, which she lovingly referred to as her grupito ("small group" in Spanish), included seven students whose information is outlined in Table 5.1.

The grupito's home language proficiency was determined by the Developmental Reading Assessment (DRA), which evaluates students' instructional level in Spanish. Their English proficiency level was determined via the Student Performance Task Assessment and Placement, which is part of the Core Knowledge Language Arts program, a comprehensive curriculum focused on reading, writing, listening, and speaking skills.

All the students had a higher level of proficiency in Spanish, their home language. They have all been in U.S. schools since kindergarten, when they were 5 years old, and some also attended prekindergarten at the age of 4. Of the seven emergent bilinguals in the grupito, two also had identified disabilities and all students struggled with the variety of English that was required of them in schools and on standardized assessments. All but one of the students were of Puerto Rican descent (the other was Dominican) and had been placed in Ms. Yau's group because of their English proficiency levels.

TABLE 5.1 Characteristics of Students in the Grupito

Pseudonym	*Spanish Proficiency: Grade Level*	*English Proficiency: Grade Level*	*Years in U.S. Schools*	*Categories*
Sonia	1st	K	K–2	EBL & SWD: Speech and Language Impaired
Daniela	2nd	2nd	PreK–2	EBL
Lorenzo	1st	1st	PreK–2	EBL
Ada	1st	K	K–2	EBL & SWD: Attention Deficit Hyperactivity Disorder
Pricilla	2nd	2nd	K–2	EBL
Inez	2nd	K	K–2	EBL
Carlos	2nd	2nd	K–2	EBL

Lesson Design and Moves

The focal lesson stems from the Core Knowledge curriculum (2013), which consists of skills and language arts listening and learning strands at the lower elementary level. This curriculum has been adopted in some schools and districts across New York State because of its direct alignment to the Common Core State Standards. The focal lesson comes from a larger unit on Greek Myths and comprises 10 highly scripted lessons, to be taught over a two-week period. Following an introduction to Greek myths, students listen to stories about gods and goddesses such as Zeus, Hera, Apollo, and the protagonist of this lesson, Hercules. The Hercules read-aloud text focuses on his strength to defeat others, as well as his lack of self-control, which puts him in a position where he defeats himself. At the conclusion, after being rejected from living among the community by the Greeks due to his temper, Hercules is given another chance by Theseus. This lesson, intended to last approximately an hour, includes seven content objectives and five language arts objectives, which are mostly taken from the Reading and Writing Common Core State Standards (they appear below in parentheses):

Content Objectives

- Explain that the ancient Greeks worshipped many gods and goddesses
- Identify Mount Olympus as the place believed by the ancient Greeks to be the home of the gods
- Identify Greek myths as a type of fiction
- Demonstrate familiarity with the myth "Hercules"

- Identify the elements of character, setting, plot, and supernatural beings and events in "Hercules"
- Identify common characteristics of Greek myths (e.g., they try to explain mysteries of nature and humankind, include supernatural beings or events, give insight into the ancient Greek culture)
- Describe some of the many different types of mythical creatures and characters in Greek myths, such as Atlas, Pan, Cerberus, Pegasus, and centaurs

Language Arts Objectives

- Recount information from "Hercules," a Greek myth, and determine the central message of the myth (RL.2.2)
- Describe how Hercules responds to challenges in "Hercules" (RL.2.3)
- Plan, draft, and edit a narrative Greek myth, including a title, setting, characters, and well-elaborated events of the story in proper sequence, including details to describe actions, thoughts, and feelings, using temporal words to signal event order and providing a sense of closure (W.2.3)
- Make a personal connection to friendship as it is depicted in "Hercules" (W.2.8)
- Identify how Hercules feels when he was feared by Greek citizens

(Core Knowledge, 2013, pp. 129–130)

Aside from the text that the teacher must read aloud, each lesson has accompanying pictures for students to view during the lesson, as well as discussion and comprehension questions and extension activities, all in English. Vocabulary words are also identified for each lesson, and for the Hercules lesson the 2nd graders were to learn the words "aimlessly," "commotion," and "dreadful." The units are fully inclusive in that teachers can follow them without additional resources. However, when addressing new content with students who are emergent bilinguals, Ms. Yau knows that these lessons—in their original format—are not comprehensible to her students. She and I collaborated on planning and teaching the lesson about Hercules using translanguaging. We took steps to modify the lesson in a way that would give the grupito greater access to the language and content.

Unlike most of the other lessons in this unit, where students had little to no background knowledge, many of the students either had heard of Hercules or had seen the movie named for him. This made the content seem less foreign, but it still required a significant amount of scaffolding. In the dialogue that follows, Ms. Yau explains how she goes about planning for and implementing an English-only read aloud text for emergent bilinguals who are at different progression stages in English:

MS. YAU: At home when I am reading this and I know there's certain academic vocabulary that is going to be challenging for them, other than the vocabulary that we have to review prior to the lesson, I look into that and so I make little notes on it . . . And especially when I am here and it's show time and we're having that conversation and I have blank stares, or I know right off the bat the kids are not getting it, I make a point of immediately going into Spanish, and I take a quick glance at my notes and boom, there I go.

T. KLEYN: Are there ever times when they are getting it and you do Spanish anyways?

MS. YAU: I do, even when they're getting it, it's just more like what's comfortable for us, and a lot of the kids come from the Caribbean; they are a little more engaged and it changes their affect.

In planning the lesson, Ms. Yau reads through the full text and identifies words and phrases the students would have difficulty with, especially in English, and notes how to say the words or explain the concepts in Spanish. But she also includes Spanish as a way to make the students feel more connected and engaged with the text, so that both languages have multiple purposes. Spanish is a valid resource that is not simply viewed as a temporary bridge or crutch to English. With this framework, Ms. Yau and I then divided the read-aloud lesson into three parts with the following translanguaging moves:

Pre-Read-Aloud

- Vocabulary Preview: Which words are cognates? Which aren't?
- Ask for examples from students' own lives (i.e., Do you ever feel like we have a commotion in our classroom? Why? Have you ever had a dreadful day? What happened?) These can be to the full group or via "turn and talk" to partners, that is having students talk to each other, in English or Spanish.
- Ask students if they have ever heard of Hercules before and, if so, where and what do they remember about him.

During Read-Aloud

- Every so often pause and ask a student to summarize what was read in Spanish
- Explain challenging concepts in Spanish

Post-Read-Aloud

- Accept answers in Spanish and have peers summarize in English
- After posing some questions, allow students to turn and talk in Spanish—and share out in English (or Spanish if needed)
- Allow students to write about the text in the language(s) they select

The final writing activity asks students to draw a picture and then recount the myth and its importance. Students do this by completing the following sentence starters:

My Greek myth character is _______________.
In this myth _______________________________.
This myth is important to the ancient Greeks because _________________.

The lesson went according to our plans and the students were generally excited about it, partly due to their familiarity with Hercules, as well as the special circumstances under which it was held, in the principal's office (so we could document the lesson without noise from the other students/groups). What we will show below is that whereas the lesson followed our design and—to a significant extent—the prescribed script, we allowed for flexibility throughout, so that translanguaging provided the support some students needed to access the content.

Taking Up Translanguaging

Although Spanish, or any other language other than English for that matter, was absent from the prescribed curriculum, the instruction that Ms. Yau and I designed introduced many rich instances of translanguaging throughout. Many of these moments were planned, although some arose spontaneously based on students' needs and reactions to the lesson, not unlike any other "planned" lesson. Here we focus on a few critical moments to delve deeply into understanding how translanguaging was instrumental in helping students access an English-only text and expand their linguistic repertoire.

Permission to Translanguage

Although this is a (transitional) bilingual classroom where English and Spanish are used, the students and their teachers have become accustomed to clear demarcations of when each language is to be used, and crossing these artificial borders is often looked down upon. Through her work with CUNY-NYSIEB, Ms. Yau has come to see the benefits of using languages more dynamically in her instruction, albeit still following a macro-language allocation policy grounded in days, times, and subject areas that dictate when to use one language or the other. The class follows a 70:30 language allocation policy, with approximately 70% of the instruction in English and 30% in Spanish. Languages are also divided by content area with English used for English Language Arts, math, listening and learning skills, and Spanish for social studies and science. The new normal of translanguaging is something Ms. Yau was still getting accustomed to and also something she often had to remind her students about, as she explicitly gave them permission to use, rather than suppress, any given language.

Starting in the beginning of the lesson, and reinforcing it a few times throughout, Ms. Yau was often heard saying "So here we go . . . You can say it in Spanish or in English." Just as bilingual teachers have learned to function within a double monolingual world (García, 2009), students have also internalized this language separation approach, although they may not have been able to follow the firm rule imposed upon them. Ms. Yau is herself unlearning this unnecessary rigidity and is constantly reminding students that their participation in this lesson is welcomed in any and all named languages that would permit them to be active learners and participants.

Student Translanguaging

Translanguaging can take a variety of forms—from teacher to student, student to teacher, student to student, and even student to self. Student-to-student translanguaging emerged in the review phase of the lesson when Carlos, the sole student in the grupito who spoke only in English throughout the entire lesson, offers a suggestion about what may have happened to the Minotaur in the story that was read in the prior lesson, and Ada, another student, joins in and extends Carlos's thought:

MS. YAU: The sun melted the wax. The feathers came out and he fell into the ocean. You are absolutely right.

CARLOS: Maybe he died?

ADA: Maybe he died cuando le dio al sol con la mano [when he hit the sun with his hand].

MS. YAU: Maybe. The story doesn't give us that detail, but you are right.

Ada, who is still at the very early stages of English acquisition, understands Carlos's idea and adds to it. And although this discussion is taking place in English, she is only able to use Carlos's words to start her thought, but must turn to Spanish to complete it. Had students only been permitted to participate in the discussion in English, Ada would have likely not spoken up at all and the teacher would not have been able to gauge her understanding, which we can see is strong. The teacher then acknowledges Ada's response as valid and continues to use English, which was the primary language used during the review segment of the lesson. Ms. Yau explains, "When I do the review, I pretty much go full on in English and when it's a new lesson I go back into Spanish for the concepts like the vocabulary words and things like that."

This example illustrates how in a lesson that takes up translanguaging, students can serve as linguistic resources to one another, helping to build off their ideas and language. The teacher's role here is to stand back, listen, and accept students' responses across languages, with the larger goal of having them comprehend the story and make inferences.

Playing With Language

When a classroom is open to different languages coming into contact with one another, students are able to play with language as they are given free range to explore and make connections. This happened during the vocabulary section of the lesson when students learned a new word, in both English and Spanish:

MS. YAU: Here is another one. Say it after me, "commotion."
CLASS: Commotion
MS. YAU: Ooooh and this sounds like a word in Spanish.
ADA: Commoshannnnnte
MS. YAU: Commoshante? Jajajaja almost. Digan conmoción [Say commotion].

Cognates are often touted as a way for Spanish-English bilinguals to easily access and make meaning of new words across languages (Bravo, Hiebert & Pearson, 2007). In the case of the word "commotion," the students had not known the word in English or Spanish. However, Ms. Yau's prompting of a similar sounding word in Spanish gave them a chance to try it out in that language, albeit unsuccessfully. The trial provided students a space for experimentation as they built off one language and connected it to another. It was done in a playful and low-stress way, without penalty. Students were able to experiment with language in the absence of a right–wrong binary as they saw that play and laughter could be a part of learning.

The focus on cognates cannot just focus on word pairs. Simply knowing how to say a word in two languages—cognate or not—is insufficient without knowledge of its meaning. This was how the grupito came to understand the meaning of "commotion":

T. KLEYN: ¿Y qué significa conmoción? ¿Quién sabe? Está difícil, ¿no? [And what does commotion mean? Who knows? It's difficult, no?]
CLASS: Conmoción
MS. YAU: Conmoción, when there is a lot going on in the cafeteria there is quite a commotion when you go in there.
ADA: I know! I know! When there is a lot of noises.
MS. YAU: Right, when there is a lot of noise. Como decimos en Puerto Rico hay un alboroto, mucho ruido, sí [Like we say in Puerto Rico there is a racket going on, lots of noise, yes].
LORENZO: Aquí en la ciudad [here in the city].

In this explanation, Ms. Yau takes two approaches to showing students what commotion means, both through connecting to what students already know. First, she locates an example with an experience students are all too familiar with—the school cafeteria. This example is given in English as the experiences students have in the school, especially those outside of their bilingual classroom, are mostly in English. Then, as a teacher sharing Puerto Rican descent with all but one of the students in the grupito, she offers a cultural example of what one may refer to as commotion there, an "alboroto."

Ms. Yau later reflects on her own changes in teaching and her students' progress in learning as she has started to take up translanguaging:

> Even though the concepts are in English and everything is in English, I go into Spanish and I make sure I point out those words in Spanish and have them participate. I don't remember ever saying anything in Spanish before because I thought I don't want to confuse them. . . . Now I feel like it is going to be more vocabulary for them to learn in English and Spanish, but it's really about the concepts. They have that capacity to take it all in and use both.

Ms. Yau's unique translanguaging for play and explanations across languages and cultures provides students the chance to learn a new term in two languages as they build off one language in an English-only scripted lesson (Graves & Watts-Taffe, 2009). As she says, "they have that capacity to take it all in," and they do.

Necessary for Some; Useful for All

Over the 40-minute lesson that we documented, each student had an average of 13.5 turns to speak, usually after being called on or calling out, and sometimes after being prompted from Ms. Yau to contribute. This was not so in the case of Sonia, one of two students with disabilities in the grupito, as well as Inez, a student who has to be pushed to speak and when she did, responded primarily in Spanish. These two students only spoke seven times throughout the lesson, about half of the average number of turns the other students took. Sonia's contributions were divided almost evenly with three English and four Spanish utterances, while Inez only spoke in English once.

Prior to Ms. Yau's use of translanguaging strategies in her English-focused content areas, Inez and Sonia were almost never heard from during these times and were essentially made invisible through the constraint of using English only. However, the following instance shows how Ms. Yau now invites Sonia to participate via the acceptance of Spanish as it relates to the English read-aloud:

MS. YAU: ¿Qué más sabemos de Hercules? ¿Qué más ha pasado en el cuento hasta ahora? Dímelo en español, Sonia. [What else do we know about Hercules? What else has happened in the story up to now? Tell me in Spanish, Sonia.]

SONIA: Porque era fuerte. [Because he was strong.]

PRICILLA: Porque él, cuando el se pusía, when he was getting angry, él se, he uhm, he uhm, he pushed the, uhm, the houses.

MS. YAU: Yea, you're right. He would destroy things so things would happen.

In this exchange Ms. Yau not only invites Sonia to contribute, but gives her permission to do so in Spanish. Although Sonia's response is short and lacking in detail, she is speaking and participating. This has rarely occurred prior to the use of translanguaging. We also notice that Sonia's Spanish spurs Pricilla to answer in Spanish, but she struggles to complete her thought and switches to English. Therefore, the accommodation to use Spanish was not only useful for Sonia, but pushed others in the class to discuss the English story in Spanish. Sonia's prompting of the use of Spanish by Pricilla shows that translanguaging is not merely an accommodation made for Sonia, but also a way to support the Spanish development of all students in the grupito. As young 2nd graders, all students, including emergent bilinguals, need support developing their home languages. Translanguaging supports the development of bilingualism by giving all students opportunities to use the minoritized language.

In the debriefing conversation following the lesson, Ms. Yau sheds light on how Spanish is needed more for the comprehension and participation of certain students such as Sonia and Inez, but is used and useful for all:

MS. YAU: Before, I could tell that Inez felt on the spot like, "Why are you only speaking to me in Spanish." Yet I was like, "But it's what you speak, why aren't you speaking?" . . . Even though she doesn't say, "You spoke to everyone in English and now you are changing for me and Sonia." I could see that she felt like that. She felt singled out, she was like, "I am still feeling uncomfortable so I am not even going to speak in Spanish."

T. KLEYN: So what has changed?

MS. YAU: [It's important to have the] conversation flowing because if I don't translanguage the kids like Inez and Sonia are not going to feel comfortable speaking . . . For once there are full conversations and we are all engaged in a question, and if it's Spanish, I notice that they come alive a little bit more. That was a big "aha" moment for me once I started.

Here Ms. Yau speaks to the way she has modified her approach to supporting students like Inez and Sonia. She has moved away from singling them out by speaking in Spanish only to them, and toward making Spanish, and dynamic language use specifically, more of a rule rather than an exception. This way Spanish is not only for students struggling with English, but a valid language to communicate with all students along the bilingual continuum.

Translanguaging as Amplifying

When students are learning in a new language, the curriculum or content is often watered-down or simplified, especially in a monolingual context. Walqui and van Lier (2010) stress the importance of amplification, or increasing language use and stating concepts or ideas in multiple ways, so that language is increased, rather than decreased. Although amplification *can* take place only in English, and is often conceived of in that way, translanguaging allows for a higher or at least different amplification for students. It opens up multilingual spaces to amplify, rather than simplify, both language and content.

The listening and learning strand of the curriculum that Ms. Yau is implementing presents students with challenging information, often written above their (English) reading level, although students are able to listen to texts at higher levels than they can read them. This reality, conflated with the often-unfamiliar topics for students whose English is emerging—and who are not the primary audience for this curriculum—make this listening and learning experience a most challenging one. To overcome these numerous obstacles, Ms. Yau uses translanguaging to provide students access to the content by amplifying the language(s) themselves. The three examples below show what Ms. Yau read, in quotation marks, and what she added to help her students understand the content:

> *Example 1*: "It's Hercules!!! a boy shouted. His father stopped in the middle of plowing . . ." Estaba arando, that is, when you turn the dirt so it gets ready to put the seeds there. *(Demonstrates using her hands)* Ok?
>
> *Example 2*: ". . . but there was one thing that Hercules could not defeat." Era algo que él no podía derrotar. El no podía. He could not defeat it. El no podía.
>
> *Example 3*: "But it was always too late; he had hurt someone. Alas, the other Greeks they told Hercules." This is what happens when they couldn't take it anymore. They said, "You have done many great things for us, but now you are a threat to our safety." Nuestra seguridad está en peligro.

Each example shows how Ms. Yau amplified the language of the text, sometimes in Spanish, sometimes in English, and occasionally bilingually. These additions, followed by comprehension and discussion questions, give students additional opportunities to access the content being read to them.

In the first example, Ms. Yau deviates from the text to explain the word and concept of plowing. Her rationale was described as we debriefed this segment:

T. KLEYN: You gave them the word for plowing in Spanish and then you gave the definition in English.

MS. YAU: Yes, arando. What I assume is because they come from the Caribbean and many people have a finca [farm], so I am thinking that maybe

> they have a sense of what it is, if I say it in Spanish. When I grew up, it was very rural, and so a lot of the kids I can tell if they are from that area because of the way they speak their Spanish. But after I say it, I look at their little faces to see if they get it. I was hoping that somehow someone would make a connection like, "oh yea, I lived next to a farm" or something like that.

Again, Ms. Yau uses her own background and that of her students to make connections between two seemingly disconnected cultures: Greek and Puerto Rican. She mentions that where students currently live in New York, plowing mostly takes place with snow, but uses the Spanish word ("arando") and an English definition—grounded in warm weather—with a bit of body language to help students understand this concept.

In example #2, Ms. Yau aims to help students understand one of the most challenging concepts in the text: self-defeat. By paraphrasing the first sentence and then restating that he "could not" both in English and Spanish, there is more contextualization of the written text. In questioning students and asking them to give an example of a time when they defeated themselves, Carlos shared that he experienced self-defeat by "punching myself." Clearly, the students needed more amplification here, as this concept is very difficult to grasp for a 7- or 8-year-old emergent bilingual.

Example #3 shows how languages are used flexibly to expand upon a concept and rephrase it in Spanish to create multiple access points for students. These small, yet powerful, excerpts illustrate how Ms. Yau uses translanguaging to amplify the text and context in the name of students' comprehension, connections, and extensions.

Holistic Assessment

Any content assessment administered in English is first and foremost a test of English proficiency (Menken, 2010). If we want to truly evaluate student understanding of content, they must be free to use their full linguistic repertoire. This lesson not only fluidly embedded English and Spanish during the instructional segment, but also permitted students to continue to use both languages, as needed, to be assessed on what they had learned. There was a direct correlation between the way students used language(s) during the lesson in their speaking and then in their writing. Following the lesson, students were asked to complete sentence starters that addressed key concepts of the text. Table 5.2 outlines the primary languages students selected to use in their speaking turns with the group and then in their writing of the text.

Over half the grupito, or four students, used both English and Spanish to complete the English sentence starters about Hercules. Most started with English to continue the flow of the sentence, but when they no longer had the English

TABLE 5.2 Language Use (Speaking & Writing) of Students in the Grupito

	Speaking			*Writing*		
Student	*English Turns*	*Spanish Turns*	*Total Turns*	*English Text*	*Spanish Text*	*Bilingual Text*
Sonia	3	4	7			X
Diana	12	1	13	X		
Lorenzo	15	4	19			X
Ada	13	3	16			X
Pricilla	9	4	13			X
Inez	1	6	7		X	
Carlos	16	0	16	X		

language to finish their thoughts, they turned to Spanish. Had they been required to stay in English only, they would likely have either stopped mid-sentence or written a watered down version of their original thought.

Pricilla's text in Figure 5.1 shows her flow from English to Spanish to express her understanding of what happened in this myth and why it was important (it also shows her misunderstanding, where she conflates Hercules with the tall tale of Paul Bunyan, which they had also read recently, who made rivers and was always with his friend, a blue ox).

Here we have written Pricilla's words in Figure 5.1 and translated the Spanish:

> My Greek myth character is Hercules. In this myth Hercules was distroi the hous y hercules isia rios y tenia un amigo y hercules cuando era un bebe cojio dos sembiente y cojio un oso y lo mato [made rivers and had a friend and Hercules when he was a baby he took two snakes and a bear and killed them.] This myth is important to the ancient Greeks because cuando ropia las cosas las personas se nojaban y no es bueno enojarte [when he broke things people would get mad and it's not good to get mad.].

Most students followed a similar English-to-Spanish pattern like Pricilla, while three decided to write monolingually. Diana and Carlos stayed in English throughout, just as they did during the lesson (with the exception of one Spanish turn by Diana), while Inez wrote completely in Spanish.

The essays by the grupito show what students were able to comprehend from the read aloud, and the areas where they struggled as well. As a group, they were able to understand the literal parts of the text, but did not grasp the more abstract concepts and lessons to be learned from the myth. There could be many reasons for this, including the challenging concepts, their need for additional scaffolding, and/or the developmental disconnect between the larger ideas and the age of the 2nd graders. Nevertheless, providing students choice, or at least not mandating their language use, created more opportunities for them to explain their

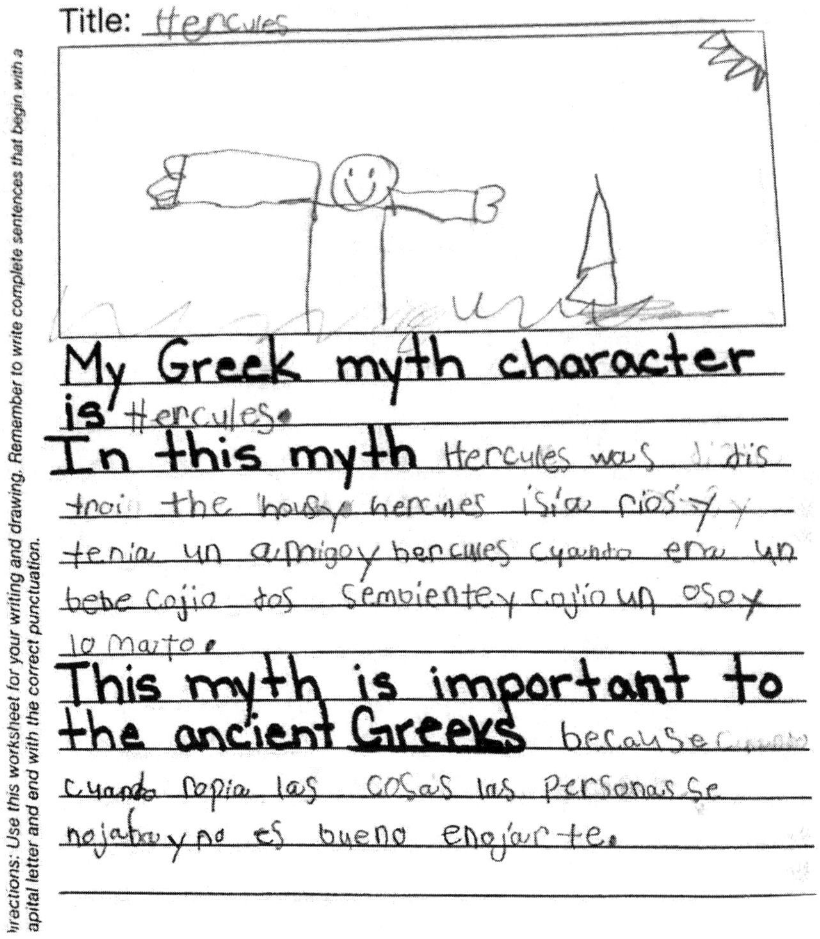

FIGURE 5.1 Pricilla's Work

understandings. In the absence of limitations to use any one language, they were able to use all the linguistic resources available to them to express themselves so their teacher could assess their understanding of the content and gauge their language use and needs.

Larger Meanings and Implications

Although this chapter focuses on just one lesson, there are larger meanings that can be applied to (bilingual) classrooms with emergent bilinguals. Here we share four of these implications that each start with a related quote from Ms. Yau. We then provide ground-level implications for educators and their students.

Translanguaging as Becoming Bilingual While Accessing All English Texts

> I feel good that I'm getting to have these kids [who are in the early stages of learning English] be a little more engaged. They seem to feel even more alive when they are able to explain themselves in both languages. Sometimes they have these pauses when they are trying to speak in English and they are trying to look for the word, and they are like "I have to say this in English?" and sometimes they say, "Yo lo sé en español. ¿Te lo digo en español"? [I know it in Spanish. Should I tell you in Spanish?]
>
> —*Ms. Yau*

When a text or a curriculum is only in English, that does not mean all instruction, discussion, and related work needs to remain in that language as well. On the contrary, when students are able to use their full linguistic repertoire to make sense of the English text, they will have a deeper understanding of it. They will also have a chance to develop new vocabulary in the additional language, thereby becoming bilingual and, ideally, biliterate. This approach means that it is the students—and their language practices—that dictate and are at the center of instruction, rather than a top-down curriculum or text. This places the power with the students and their teacher, and allows them greater points of entry to any text—English or not.

Translanguaging as a Pervasive Part of Classroom Culture and Instruction

> I don't see any negative feelings from the students towards Spanish or English. They embrace both of them. They really do. I don't have one kid, I don't think, that does not want to embrace their native language.
>
> —*Ms. Yau*

There are always students who require additional home language support, and for them translanguaging can be a lifeline to active learning and participation. However, translanguaging is not and should not be viewed as a crutch or a transition from the home language into English (or vice versa). If it is only used with certain students who are still struggling with English, they and their classmates will see it as a remedial and unwelcome tool. Instead, all students should be in a classroom where translanguaging is the norm and speaking in multiple languages is viewed positively for students who fall along the full continuum of bilingualism. In this way, speaking, reading, and writing in many languages becomes the expectation and a point of pride, rather than shame. Classrooms where translanguaging is the norm no longer create artificial boundaries between languages and their speakers, but mirror real world environments where linguistic contact zones, and also separations, exist. It is the educator who must set this tone from the very beginning, in both implicit and explicit ways, so students are clear that their learning space is one where all languages are valued and used for multiple educational purposes.

Translanguaging as Planned and Instinctual

> I read the facial expressions. It gives me an idea of what is going on, who is getting what, and I go in and out of English and Spanish based on what I see so it's not always something that I preplanned. Yes, I do have the vocabulary words and little notes in Spanish and in English, but it doesn't mean that's all I do.
>
> —*Ms. Yau*

Just like a teacher plans for content, she must plan for language as well. Planning for translanguaging requires an in-depth understanding of students' content knowledge, language practices, cultural backgrounds, strengths, and struggles. It sometimes requires letting go of teacher control so that students can take charge of their learning through their full linguistic repertoire. Other times it means becoming familiar with words or terms in a different language or searching for multilingual resources. But in spite of the most careful planning, moments will arise when deviation from the planned path is required. This means reading students and making on-the-spot decisions that may deviate from the plan. It means sometimes quickly explaining a concept in a student's home language or asking another student to do so. Just as translanguaging is dynamic, so too is the approach for enacting it. While translanguaging is planned and purposeful, it can also be spontaneous during big and small classroom moments. This is what García, Johnson, and Seltzer (2016) refer to as the translanguaging shifts.

Translanguaging as Building Fluid Language Practices in Bilingual Programs

> My students let me know if they understand. I don't have to translate back and forth. Everything just flows.
>
> —*Ms. Yau*

The term "flow" kept coming up in the debriefing conversation with Ms. Yau. This flow, or fluidity, is just the opposite of what many bilingual classrooms have become. Instead of being a safe haven for all languages, they have become policed language zones. Through translanguaging, the natural flow that is a part of being bilingual can emerge with the goal of viewing students in a holistic way—especially when it comes to their languaging and cultural practices—and supporting their content and language learning. Through the act of translanguaging, the overarching structure of how bilingual programs are conceptualized and enacted can become freer, more open spaces for learning across languages.

Conclusion

Ms. Yau's work with her grupito shows the promise of translanguaging, even within a curriculum that was not intentionally designed for it. The grupito, emergent bilinguals with and without disabilities along a continuum of English and Spanish development, were given multiple ways to access an English-only curriculum. The freedom they were offered to bring in their language practices and to use their bilingual voices opened up spaces for learning both content and languages. The teacher's careful planning and integration of translanguaging, combined with her knowledge of each member of the grupito and her flexibility around areas she could not plan nor predict, contributed to a learning experience that let the students drive the lesson, while still meeting the prescribed instructional goals. Ms. Yau's newly found translanguaging approach and culture of linguistic inclusion has drastically changed the way she teaches and how her students learn by bringing their full selves into each lesson.

TEACHER'S VOICE BY HULDA YAU

When I was first introduced to translanguaging, I understood it as "code-switching," going from one language to the next. I didn't understand how promoting students' full linguistic repertoire would benefit all my students. I shortly realized that using both languages in a very intentional and strategic way helped to facilitate the learning of content and language for my emergent bilinguals.

With this new insight, I began to use my students' home language as a resource rather than something they needed to transition away from. Through the implementation of translanguaging strategies, I was able to teach rigorous content in a way that was comprehensible to my students as their home and new language were being developed for academic purposes. For translanguaging to become an effective instructional tool, I had to create a new normal in our classroom culture. This meant placing student languages and learning at the front, instead of just exposing them to content and moving on with the pacing guide. I had to stop doing business as usual and center myself on students.

Based on the successes I have seen in my own teaching, I am currently working on promoting translanguaging strategies in our school and district through professional development sessions. At the school level, a colleague and I established a collaborative descriptive inquiry group. Our participants include speech therapists, special education teachers, ESL teachers, general education teachers, and bilingual teachers. This diverse group exemplifies how translanguaging can cross over many borders and benefit many types of students. Creating this type of collaborative environment pushed us to try out various types of translanguaging strategies in different settings and reflect on how they support student learning. It's been an incredibly successful experience that has shown us the power of validating and using our students' languages and cultures for learning.

Discussion Questions and Activities

1. What are the considerations for translanguaging at the elementary level given the developmental stages of students, pedagogical approaches, and set-up of classrooms?
2. What are the advantages and challenges of using translanguaging in a transitional bilingual classroom?
3. How can translanguaging support emergent bilingual students with disabilities?

Acknowledgment

We would like to thank Catherine Velasquez Leacock for her detailed transcriptions of the lesson and debriefing conversation.

References

Bravo, M. A., Hiebert, E. H., & Pearson, P. D. (2007). Tapping the linguistic resource of Spanish-English bilinguals: The role of cognates in science. In R. K. Wagner, A. E. Muse, & K. A. Tannenbaum (Eds.), *Vocabulary acquisition: Implications for reading comprehension* (pp. 140–156). New York: Guilford Press.

Core Knowledge. (2013). *Listening and learning strand: Grade 2*. New York: Core Knowledge Foundation. Retrieved on March 16, 2016, from: http://www.engageny.org/sites/default/files/resource/attachments/ckla_g2_d4_anth.pdf

García, O. (2009). *Bilingual education in the 21st century: A global perspective*. Malden, MA and Oxford, UK: Wiley/Blackwell.

García, O., Johnson, S., & Seltzer, K. (2016). *The translanguaging classroom: Leveraging student bilingualism for learning*. Philadelphia: Caslon.

Graves, M., & Watts-Taffe, S. (2009). Fostering word consciousness. In M. Graves (Ed.), *Essential readings in vocabulary instruction* (pp. 114–123). Newark, DE: International Reading Association.

Menken, K. (2010). No Child Left Behind and English language learners: The challenges and consequences of high-stakes testing. *Theory into Practice*, 49(2), 121–128.

Walqui, A., & van Lier, L. (2010). *Scaffolding the academic success of adolescent English learners: A pedagogy of promise*. San Francisco, CA: WestEd.

6

DECLARING FREEDOM

Translanguaging in the Social Studies Classroom to Understand Complex Texts

Brian A. Collins and María Cioè-Peña

Introduction

Students in the U.S. are increasingly being held to higher standards as part of national education reform initiatives such as the Common Core State Standards (CCSS). These standards serve as a set of expectations for what all students should know across the United States, and for developing college and career readiness skills, and as requirements for academic achievement and high school graduation. School curricula and assessments are being redesigned to meet the CCSS recently implemented by the majority of states across the nation. As the requirements and materials in schools continue to change and become increasingly more complex, there has been limited focus on how to adapt instruction for our rapidly shifting school population, which includes substantial and growing numbers of emergent bilingual students. How do we support emergent bilinguals and ensure their success within a rigorous standards-driven curriculum? Research has evidenced that using students' home language within the learning environment leads to stronger academic outcomes for emergent bilinguals (Collins, 2014; Rolstad, Mahoney & Glass, 2005). Using the home language in the classroom helps emergent bilinguals better understand new content, as well as build their comprehension and production in the new language (August & Shanahan, 2006; Cummins, 2007). Likewise, continued development of the home language supports bilingualism and biliteracy, essential skills of the 21st century. To this end, translanguaging provides a viable pedagogical approach to support emergent bilinguals' linguistic and academic development and prepares students for the educational demands and opportunities of today's progressively globalized and multilingual world.

Many of the new standards and aligned curricula focus on close readings of complex texts, including seminal U.S. documents and classics of American literature. Emergent bilingual students often have limited familiarity with these types of texts and historical events and documents (i.e., the Gettysburg address). Furthermore, much of the curriculum being used in U.S. schools, including that which is aligned to the CCSS, is in English and relates to a U.S. cultural context. This type of curriculum is likely challenging for all students, but especially for emergent bilinguals who may have less related background knowledge and are in the process of developing English literacy skills. Translanguaging can be used as an instructional strategy to bolster comprehension of these complex materials through multimodal activities. Encouraging emergent bilinguals to translanguage in their discussions and group work as they reflect, share, speak, read, and write promotes their engagement (Flores & García, 2013). Translanguaging allows students to actively participate in lessons and simultaneously use more complex language practices to comprehend, evaluate, synthesize, discuss, and engage with complex content, as well as to develop reading and writing skills in multiple languages (Celic & Seltzer, 2012).

Rather than substituting difficult curriculum and lessons with lower-level materials and overly simplified content, it is important to maintain rigorous standards and make lessons accessible for emergent bilinguals. In this chapter, we describe a lesson that was designed to introduce a historical and complex primary document, The Declaration of Independence, to develop emergent bilingual students' higher-order thinking skills and build their content knowledge. Translanguaging practices were integrated into the lesson as a means for emergent bilinguals to successfully participate and learn. The lesson presented here was designed, implemented, and analyzed to better understand how, when, and why translanguaging is taken up or resisted by students and teachers. Here we identify prevailing themes throughout the lesson and analyze how translanguaging was used to engage students' critical thinking.

The School, Students, and Program

Villaverde Middle School (pseudonym) includes grades 6 through 8 and is located in an outer borough of New York City. Villaverde serves approximately 420 students, who are almost exclusively Latino, the majority (94%) of whom are emergent bilinguals and from Spanish-speaking backgrounds, primarily from the Dominican Republic, Mexico, and Ecuador. The school offers two program options for emergent bilinguals whose home language is Spanish: transitional bilingual education (TBE, one classroom per grade level based on enrollment) and English as a second language (ESL). The TBE program at Villaverde Middle School is an option for those students who have been identified as emergent bilinguals with lower levels of English proficiency. At present, the school only has two TBE classes: a 6th/7th-grade bridge class and an 8th-grade class. Emergent bilinguals who speak Spanish at home, but are deemed to have a middle to high level of English proficiency, are placed in the general education classes and receive pull-out ESL services.

The research presented and discussed in this chapter was collected within the 8th-grade self-contained TBE class. In this classroom, the formal language allocation policy stipulates that all the subject areas are taught primarily in either English or Spanish; however, within these spaces both languages are used, with the teacher assigning work in English and Spanish based on the students' level of bilingualism. The teacher assigns work to students in either English or Spanish depending on how dense the content is, the students' proficiency, and the materials available. For example, during a social studies lesson in which the instruction and textbook are in Spanish, some students may respond to questions in their notebooks in English and others in Spanish. The classroom is very colorful and rich. There are Spanish and English vocabulary words posted throughout, intermingled with student- and teacher-made charts, along with commercial posters. There is a fairly even distribution of English and Spanish materials in the classroom. The classroom has a library that contains both English and Spanish books, as in Figure 6.1.

Students in this class spend their entire day together and receive at least half of their instruction from their homeroom teacher, Mr. Vásquez, and an ESL teacher, Ms. Arias. Both educators are bilingual and from the Dominican Republic. Mr. Vásquez teaches Spanish Language Arts and social studies mostly in Spanish and Ms. Arias teaches English Language Arts. Combined, these courses represent three to four periods in the day. The other periods include lunch, math, science, gym, and technology, all of which are taught in English by content area teachers. The class is composed of 17 students, 10 boys and 7 girls. All of the students are Latino immigrants with the majority (11) originating from the Dominican Republic. In addition, there are two students from Ecuador, two from Honduras, one from Mexico, and one from Peru. Twelve of the students recently immigrated to the U.S., six of whom have incomplete/interrupted formal educations (SIFE). There are six students in the class who are overaged, that is, older than the typical middle school student.

Translanguaging Design

The Lesson

The social studies lesson that is the focus of this chapter was conducted mid-year as an introduction to a unit on the American Revolution. The focus of the lesson was on the Declaration of Independence, which was chosen because it is part of the 8th-grade curriculum and Mr. Vásquez had expressed concerns about students being able to access historically based content. The objectives of the lesson were to: (1) identify reasons why the founding fathers declared independence from Britain, (2) paraphrase details from a primary source, and (3) translanguage to engage with the content. This lesson was taught by one of the authors (María) in a classroom in which both Brian and she had worked throughout the year.

The lesson was video recorded, as were the student-group discussions, and then transcribed. The authors analyzed the transcripts for evidence of how, when, and why translanguaging was taken up by students and teachers. The lesson design appears in Table 6.1.

As the translanguaging column in Table 6.1 shows, the teacher had predetermined the use of one language, the other, or both for different tasks, and for

FIGURE 6.1 Multilingual Classroom Library

TABLE 6.1 Lesson Design

Common Core English Language Arts—History/Social Studies Standards:

CCSS.ELA-LITERACY. RH.6–8.1	Cite specific textual evidence to support analysis of primary and secondary sources
CCSS.ELA-LITERACY. RH.6–8.2	Determine the central ideas or information of a primary or secondary source; provide an accurate summary of the source distinct from prior knowledge or opinions
CCSS.ELA-LITERACY. RH.6–8.6	Identify aspects of a text that reveal an author's point of view or purpose

Task	*Materials / Resources*	*Translanguaging*
Overview of American Revolution	• "Brainpop" video overview of American Revolution (English and Spanish versions)	• First viewing in English, second in Spanish • Students take notes in English or Spanish
Review primary/secondary documents: Declaration of Independence (DoI) and painting depicting the signing of the DoI	• Image of the original DoI • Trumbull's painting of the signing of the DoI	• Teacher presents in English • Turn & Talk in English or Spanish • Class share in English or Spanish
Introduction of the DoI—structure and purpose	• English printed version of the DoI	• Teacher presents in English • Turn & Talk in English or Spanish • Note taking in English or Spanish
Break up into small groups of four to analyze and paraphrase sections of DoI (each group had different sections focused on reasons for succeeding from England)	• English printed version of the DoI • Spanish translation of the DoI • English/Spanish glossaries	• Group discussions in English or Spanish • Assigned sections of text based on English proficiency
Whole group share	• Spanish/English parallel sentence frames	• Students required to share in English
Individual exit slip (end of lesson assessment) completion	• Prompts written in both English and Spanish	• Students encouraged to complete the exit slip in English, but could incorporate Spanish vocabulary if needed

the students or herself. That is, the language use was intentional, as the teacher had planned when and why each language was to be used. We first discuss the intentional language use of the lesson, and then we present the fluid language use that we observed, especially by students, as they made meaning of the lesson. These two characteristics—the design of intentional language use and the shifting to fluid language use—were part of the translanguaging design of the lesson. Each of these characteristics is discussed below.

Intentional Language Use

Translanguaging in the classroom involves the intentional use of bilingual students' fluid language practices and their multiple languages in one space. By intention, we mean that language use is not random, but rather languages are used strategically and allocated to particular tasks in advance. The teacher constructs translanguaging spaces intentionally and maintains them through teacher-led specific activities, pedagogical strategies, and the use of multilingual and multimodal resources (García, 2014). We call this planned design by the teacher the *intentional translanguaging design.*

For this lesson, the translanguaging design was planned in advance. External factors determined certain language use for specific parts of the lesson. For example, primary documents were in English. It was important that the students be exposed to the original document, which in this case, the Declaration of Independence, was an English text. Additionally, since the students were preparing for the social studies standardized test in English, it was important that one of the final products be completed in English. In planning the lesson, decisions about intentional language use were made for the different parts of the lesson: teacher-led instruction, student processing, and the final product. But in addition to this, the decision was made to make materials available to the students in both English and Spanish as a way to support the bilingual/biliterate goals of the lesson. Thus, students were provided with

- English and Spanish versions of the Declaration of Independence,
- A video about the American Revolution in Spanish and English,
- Handouts with English and Spanish directions and questions, and
- English sentence frames with parallel Spanish translations.

Although it is important for the teacher to decide in advance which languages will be used when and how, it is even more important that the students understand the intentional language use as well. Although this class had experience using translanguaging in past lessons, it was essential to begin the lesson with an open discussion with the students about language use. At the onset, the students understood that all of the instruction from the teacher would be given in English, but that they could turn to their partner for assistance and employ all their meaning-making resources from their extensive language repertoire. In the following excerpt, the teacher and students discuss the languages to be used to take notes on the information they learn from a short video (BrainPOP, 2015) about the American Revolution.

TEACHER: I'm writing down the information of the story. Do I have to write it in English or Spanish?
STUDENT: En español [in Spanish].
TEACHER: In Spanish? Everybody has to write in Spanish?
STUDENTS: No.
TEACHER: Then what?
STUDENT: In English.
TEACHER: Everybody has to write in English?
STUDENT: It can be in English or Spanish.
TEACHER: It can be in whatever language you need in order to take the notes. You can write in English or Spanish.

In instances when the use of multiple languages is made available to students, it is important to remind them that one size does not fit all. Although some students may choose to write in the home language, not all of them will need to or want to. Similarly, to ensure that students know when they have the space to use all of their linguistic resources, it is also equally important to let them know when there are specific linguistic expectations. In the following passage, the teacher is making sure that the students understand what is expected of them at the end of the lesson:

TEACHER: What language are we going to share in?
STUDENTS: English.
TEACHER: In English. But as a group, you can work in what language?
STUDENTS: Spanish or English.
TEACHER: But when you share [with the whole class], you need to share in English.

Students were reminded of the intentional use of language in this lesson not only during the whole class introduction to the tasks, but also throughout the small group and independent work. The teacher traveled from table to table, listening to the students' group shares in both English and Spanish. She also provided students with English and Spanish sentence frames that the groups could use to prepare the sharing of ideas in English with the whole class. Figure 6.2 presents how a student from one group had started writing in Spanish, but ultimately completed the English sentence frame.

Some teachers worry that if given too much linguistic freedom students who are dominant in one language, but learning another, will rely too heavily on the

The founding fathers felt that

independence from Britain was necessary

because The british raise the taxes without ask the colonist and for not allowing us to trade w/ the all parts of world. Declaim our most valuable laws

Los padres fundadores de los Estados

Unidos sintieron que la independencia de

Bretaña era necesaria porque

los br

__________ y __________.

FIGURE 6.2 A Student's Response Using Sentence Frames

language in which they are proficient, thus hindering their progress in the other language. By making linguistic expectations clear, teachers give students opportunities to use their home languages in ways that are constructive and focused on the task at hand. Otherwise, students may be left neither grasping the language nor the content. Translanguaging allows students to access and develop content area knowledge while also encouraging their bilingual and biliterate practices.

Beyond planning the intentional use of English or Spanish, this lesson design also provided space for the fluid use of language features from the students' entire linguistic repertoire. This is further discussed in the next section.

Language Fluidity

Translanguaging is a common discourse practice of bilinguals in many contexts. Bilinguals often use their language features dynamically in order to communicate in effective ways. To extend these practices into academic contexts, it is key to create space for language fluidity in the classroom where bilinguals are empowered to translanguage (García & Leiva, 2014). Translanguaging can be then used as an instructional strategy that allows bilingual students to flexibly access their entire linguistic repertoire in order to understand rigorous content and use language in the ways desired in academic contexts. When bilingual students are encouraged to use their language strengths to discuss and reflect on concepts, they are able to gain a deeper understanding and comprehension of new content. They also develop subjectivities that empower them as bilingual people, not as English speakers only or Spanish speakers only.

In this lesson, most of the teacher-led discussion and instruction was in English, whereas most of the small group student discussion was in Spanish. However, within each of these spaces there was evidence of language fluidity where students and the teacher used English and Spanish to analyze and find meaning in the text.

While students worked in small groups, there were no restrictions of which language the students should use; rather, they utilized their full linguistic repertoire to understand the text. In the following exchange, we see how the teacher leads a class discussion in which she asks a student in English why the Founding Fathers declared independence. The student responds in English and in Spanish.

JOSÉ: The [king] dissolved representative houses repeatedly.

TEACHER: Ok say it again. First start here (pointing to sentence frame), *The Founding Fathers . . .*

JOSÉ: (reading from sentence starter) *The Founding Fathers feel that independence from Britain was necessary because . . .* the king dissolved the representative houses repeatedly.

TEACHER: So the king dissolved the representative houses repeatedly. What does that mean?

JOSÉ: Que no dejaba que de las cámaras se reúnan. [That he didn't let the houses meet.]

TEACHER: OK, so people weren't allowed to meet and get together (gesturing with hands/fingers to "get together"). Ok, second reason . . .

JOSÉ: He refused other houses to be elect.

TEACHER: So, what does that mean then?

JOSÉ: No dejaba tampoco que escogieran a otras cámaras de las colonias. [Neither did he let them choose other representatives from the colonies.]

TEACHER: So you couldn't vote for your own representatives.

JOSÉ: The king has allowed the population to go up. No dejaba que personas de otros países llegaran a las colonias. [He didn't allow people from other countries to come to the colonies.]

TEACHER: So those are three reasons. Three reasons why it didn't work. The first one was, there was no representation so they wouldn't let them meet, the second one, you could not vote for people to represent you and the third was . . .

JOSÉ: No dejaban que otras personas llegaran a las colonias.

TEACHER: So he wasn't allowing people to come to the colonies. Does that make sense?

STUDENTS: Yes!

In the example above, the teacher is supporting José, an emergent bilingual who recently immigrated and had been in the U.S. school system for less than one year. José has high proficiency in his home language, Spanish, and beginning proficiency in English. It is evident from the dialogue with the teacher that he was able to find three reasons to justify independence from Britain in the text and had a good understanding of them. He used English to *identify* the reasons and Spanish to *demonstrate* his understanding. The teacher translated and shared his Spanish response in English, adjusting the language of the task for the others. During this time, the other students in the class were fully engaged and listening to the dialogue (even as the class bell rang and there were other distractions in the classroom).

José was grouped with two other recent immigrant students with similar language abilities. These other students decided to use the English version of the Declaration of Independence, as well as English sentence frames to prepare their responses, yet they discussed the meaning of the text primarily in Spanish. In the groups, we noticed that the work completed in English tended to be more closely copied from the text, while when they were using Spanish they paraphrased and the answers were more creative and elaborate, which was one of the objectives of the lesson. For example, the response in English in the sentence frames that appear in Figure 6.2 is much less developed than the paragraph response primarily in Spanish that appears in Figure 6.3. In the student's paragraph response that appears in Figure 6.3, we see that the first and last line written in English is copied from the text, whereas the rest of the response in Spanish is paraphrased.

As is often the case, the emergent bilingual children in this classroom have different bilingual abilities, and therefore flexibility in language practices is necessary. The fluid use of language across contexts (English text, Spanish group discussion, Spanish response to teacher, teacher recast in English), depending on the needs of specific children, supports the common goal of students engaging with, and understanding, the text. Taking up translanguaging allows the teacher to adapt and provide the appropriate language input for individual children and differentiate the instruction, while ensuring that all students are working towards achieving skills reflected in the lesson standards and objectives.

The American Revolution

Write a brief paragraph where you identify three reasons why the founding fathers went on to declare independence against Britain and King George. Be sure to support it with evidence from the text.

For not allowing os trade whit
all Parts OP the word. Esto quiere
decir que las Personas traian Productos
Para venderlos Pero el gobierno les
Proivian venderselos a otras Personas.
solo que se quedaran con ellos
y que no lo Repartieran a los
demas. For suspending our Legislatures,
and declaring themselves invested whit
Power to legislate For us in all
cases whatsoever.

FIGURE 6.3 A Student's Paragraph Response

During the lesson, there were many instances of students paying attention and listening, even when they were not able to respond in English. This is the case in the following dialogue where students respond in English and Spanish. We can see that students are not only answering with intention, but they also do not repeat what others have said in the other language, which demonstrates a collective understanding.

TEACHER: OK, so a primary document, what are some examples of a primary document?
STUDENT 1: A letter?
TEACHER: A letter. That's a great example. What else?
STUDENT 2: A diary.
TEACHER: A diary, ok.
STUDENT 3: A newspaper.
TEACHER: A newspaper, anything else?
STUDENT 4: Picture.
TEACHER: A picture, so it could be from that time period.
STUDENT 5: La ropa.
TEACHER: So clothing from that time period, anything else? Could be artifacts right?
STUDENT 6: Artes.
TEACHER: ¿Artes? So art from that time period.
STUDENT 7: Monedas.
TEACHER: Money from that time period. So, different things as long as it comes from that time.

The teacher used students as resources to listen to each other and she reiterated what they said in English. This is another example of how translanguaging within the lesson allows students to participate and engage. Teachers who do not share the language with their students, however, may need to support students' language needs and abilities in ways other than reiterating student responses back in English. For example, these teachers may have to ask another student who shares that language to recast or translate the response. Translanguaging allows students the space to take control of their own learning and make sense of content and language (García, Johnson & Seltzer, 2016).

Students' engagement in learning increases through translanguaging. An example from our lesson is when the teacher asks a question in English and the students discuss in Spanish in small groups.

TEACHER: Turn and talk to your partner. What is it that they [the Founding Fathers] think a government should look like?
ISABEL: Ellos tienen que elegir como quieren que el gobierno sea, como les gustaría. [They have to elect how they want the government to be, how would they like it.]

RAÚL: Entendí. [I understood.]
ISABEL: Dime. [So tell me.]
RAÚL: Quieren que el gobierno sea justo y los tome en cuenta. [They want the government to be fair and take them into consideration.]
ISABEL: Y que sea elegido por ellos mismos (pause) y los tomen en cuenta y las leyes sean por ellos mismos. [And that they be elected by the people and that they take them into consideration and make laws for themselves.]

We see that students are motivated to discuss the text and are accountable to their small groups when they are using their home language. In this example, Isabel is checking to make sure her partner, Raúl, fully understands and participates in the discussion by responding to the teacher's question. Isabel will not take a superficial answer from Raúl and presses him to fully answer the question, which she then reiterates. Allowing students to use language flexibly, to discuss the content in Spanish, and to answer the question posed in English by the teacher increased the depth of the conversation in this group. By discussing the content in Spanish, they are better situated to answer the English questions, whereas if their discussion had been in English the depth of the conversation would have been more superficial.

As this lesson was in a bilingual classroom, students were able to use language features fluidly because their peers shared the same home language and had similar language experiences and linguistic features in their repertoire. Students used language fluidly during discussions about the reading and while speaking to others within the classroom. The fluid use of English and Spanish within the same lesson allowed students to draw on their full knowledge to contextualize their linguistic development in English, as well as the development of their bilingual and biliterate abilities. At the same time, students were able to gain critical content knowledge.

The translanguaging design of this lesson, both in intentional language use and in fluid language use, was supported through two other principles of translanguaged classroom structures—the availability and use of multilingual and multimodal resources and collaborative grouping.

Instruction in Translanguaged Classrooms: Resources and Grouping

A successful translanguaging design depends not only on the teachers' capacities to plan an effective lesson thinking about intentional and fluid language use, but also on her ability to provide students with effective instructional resources, as well as effective instructional grouping. How this teacher was able to shape these two features of translanguaged classrooms is discussed in the next section. We turn first to the multilingual/multimodal resources, before we discuss collaborative grouping.

Multilingual/Multimodal Resources

Multilingual/multimodal resources refers to the use of multiple media (written, oral, visual, virtual) in order to provide students with various entry points into a lesson. Incorporating multilingual, multimodal texts increases the comprehension of complex content. The content of this lesson was expected to be extremely challenging for the students because of language demands as well as the complexity of the subject; therefore, a great deal of attention was paid to the types of supporting materials that would be used during the lesson.

At the start of the lesson, the teacher used a BrainPop video (online animated, curricular content-based videos), first shown in English and then in Spanish, to contextualize the work around the Declaration of Independence. The rationale for the language order of the videos was to ensure student engagement during both viewings, and so that the Spanish video could serve as reinforcement of student understanding and ability to grasp concepts, ideas, and language features from the English version. The students were also shown a painting depicting the signing of the Declaration of Independence, as well as a picture of the original document to differentiate primary and secondary sources of information. During group work, students were given print versions of the Declaration of Independence in English and were provided with corresponding page numbers to access a Spanish version in their textbooks. Additionally, a handout with questions about the text in both languages was provided, with English as the primary print and Spanish translation as a subscript (see Figure 6.4). Lastly, in order to facilitate the whole group share of

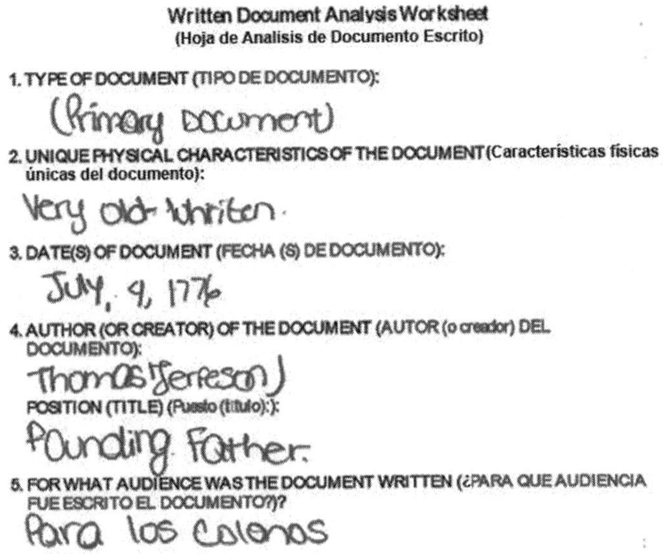

Written Document Analysis Worksheet
(Hoja de Analisis de Documento Escrito)

1. TYPE OF DOCUMENT (TIPO DE DOCUMENTO):
   (Primary Document)
2. UNIQUE PHYSICAL CHARACTERISTICS OF THE DOCUMENT (Características físicas únicas del documento):
   Very old written.
3. DATE(S) OF DOCUMENT (FECHA (S) DE DOCUMENTO):
   July, 4, 1776
4. AUTHOR (OR CREATOR) OF THE DOCUMENT (AUTOR (o creador) DEL DOCUMENTO):
   Thomas Jefferson)
   POSITION (TITLE) (Puesto (titulo):):
   Founding Father.
5. FOR WHAT AUDIENCE WAS THE DOCUMENT WRITTEN (¿PARA QUE AUDIENCIA FUE ESCRITO EL DOCUMENTO?)?
   Para los Colonos

FIGURE 6.4 Student Handout: Written Document Analysis Worksheet the lesson, each group was provided with an English sentence frame that was to be used to help them organize their English statements to the whole class (see Figure 6.2).

Although this lesson was conducted primarily in English, the fact that it was a content area lesson meant that the teacher had to ensure that all students would be able to access and engage with the subject matter regardless of their English proficiency level. Since the teacher gave most of the instructions in English, the availability of Spanish-language materials supported students who otherwise may have disengaged from the lesson. The visuals and support materials in Spanish provided students the ability to keep up and participate in the class discussion and to work independently and in their groups. The use of the parallel Spanish text allowed students to use their home language skills to help them comprehend complex words, sentences, and/or ideas. We see this illustrated in the following example taken from discussion in one of the groups.

KELIANI: Son tres razones por las que tienen que tener, porque escribieron la Declaración de Independencia. [There are three reasons why they have to have, why they wrote the Declaration of Independence.]

JUAN: Una es por los impuestos, por la aumentación de impuestos. [One is because of the taxes, because of the increase in taxes.]

KELIANI: Y ¿dónde dice esto? Léelo en inglés. [And where does it say that? Read it in English.]

JUAN: (Reading the text) "For imposing tax without our consent."

KELIANI: Entonces ¿Qué significa? Los británicos ponían impuestos sin consentimiento. [Then, what does that mean? The British added taxes without consent.]

These students used the multilingual text as a way to not only ensure that they were all participating in the discussion, but also that they were holding each other accountable for developing meaningful understandings beyond parroting the text. In follow-up conversations with the students about which components of the lesson they found most useful or beneficial, students frequently mentioned the availability of the Spanish materials. The students commented that access to the materials in both languages allowed them to learn new vocabulary, to be more self-sufficient, to engage in group discussions, and to feel connected to the lesson. These conversations also highlighted that by giving students materials in both English and Spanish, they were provided with a sense of choice, which in turn allowed learning autonomy. Even though students were in groups, they weren't totally dependent upon their peers. Multiple students stated that having the materials available in both languages allowed them to learn a lot of new words because they were able to use the Spanish text to provide not only a direct translation, but also examples of the ways in which words were used.

ABEL: Para mí fue importante porque me ayudó a comprender algunas palabras que no entendía muy bien [en] inglés. Como "consent," no sabía muy clara esa palabra, así que busqué el texto en español. [For me it was important because it helped me understand a few words that I didn't understand very well [in] English. Like "consent," I did not know very clearly that word so I looked in the Spanish text.]

TEACHER: Consent.

ABEL: Busqué la palabra correctamente y me dijo que es consentimiento, entonces me ayuda a comprender más, tenerlo más claro el texto o cualquier cosa que estoy leyendo en inglés. [I looked for the word correctly and it told me it was consent, so then it helped me understand better, understand the text more clearly or anything that I may be reading in English.]

The above example not only highlights the student's ability to learn new vocabulary in both languages, but is also evidence of Abel's self-motivation and self-monitoring as he engages with the text. One concern for teachers when providing home language materials is the fear that this will lead to students becoming too dependent on the home language and as a result hinder their English language development. But, on the contrary, this example showcases a student who used the English materials and only turned to the Spanish material when he felt he needed more linguistic support.

Other students read the English text, mentally translated it to Spanish, and subsequently read the Spanish in order to monitor their own understanding. This was the case for the student who told us:

> Creo que fue importante porque yo leía todo en inglés, y lo traducía en mi mente y luego leía en español para ver si estaba bien lo que había traducido. [I think it was important because I would read everything in English and I would translate it in my mind and then I would read it in Spanish to see if I had translated it correctly.]

By using multilingual/multimodal texts, the teacher was able to give students multiple points of access for them to participate and engage with the content, the materials, and their peers. Ultimately, the goal of the lesson was to teach the students about the Declaration of Independence. The Spanish-language materials did not distract from the goals established by the teacher, but, on the contrary, supported them. Additionally, the use of multilingual, multimodal texts facilitated students' abilities to work collaboratively in multiple languages, the topic to which we turn next.

Multilingual Collaborative Work

Collaborative learning is an important component of a student-centered classroom and increases engagement and learning. In a translanguaging classroom, students are provided the opportunity to use multiple languages when collaborating to complete work. When students use their entire language repertoire in collaborative work at school, they are able to communicate in ways that are similar to the ways they use language in other settings. For some students, this allows them to shift from a more passive to a more active role and engage collaboratively in rigorous academic activities. Working in collaborative groups extends and deepens the thinking of students, while also enabling students to gain different perspectives. Translanguaging in collaborative group work affords students the space where all of their language skills are utilized to communicate their understanding, find meaning, and model and support each other's learning (Celic & Seltzer, 2012).

In this lesson, we observed students actively participating when working collaboratively. We saw that the use of translanguaging was encouraged by the social dynamic of children seated with peers who shared the same home language. In addition, the lesson was structured so that there were plenty of moments for collaboration (i.e., whole class sharing, debriefing, reiterating ideas). Long periods of sustained teacher-focused instruction may limit students' engagement with new content. Giving students the time to work collaboratively allows them to build on each other's knowledge and receive individual assistance from peers. For example, in the following interaction, three students discuss a complex sentence in the text and work together to decipher the meaning:

ANA: (reading from the Spanish-language text): "Transportándonos más allá de los mares para ser juzgados por delitos supuestos," ¿Qué significa eso? ["Transporting us beyond seas to be tried for pretended offences," What does that mean?]

MANUEL: Lo que yo entendí de la oración, es que por llevarlos a otro lugar para interrogarlos, a ver si, para ser juzgados como dice aquí, para interrogarlos sobre algunos delitos o . . . [What I understood from the sentence, is that by bringing them to another place to interrogate them to see if, to be judge, like it says here, to interrogate them over some offense, or . . .]

FELIX: Los llevan a otro lugar para juzgarlos. [They took them to another place to be judged.]

In this example, Ana orally reads a complicated section of the text from the Declaration of Independence in Spanish and asks her peers to help with the meaning. Manuel shares his understanding by elaborating and correctly paraphrasing the text into more common and comprehensible language. Then Felix succinctly summarizes the meaning. The students in this example are not talking over one another; rather, all the students in the group are working together to decipher the complex discourse presented in the text. The collaborative group learning structure of the lesson helped to facilitate students' use of their home language practices to make meaning. Many aspects of this task may not have been possible to complete if the students were working individually. As a group, students were parallel-reading a text in English and Spanish, discussing in Spanish, taking notes in English and Spanish, and sharing with the whole class in English. This dynamic use of language features truly takes advantage of their linguistic abilities while learning new content. In collaborative groups, emergent bilinguals feel empowered in what they know, and are therefore more comfortable appropriating English features into their linguistic repertoires (Flores & García, 2013). Furthermore, students recognize that collaboration is valuable. They appear to enjoy helping one another.

During the students' post-lesson reflections, we heard how they appreciated working together and helping classmates to improve and build upon their language abilities, while learning new content. Furthermore, students were empowered to help one another in the learning process. At the end of the lesson, we asked students to share their views on whether translanguaging is important for their learning. One student told us:

> Yo me sentí como inteligente y también. . . . como capaz para ayudar a mis amigos, mis compañeros; los que estaban en el grupo no saben hablar inglés y les traducía, los ayudaba. [I felt smart and able to help my friends, my classmates; those who were in the group and don't speak English, I translated for them, I helped them.]

By giving emergent bilingual students the opportunity to translanguage, they develop a more assertive identity, one that shows them as being more intelligent. In the quote above, for example, this student feels capable of helping others. Through translanguaging, this student finds a way to be smart, helpful, and competent. Rather than "limited," or a "learner," this emergent bilingual student can identify and leverage language resources that make him feel smart, useful, and caring.

As this class is accustomed to working in groups collaboratively, they are well versed in understanding one another's needs. At the same time, they also hold each other accountable for learning, as demonstrated in the following passage:

BETICIA: OK, tenemos que hacer anotaciones, verdad? [OK, we have to take notes, right?]

CONSUELO: Sí, porque cada vez que leemos tenemos que hacer anotaciones [Yes, because each time we read we need to take notes.]

BETICIA: No, pero no nos queda más tiempo. OK, vamos a hacer esto, mira, entonces preguntamos anotaciones pero del documento, dialogando. Entonces ¿tú quieres decir que ellos ya se cansaron de tener tantas leyes que ellos les pusieron en ese tiempo, y el actual rey siempre está en desacuerdo por lo que ellos querían ? [No, but we don't have much time. OK let's do this, look, let's ask ourselves the notes but from the document, talking to one another "dialoguing." So, you want to say that they got tired of all the laws to which they had been subjected during this time and the King was always in disagreement with what they wanted?]

STEFAN: Ellos no tenían como una voz, como demanda. [They didn't have like a voice, like a demand.]

CARLOS: Ah, un representante. [Oh, a representative.]

CONSUELO: Sí exacto. [Yes, exactly.]

BETICIA: Un delegado. Entonces se cansaron y para eso escribieron esto, para que ellos los escucharan, y para tener y hacer todo lo que ellos quieran. ¿Entienden? ¿Van entendiendo? [A delegate. So they got tired and that's why they wrote this, so they would be heard and to have and do everything they wanted to. Do you understand? Are you all understanding?]

CARLOS: Sí, yo entiendo. [Yes, I understand.]

BETICIA: Hay que hacer lo más que podamos. [We have to do the most that we can.]

Here, students worked together in their home language and diligently followed the instructions of the lesson. They recognize the expectation of taking notes and suggest note taking "orally" through their dialogue because there wasn't enough time. This effective time saver of dynamically discussing the reading with their peers was possible because students were given the opportunity to work together and to be in charge of their learning. We can see that they do not take this opportunity lightly and work together to gather information from the text. One student reminds the group that they must do as much work as they can ("Hay que hacer lo que más podamos"). Accountability is a major part of the group dynamic. We observed students checking with each other to make sure they understand, as Beticia asks: "¿Entienden? ¿Van entendiendo?" In other examples, classmates use each other to understand where to find the text-based evidence of what a classmate is saying: "Show me, show me where it is."

A common concern of teachers with group work may be that students will not put in a full effort or engage with the task. This is especially a concern when students are using their home language and the teacher may not be able to understand them. However, as these multiple examples demonstrate, when the tasks and expectations are clearly stated and understood, students in collaborative groups work diligently and hold each other accountable.

Impact of Translanguaging

In this lesson, translanguaging was used as an effective tool to engage bilingual students in higher-order thinking skills and the comprehension of historical texts. Translanguaging strategies that were purposely integrated into the lesson allowed students to build content knowledge around an unfamiliar topic and understand a complex text of a primary historical source. It was encouraging to see the level of understanding of extremely dense passages from the Declaration of Independence that students were able to construct by translanguaging. Students readily listened in English and responded in Spanish, as well as read and discussed parallel texts in English and Spanish. By providing space for students to work in both languages, they were able to engage and understand material that they may not have been able to access if these had been provided only in English. For example, after viewing the "BrainPop" video on the American Revolution in English, one student shared that she was confused "and didn't understand much," whereas after viewing it in Spanish she "was able to understand the events that had happened and answer the questions."

Translanguaging in the lesson supported students along different stages of bilingual progressions to participate, complete work, and share new knowledge with the whole class in English. Students worked collaboratively in their groups constructing responses in English, which were often shared with the whole class by students with beginning English proficiencies. These students with lower English proficiency were supported by their classmates as they developed their responses, so they were confident that what they were sharing was accurate and met the requirements of the task. The lesson utilized small groups as a space for students to work collaboratively to support one another's learning while translanguaging. Students were very much on task in their small groups and demonstrated strong collaboration, as well as peer-to-peer accountability. Overall, the use of translanguaging strategies allowed students to engage with a more complex text and have a greater level of interaction with their teacher and their peers, which resulted in more time on task. Students discussed the complex texts, making notes of the events through the dialogue and were conscious to do "the most we can."

A central aim of this lesson was to utilize translanguaging as a strategy to allow emergent bilinguals to achieve the rigorous curriculum standards through practice with materials and activities that leveraged their current strengths and abilities. Through the use of translanguaging, this lesson upheld the required abilities outlined in the Common Core State Standards.

The use of primary documents in multiple languages allowed students to accurately cite and analyze specific sections of the text. Students identified the reasons why the colonists wrote the Declaration of Independence by using primary documents. We observed that students used the Spanish version to find facts and evidence, while also using the English version to help formulate their responses. The students did not stop after finding the same text in English; rather, they went on to question one another.

Working in multilingual collaborative groups gave students with different readiness levels the opportunity to assist one another in understanding the complex content. Having access to their peers' multiple language resources allowed them to discuss and collectively determine the central ideas and author motivations found within the Declaration of Independence. Students used their home-language skills to help them understand the content and further develop their English abilities for academic purposes. Through collaborative work with peers, we saw that students were able to successfully share their findings with the class in English.

The lesson also provided students with the opportunity to demonstrate their summarizing and paraphrasing abilities. Students cited passages directly from the historic text with one student paraphrasing another, and a third student summarizing. They worked collaboratively in Spanish to analyze and understand the text, using translanguaging to find meaning. Had these students only been granted access to this lesson in an English-only learning environment, their ability to meet these standards would have been greatly hindered.

Students felt empowered through using their full linguistic repertoire to participate in the lesson, as well as support one another. After the lesson, several students expressed how the use of Spanish and English both increased their understanding and built their self-confidence as active learners. By providing the opportunity for students to translanguage in this lesson, they were able to strengthen their academic abilities, deepening their content knowledge and language and literacy use. The impact of using translanguaging strategies in this bilingual classroom of diverse learners proved to be an effective resource in meeting the rigorous demands and standards that are a required part of the school's mandated curriculum. By giving students the tools to access this challenging material, they were motivated to complete the work and actively maintain engagement throughout a lengthy and demanding lesson.

Conclusion

In the current academic climate, with high demands placed on demonstrating yearly progress, many students struggle to meet rigorous learning standards and expectations. Many of these standards and reforms do not take into consideration the rapid demographic changes in school populations, which include increasing numbers of emergent bilinguals. As a result, much of the standards-aligned curricula have been rapidly produced with little consideration of the students who will be using it. The lesson described in this chapter demonstrates that the rigorous standards do not need to be discarded or lowered, but rather the instruction and support must be adapted to the unique learning strengths, needs, and abilities of emergent bilingual students. As more and more of our students come from homes where languages other than English are spoken, it is recommended that we identify strategies and approaches that leverage and build upon children's bilingualism rather than blindly instruct students as though they were English monolinguals.

Based on our observations and work described in this chapter, we have identified a specific translanguaging lesson design and classroom structures, which effectively engage and support emergent bilinguals in attaining the necessary abilities outlined by the Common Core State Standards. In the described lesson, the standards were aligned with the same rigorous texts that are utilized in many state-developed curricula and assessments. What changed was the translanguaging pedagogy that was used in the lesson. Following are some recommendations for using translanguaging to strengthen the language and content development of emergent bilinguals:

A translanguaging *lesson design* should include:

1. the intentional language use of the lesson
2. space for language fluidity whenever it is appropriate to deepen understanding of both content and language

A translanguaging *classroom structure* should include:

1. the provisions of multilingual and multimodal resources
2. collaborative working groups

We recognize the challenges placed on teachers today and understand that the integration of these four components that make up the lesson design and the classroom structure do not necessarily come easily. Nevertheless, we feel that the diligence and level of understanding demonstrated by the students during this lesson attest to the value of translanguaging.

Discussion Questions and Activities

1. How could additional adult support have been incorporated into this lesson? Consider support from co-teachers, ESL, English Language Arts, or special education educators and paraprofessionals. Also consider possible support from families.
2. Based on the strategies discussed in this chapter, write three language objectives for the lesson described.
3. What would be an appropriate final product for a unit of study that includes this lesson on the Declaration of Independence? How could students' translanguaging be used in creating this final product?

References

August, D., & Shanahan, T. (2006). *Developing literacy in second language learners: Report of the national literacy panel on language-minority children and youth.* Mahwah, NJ: Lawrence Erlbaum Associates.

BrainPOP. (2015). American Revolution/Independencia de Estados Unidos. Retrieved on March 16, 2016, from: https://www.brainpop.com/socialstudies/ushistory/american

revolution/ and https://esp.brainpop.com/ciencias_sociales/la_historia_/independencia_de_estados_unidos/preview.weml

Celic, C., & Seltzer, K. (2012). *Translanguaging: A CUNY-NYSIEB guide for educators.* New York: CUNY-NYSIEB, The Graduate Center, The City University of New York. Retrieved on March 16, 2016, from: http://www.nysieb.ws.gc.cuny.edu/files/2013/03/Translanguaging-Guide-March-2013.pdf

Collins, B. A. (2014). Dual language development of Latino children: Effect of instruction program type and the home and school language use. *Early Childhood Research Quarterly*, 29(3), 389–397. DOI: 10.1016/j.ecresq.2014.04.009

Cummins, J. (2007). Rethinking monolingual instructional strategies in multilingual classrooms. *The Canadian Journal of Applied Linguistics*, 10(2), 221–240.

Flores, N., & García, O. (2013). Linguistic third spaces in education: Teachers' translanguaging across the bilingual continuum. In D. Little, C. Leung, and P. Van Avermaet (Eds.) *Managing diversity in education: Key issues and some responses* (pp. 243–256). Clevedon, UK: Multilingual Matters,

García, O. (2014). TESOL translanguaged in NYS: Alternative perspectives. *NYS TESOL Journal*, 1(1), 2–10.

García, O., Johnson, S., & Seltzer, K. (2016). *The translanguaging classroom: Leveraging student bilingualism for learning.* Philadelphia: Caslon.

García, O., & Leiva, C. (2014). Theorizing and enacting translanguaging for social justice. In A. Creese and A. Blackledge (Eds.), *Heteroglossia as practice and pedagogy* (pp. 199–216). New York: Springer.

Rolstad, K., Mahoney, K., & Glass, G. V. (2005). The big picture: A meta-analysis of program effectiveness research on English language learners. *Educational Policy*, 19(4), 572–594.

7

NAVIGATING TURBULENT WATERS

Translanguaging to Support Academic and Socioemotional Well-Being

Kate Seltzer and Brian A. Collins
with Katrina Mae Angeles

Introduction

Some emergent bilinguals are labeled by the school system as students with incomplete/interrupted formal education (SIFE). This includes immigrant students with low English proficiency who have had limited or interrupted formal education and perform below grade level in literacy and math (DeCapua & Marshall, 2011). Along with academic demands, students labeled SIFE often encounter a number of social and emotional challenges, such as separation from family, discomfort with new cultural norms and a new language, and post-traumatic stress brought on by war or violence (DeCapua, Smathers & Tang, 2007). Despite the fact that 10% of emergent bilinguals in New York City schools are labeled as having incomplete/interrupted formal education (Office of English Language Learners, 2013), educators continue to struggle to successfully educate this population. In this chapter, we explore the experiences of these students in an 11th/12th-grade English Language Arts (ELA) classroom. Specifically, we are interested in understanding how translanguaging can provide immigrant students with low literacy in their home languages the type of support they need to tackle difficult academic and socioemotional challenges. Research has evidenced substantive links between children's social and emotional well-being and school success (Greenberg et al., 2003). Students provided with the opportunity to express themselves and relate to others are able to build a stronger sense of belonging at school and engage academically.

For this lesson, we worked with a teacher of English Language Arts to design lessons around three poems that drew on students' prior knowledge and experiences. Although we had worked with this teacher for over six months, here we report on data gathered during two English Language Arts periods where we acted as participant observers. Both of the authors are former teachers of bilingual youth and speak English and Spanish. Besides collaborating with the teacher in the planning of the lessons, we also facilitated small-group discussions and talked with students about their connections to the poems. When opening up conversations around the poems, which we audio recorded, we were explicit in our invitation to use either or both English and Spanish. We also conducted interviews with the teacher, school principal, and several focal students. Our methodological approach included analysis of student work and of students' discussions during the lessons. The transcripts of the lessons and discussions with students were coded for themes, which arose inductively. In the following sections, we present background information about the school, teacher, students, and the lesson. We then analyze how the use of translanguaging served the dual purpose of gaining students' access to English texts and grade-level English Language Arts tasks, as well as enabling them to share their own experiences and feelings around school and their own lives through the vehicle of their home language, Spanish.

The School

Kings High School (pseudonym) is a small school serving students in grades 9 to 12 in a low-income outer borough neighborhood. Kings is housed in a building that was once one of New York City's largest high schools, and which is now home to five different high schools, a result of policy to close down large underperforming high schools and replace them with small schools. Kings has about 300 students, almost all of whom are Spanish-speaking Latinos, mostly from the Dominican Republic, who have been in the country less than three years. In the 2013–14 school year, 94% of the population was labeled English language learners and 35% of those were labeled as "SIFE".

Due to its small size, all of the students know one another well and are well acquainted with the school's teachers and administrators. In between classes, the hallways are loud, boisterous, and filled with the sounds of laughter, teasing, and gossip, almost all of which takes place in Spanish. The classrooms, too, are mostly Spanish-speaking spaces. Almost all of the teachers speak Spanish. Kings has a school-wide transitional bilingual education program, thus most of the content area classes are offered in Spanish. For a time, the school established what they called "English-only zones" in the English Language Arts classrooms in order to push students to speak English. However, in part because of the school's involvement with CUNY-NYSIEB starting in 2013, these "zones" have been abolished and the English Language Arts classrooms are now more flexible spaces, where students can draw on their home languages to help them read and write in English. It is in one of these ELA classrooms that we spent time in the winter and spring of 2014. To help set the scene for our study, we next introduce you to teacher Katrina Angeles and some of the students in her classroom.

The Teacher

Katrina Angeles is Filipino and began her teaching career in the Philippines, where she taught high school English literature. When she immigrated to the United States, she got her teaching certification and master's degree and began teaching at Kings High School in 2007, the year the school opened. Ms. Angeles speaks English, Filipino, and, since starting at Kings, has learned enough Spanish to help her students and communicate with their families. She says that when she began teaching at Kings, she spoke no Spanish and was insecure about her inability to understand or communicate effectively with her students. With the help of her students, after a few years she was able to speak, as she calls it, "school Spanish."

The Students

At the end of the 11th grade, all students—those labeled SIFE included—have to take the English Regents, a state-level standardized test that is a requirement for graduation. If passing this exam is difficult for many, add in issues faced by students who are in the early stages of learning English and have low literacy in Spanish and little familiarity with school-based tasks, and the English Regents becomes equivalent to scaling Mount Everest. The most common of these issues, according to both Ms. Angeles and Principal María González (pseudonym), is the transition to a new country. For example, many students come to the U.S. and move in with family they have never met. Some have a parent who has lived in the U.S. for years without them, and with whom they are expected to share a small apartment. Others move in with aunts, grandparents, or other extended family members. Still others live with siblings or even on their own. According to Angeles and González, other issues that seem small—cold weather, riding the subway, a longer school day—impact students in huge ways and lead to high levels of absenteeism, tardiness, frustration, and disengagement. For students with an incomplete education in their countries of origin, their lack of exposure to school scripts and literacy practices expected of them in U.S. classrooms make their day-to-day lives at school an uphill battle (DeCapua & Marshall, 2011).

Though Ms. Angeles's class roster listed upwards of 30 students, there were usually between 10 to 15 students present during her morning class. During our time in the classroom, there was an almost even breakdown of male to female students, all of whom were labeled as SIFE. Nearly all of the students in the class came from the Dominican Republic (one female student was from Puerto Rico) and all spoke Spanish. Though many struggled academically and with such school habits as timeliness and homework, there was a clear sense that the students were comfortable in Ms. Angeles's classroom. Ms. Angeles cultivated the collegial, even familial tone in the classroom through her respectful interactions with her students, who responded in kind. Next, we introduce you to several of the students from Ms. Angeles's classroom, whose voices you will hear throughout this chapter.

Genesis

Genesis is an 11th grader from the Dominican Republic. She has been in the U.S. for four years, but is still labeled a "beginner" English speaker as per the NYSESLAT (New York State English as a Second Language Achievement Test). On our first day in Ms. Angeles's classroom, Genesis arrived to class late and immediately made an impression. She joked with Ms. Angeles in English, amiably made fun of her friends in Spanish, and spoke openly with us in both languages. Genesis was one of the more outgoing students, participating in discussions and sharing personal connections. Genesis is bright and funny, though we saw that her wit and humor could have a sharp edge. While she can seem harsh or combative, according to Ms. Angeles, her comments are not taken personally by those on the receiving end. Genesis is very close to her mother, and, according to her, their relationship motivates Genesis to do well in school.

Haidy

Haidy is an 11th grader from the Dominican Republic and older than her classmates, as she had to repeat 8th grade when she arrived four years ago. According to Ms. Angeles, Haidy is one of the most driven students in the class. Though her overall attendance in school is spotty, Haidy is almost always present in this class and usually one of the first to arrive (and often with a reluctant friend or two in tow). This is impressive, given the fact that she lives over two hours from the school. Despite attempts to convince her to transfer somewhere closer to home, Haidy refuses, citing her deep friendships and comfort at the school as her reasons for staying. Whenever we observed her, she was hard at work, doing her best with any assignment. However, Ms. Angeles and Haidy herself say that when it comes to taking tests, she frequently gets discouraged and gives up.

Ileana

Ileana is a 12th grader who moved to the U.S. from Puerto Rico after 9th grade, which she had to repeat once she arrived. In addition to being labeled as SIFE, Ileana also has an individualized education plan (IEP) for a learning disability. Ileana is quiet and reserved, but kind and friendly to everyone in the class. Though she participated very little in the lessons and produced almost no written work, Ileana pulled us aside and showed us a spiral notebook that she had filled with colorfully decorated poems in both Spanish and English. When asked what she liked to write about, she answered, "love." According to Ms. Angeles, Ileana struggles with low self-confidence and gets very nervous when taking exams.

Lena

Lena is in her fifth year of high school. She has enough credits and has passed other subject Regents necessary to graduate, but has not yet passed the English Language Arts Regents exam. For this reason, Lena comes to one class: Ms. Angeles's. Lena lives on her own, working to pay her own rent as well as send money home to her sister in the Dominican Republic. She had family issues that resulted in her being kicked out of her home, after which she lived with another student from Kings who encouraged her to keep coming to school. As Principal González told us, she is one of the many students at Kings who "found family in the community." During our time in Ms. Angeles's classroom, Lena shared many insightful comments and seemed determined to pass the ELA Regents and earn a high school diploma.

Ramón

Like Lena, Ramón is in his fifth year of high school. Though he got a 75% or better on all his other Regents exams, he has not been able to pass the English Language Arts exam, so he comes to Ms. Angeles's class for test prep. According to Principal González, Ramón is hearing impaired and could have been given more support, but his father refused to sign paperwork due to the stigma of being classified as a student with disabilities requiring an IEP. As such, early on Ramón experienced a great deal of frustration and embarrassment as he worked to learn a new language that he could not hear well. Ramón works at the nearby airport cleaning planes, but plans to go into the field of graphic design after he graduates.

José

José is a senior from the Dominican Republic who has been in the country three years, but is still labeled by the NYSESLAT a "beginner" English speaker. His attendance to school is inconsistent. According to the principal, his life in the Dominican Republic was hard. He got into fights and rarely attended school. José told us, "sometime . . . I don't understand nothing, it make me nervous and always I give up, but that's because I don't understand and I feel so angry . . . and sometime I feel like I don't belong in the school." Despite his difficult history and struggles in school, José was an active participant in classroom discussions, making connections to the content and talking honestly about his experiences.

Lesson

The two days of lessons were planned collaboratively by the teacher, Ms. Angeles, and the researchers. The lessons were designed to encourage students to make connections between culturally relevant poems about school and their own school experiences. Through close readings of three poems in small groups over the course of two days, students analyzed the characters' points of view and the themes that ran through all three poems. Students were encouraged to translanguage in their small groups and with the teacher and researchers in order to make meaning and share their connections. At the end of the second day of lessons, students were given the option to either write their own poems about school or complete a structured cloze poem.

When we arrived on the day of the first lesson, students were working on an opening activity, creating timelines indicating various "high points" and "low points" in their lives. The teacher had brought breakfast for students and there was a relaxed, familiar atmosphere in the classroom. After approximately 10–15 minutes, the teacher asked some of the students to share their positive and negative experiences with the class. Lena shared, "when I was 12, coming to NY was so bad, I didn't like the climate, the food, coming to school, people calling me names." Some students emphasized that they did not personally make the decision to immigrate and struggled with getting to know their new environment. Many marked their immigration to the U.S. as a high point on their timelines, however, after immigrating, most of their timelines were marked with low points related to their struggles at school, specifically concerning the high-stakes Regents exams that all high school graduates in New York must pass.

In 2008, Kate Menken documented how standardized testing, and the English Language Arts (ELA) Regents exam in particular, negatively impacts the lives of emergent bilinguals. Seven years later, this exam continues to be a critical factor for the students in Ms. Angeles's class—without passing the ELA Regents, they could not graduate from high school. Most of the students had already taken the exam at least once and had not passed. In fact, there were some students, like Ramón and Lena, who only came to school for Ms. Angeles's class, since they had passed all the other exams and had enough credits to graduate. The knowledge of how much control this exam had over their academic success weighed heavily on many of the students. Nearly all students cited failing the ELA Regents as a low (if not the lowest) point in their lives thus far, in ways similar to Haidy's timeline which appears as Figure 7.1.

Though all of the students we spoke with in Ms. Angeles's class had high aspirations for themselves, their timelines and their talk around the English Regents demonstrated that these goals felt out of their reach.

After working on their timelines, students moved into four groups to read the poems. We facilitated two of the small groups and Ms. Angeles traveled between the other two groups. In these groups, we discussed students' connections to the poems as well as analyzed them for literacy devices. Over the course of the two days, we read three poems.

In the book *Class Dismissed* by Mel Glenn (1982), in which a series of poems are named for different students in a school, one poem, "Franz Dominguez," paints a picture of a student who cannot read. Franz talks about the various ways

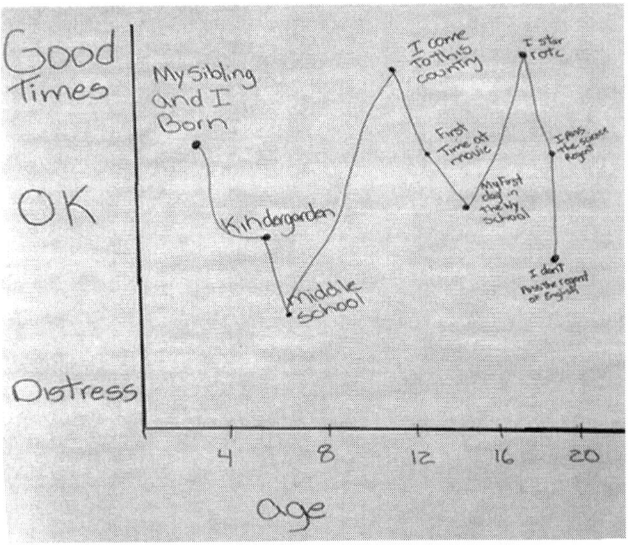

FIGURE 7.1 Haidy's Life Timeline

he hides his inability to read and relates that he isn't sure how he fell through the cracks. He thinks he could learn "if someone sat with me," but teachers don't have the time, and Franz is too embarrassed to even ask for their help. The poem ends with Franz admitting that sometimes he gets so angry that he punches a wall. Another poem, "Anna Montalvo," tells the story of a young woman who came to the U.S. from Puerto Rico and strives to graduate from high school despite a number of personal struggles, such as failing English, missing a year of school, and being overage. Finally, the third poem, "Donna Vásquez," introduces Donna, who, unlike her friend Anna, isn't interested in school—she'd much prefer to work at a salon doing people's hair. She says that when she is in school, she feels like a child, but being out in the world working makes her feel like an adult. Though all three poems are narrated by Latino characters, and Anna's poem refers to San Juan, Puerto Rico, Donna's poem is the only one that features two phrases in Spanish: ¡Qué va! and Lo siento.

Our choice of text was strategic, in that we thought the points of view and themes would resonate with students. Though the poems were written in English, save two Spanish phrases, we thought that their connections to students' own experiences would open the door to translanguaging. This was indeed the case. Having so much to say about the texts pushed students to use all of their linguistic resources to "talk back" to the poems and make their ideas understood to one another and to us. Once they were engaged in translanguaging, students were able to do *more* with the English texts than they could have done if they had only used their emerging English. Through the use of translanguaging, students were able to better understand the texts themselves, express their emotions and feelings about those texts, and support one another when the texts brought up difficult emotions. In this way, both the choice of content (the "what") and the way of engaging with that content (the "how") worked in tandem to support students academically and socioemotionally. We begin by illustrating how the texts themselves helped students make connections to their own lives and then show how these kinds of connections provided the "buy-in" necessary to motivate emergent bilingual students to use all of their linguistic resources to make meaning of English texts and express themselves.

Building "Buy-In": Making Connections to Culturally Relevant Texts in English

As students read the poems, they made connections between the narrators and people they knew—their families, friends, and classmates. These connections not only helped them engage more deeply with the poems, they also provided an outlet for students to discuss some of the difficult things they themselves encountered as recent immigrants, struggling students, and language learners. Though the excerpts below are in English, the use of engaging poems that were relevant to students' lives opened the door to more complex conversations in both languages, which we highlight later.

Some of the students connected the poems to people in their families, many of whom they saw as experiencing similar things to the poem's narrators. For example, when talking about Franz's poem and his inability to read, Ramón made a direct connection to his mother, whom he said struggled with English:

RAMÓN: This is poem for my mother.
RESEARCHER (BRIAN): It's a poem for your mom?
RAMÓN: Yeah, she don't speak English, she trying to learn the [subway] stops but she don't know what they mean.

Another student, Genesis, also spoke of her mother and her experiences as a Spanish-speaking immigrant in New York City. When speaking about what might have made Franz so angry that he would punch a wall, Genesis related that it was the fact that he couldn't understand "what the person say." The conversation then shifted to how Spanish speakers are treated in their daily lives:

GENESIS: Some people know the two languages and then they act like they don't understand.
HAIDY: Yeah.
RESEARCHER (KATE): Why would they do that? Why would someone do that?
GENESIS: I don't know why they . . . we are, like, Latinos. I don't understand.

HAIDY:	Some teacher want the student to learn English.
GENESIS:	When you go to the restaurant and they know that you know how to speak Spanish, they come talk in English [and I'm] like, "you know Spanish." I get mad when people do that to my mom . . . I always fight with the guy or the girl from the restaurant 'cause I'm like, "You know my mom don't talk English, why you don't talk to her in Spanish? To make her feel bad?"

Though the poem about Franz refers to his inability to read, Genesis, Haidy, and Ramón related it to the struggle to understand a new language. Ramón discussed how his mother, like Franz, couldn't read the English signs on the train that tell her the name of the subway stops. Genesis referred to other Spanish speakers who made her mother "feel bad" by speaking to her in English rather than Spanish. Though Haidy made a connection to teachers wanting students to learn English (and thus not allowing Spanish), Genesis stuck with her own interpretation—that there were those who refused to use Spanish simply to make others feel bad. These connections between the poem and students' mothers opened up opportunities for students to share difficult things about their lives while coming to deep, powerful understandings of the narrator's point of view.

In addition to her connection to her mother, Genesis also related Franz's experiences to one of her fellow students. Like Franz, this student struggled in school. According to Genesis, this student had "never been in school" before and was just learning his letters. When asked why teachers in the poem may not have had time to sit and help Franz learn to read, Genesis said:

GENESIS:	Cause this is what happens. There's some kid at the school who don't know how to read, he'd never been in school. And they put him in my grade but the thing is that in this school, they don't have, like, the teacher . . .
RESEARCHER (KATE):	You mean there aren't enough teachers?
GENESIS:	Yeah, so they put him in class with us and that's so hard for him and the teacher tell the principal to give him a computer, like a laptop, so he learn letters . . . [the teacher] tries to help him, but he always be like to the principal, "oh, bring him a computer and letters like ABC" so he can learn.
RESEARCHER:	How old is this student?
GENESIS:	I think he's 14.

Through this excerpt, one can see a number of issues at play. First, Genesis raised the issue that there were not enough teachers to give a student one-on-one attention. Instead, this student was put into a classroom with other students and, as one might imagine, could not keep up. The teacher, who like many teachers of immigrant students with low home literacy, did not know how to meet the student's unique needs (DeCapua & Marshall, 2011), asked the principal to "give him a computer" so he could "learn letters, like ABC." Lastly, when Genesis said that the boy was 14, one can't help but imagine the experience of being a teenager, sitting in a classroom amongst his peers, and learning the alphabet on his own. Though this was not Genesis's personal experience, the fact that she drew on it and shared it revealed its significance in her experience of school and learning, as well as her empathy for the struggles of her peers.

José, too, drew a connection between the narrator of one of the poems and his peers. He discussed his friend, who, like the character Donna, wanted to drop out and work rather than go to school:

RESEARCHER (BRIAN):	Do you know anyone like Donna?
JOSÉ:	My friends . . . they don't want to come to the school because they think that is not . . . he said that he can work. He prefer work, after stops school.
RESEARCHER:	So he didn't finish school?
JOSÉ:	No.
RESEARCHER:	What job does he do?
JOSÉ:	McDonalds.
RESEARCHER:	McDonalds?
JOSÉ:	[laughing] Yeah, the future.
RESEARCHER:	The future?
JOSÉ:	Yeah that is the future. McDonalds all the time.

José seemed to draw a direct line between his friend's departure from school and his future working in McDonalds, which José clearly saw as undesirable. The use of this poem, which mirrored his own personal experiences, encouraged José to engage with content in English and, at the same time, share an aspect of his life that might usually be left out of the classroom. Though José was not talking about himself, we can view his understanding of Donna in relation to his friend as a way of grappling with his own choices about school and the effects on his future.

In these and other moments, students related the experiences of the narrators in the poems to their own experiences. Without relevant texts that connect to their lives in socioemotional ways (in *any* language, but especially in their new language), students may not have engaged in a higher level of analysis. Next, we talk specifically about how engaging in translanguaging helped students interact with the English texts, as well as open up about their personal lives.

Translanguaging to Navigate Academic and Socioemotional Contexts

Though Ms. Angeles's class is an English Language Arts class, there is a constant flow of what García, Johnson, and Seltzer (2016) call the translanguaging corriente. This corriente, or current, of translanguaging refers to the ever-present flow of students' dynamic bilingualism that exists in all bilingual spaces. Whereas Ms. Angeles's classroom is not technically "bilingual" (in that it is not officially labeled as such by the school or district), in practice, it most certainly is. Translanguaging was used by all students for a number of reasons. It enabled them to co-construct understandings of English texts, participate in more complex discussions around those texts, and talk through emotions and feelings that came up in response to the texts. The following sections outline each of these observations.

Translanguaging to Co-Construct Understandings of English Texts

One of the reasons the students engaged in translanguaging was to explain and clarify vocabulary, new concepts, and directions. Negotiating understandings of English words using Spanish, for example, helped them co-construct meanings of these new terms. This particular use of translanguaging has the power to change the nature of traditional student/teacher roles, transforming both parties into teachers and learners (García, Johnson & Seltzer, 2016). The following excerpt captures this kind of co-construction and shift in roles:

RESEARCHER (KATE): Ok. Anyone know that word? Blame is like if I say . . . say you knock something over and I say it was Genesis; I am blaming her.

GENESIS: Oh, como que está culpando. [Oh, like someone is blaming you.]

HAIDY: Oh, culpar, culpar, culpar. [Oh, to blame, blame, blame.]

RESEARCHER: Exactly. Cuando yo digo, "es tu culpa," I'm blaming you.

Here, Haidy's understanding of the word "blame" was co-constructed by allowing her existing lexical features to emerge. Through an example, Kate provided Haidy and Genesis with the English word in context. Understanding the example, Genesis correctly rephrased in Spanish with "está culpando" [you're blaming], which led Haidy to the verb culpar [to blame]. Kate then took up the Spanish word and used both languages to solidify the group's new understanding. Similarly, in the next excerpt, Kate used both English and Spanish to facilitate a conversation around the poem with a group of students who were reticent to communicate in English:

RESEARCHER (KATE): Pero qué tipo de persona es Franz? [But what kind of person is Franz?]

STUDENT 1: Retrasado. [Delayed.]

RESEARCHER: He says, "I always order a hamburger. I can't read the menu." El no quiere decir que no puede leer. [He doesn't want to say that he can't read.]

STUDENT 2:	No sabe. [He doesn't know.]
RESEARCHER:	¿No sabe? [He doesn't know?]
STUDENT 2:	No puede leer el menú, no sabe leer. [He can't read the menu, he doesn't know how to read.]
RESEARCHER:	No puede leer. Él sabe que no puede leer, pero no quiere decir que . . . [He can't read. He knows he can't read, but he doesn't want to say that . . .]
STUDENT 2:	Quiere aprender. [He wants to learn.]
RESEARCHER:	Pero por qué no quiere decir, "yo no puedo leer"? [But why doesn't he want to say, "I can't read"?]
STUDENT 2:	Le da vergüenza. [It embarrasses him.]
RESEARCHER:	¿Tiene orgullo? Pride? [Is he proud?]
STUDENTS:	Sí, sí. [Yes, yes.]

From diagnosing Franz as retrasado [delayed] to inferring that he wants to learn despite his pride, the students used Spanish to discuss the ideas present in the English poem. Without the use of Spanish to unpack the poem, it would have been difficult to know what these students knew and understood. Thus, the use of translanguaging gave students the opportunity to demonstrate their comprehension using the linguistic tools at their disposal. In both this and the previous excerpt, the use of translanguaging was vital to both students and the researcher, and made space for a discussion that would not have been possible in English only.

Translanguaging to Participate in Complex Conversations About English Texts

In addition to demonstrating their comprehension, students used translanguaging to express themselves in conversations around the texts. These conversations were inspired by the poems, but extended past them, and enabled students to discuss the content in relation to their own lives and experiences. For example, Haidy connected the Donna Vásquez poem to her sister, who left school to be a waitress. The researcher, Brian, started the conversation in Spanish, and although Haidy began speaking with him in English, she used both languages to make herself understood and participate in the discussion:

RESEARCHER (BRIAN):	Ok, ¿Alguien tiene una experiencia así o piensa igual como [Donna]? [OK, anyone has an experience like this or thinks similarly to Donna?]
HAIDY:	No, [but] I have a lot of friends. My sister is 18 y ella se salió de la escuela and she, ella está, she's working now in the, como mesera. Ella lleva la comida a la gente en bodas. Eso es lo que hay de similar. [. . . and she left school and she, she is . . . like a waitress. She serves food to people at weddings. That's what similar.]

RESEARCHER:	Did she go to school here?
HAIDY:	Yeah, but she . . . ella se salió. [. . . left.]
RESEARCHER:	So you think that the poem is similar to your sister?
HAIDY:	Yeah.
RESEARCHER:	Any part?
HAIDY:	Yeah, my mother and my father tell her to stay in the school, but you know she don't want. She's lazy. She's lazy 'cause she don't want to wake up at 5 o'clock and then she will wake up to 9 and she don't go to the school . . . She prefer to work than go to the school.

This conversation would not have been possible or would have been much more limited without translanguaging. Though she consistently tried to converse in English, Haidy was not able to express herself fully. Because Brian opened the door to the use of Spanish in his first question, as well as the overall linguistic flexibility that characterized Ms. Angeles's classroom, Haidy was able to talk about her connection to the poem using all her linguistic resources. This made the conversation richer and helped her engage with the poem on a deeper level.

Similarly, in a conversation with Lena, Ramón, and a third student, Abigail, we can see how the use of both languages deepened the complexity of the conversation and helped Abigail become a more active participant. Here, the group discussed why Franz Dominguez didn't ask his teachers for help with reading:

RESEARCHER (KATE):	Have you ever been in that situation where you don't know, but you don't ask?
LENA:	No, I always ask.
RESEARCHER:	You always ask?
ABIGAIL:	Maybe tiene miedo, right? [. . . he was scared . . .]
RESEARCHER:	¿De qué? [Of what?]
RAMÓN:	Sometimes you don't ask—
LENA:	To be embarrassed.
ABIGAIL:	De su inglés, él no sabe. [Of his English, he doesn't know.]
RESEARCHER:	¿Y eso le da vergüenza? [And that embarrasses him?]
ABIGAIL:	In high school a lot of people they do, like, bullying.

Like Haidy's translanguaging, Abigail's use of both English and Spanish enabled her to participate in the analysis of the poem. Similarly, Kate's questions, posed in both languages in response to the language use of the students, made space for this kind of flexible use of language. This flexibility enabled all students, but especially those like Abigail, to explain connections between the content and their life experiences and participate actively in conversations around English texts.

Translanguaging to Express Emotions in Relation to Texts

For emergent bilinguals, translanguaging is a means of understanding, expressing, and building relationships. In this way, it is more than a scaffold to English—it is a way of releasing students' voices and enabling them to bring their whole selves into the classroom (García & Leiva, 2014). We observed several instances of students engaging in translanguaging in both intra- and interpersonal ways to express their emotions and connect with and support their peers.

In a conversation with Genesis and Haidy around Franz's poem, students used translanguaging to explain how they express their own frustrations similarly to Franz—with physical aggression. When talking about their connection to this moment, both students drew on Spanish and English to relay their thoughts and feelings:

RESEARCHER (KATE): What about this, what do you think he's doing at the last two lines of the poem when he says, "sometimes when no one is around I punch the wall?"

GENESIS: Cause he's angry, cause he can't read.

RESEARCHER: What does it look like to punch a wall?

GENESIS: You have to like, tiene que sacar lo que siente, la rabia [you have to get out what you feel, the anger].

HAIDY: Cuando tú estás furioso, no sientes nada, tú le das todo a la puerta [When you're furious, you don't feel anything, you give everything to the door]. When you do it and you're not angry you go, "oh my god what are you doing"?

Though the conversation started in English, both students shifted into Spanish to describe feelings of anger and frustration. The fact that Franz took out his own anger by punching a wall opened up space for students to share their responses to their own anger, which mirrored the narrator's. Though neither Genesis nor Haidy shared what exactly made them angry, their connection to the poem and their expression of their own emotions deepened the conversation and enabled students to share aspects of their emotional lives.

Similarly, when Haidy was explaining how she related to Franz's experience as a struggling student, she started explaining her connection in English, but finished in Spanish:

HAIDY: You don't understand this word and the other people, other students laugh and start laughing, oh my god. Me cuesta mucho eso [That's really hard for me].

GENESIS: Ellos son malos [They're bad], they laugh 'cause they don't do anything anyways.

RESEARCHER (BRIAN): You feel like the kids are laughing 'cause you're not reading it right or something?

HAIDY: Yeah.

RESEARCHER: Es difícil [It's difficult].

GENESIS: Don't pay attention to them.

RESEARCHER: Por ejemplo yo, cuando yo hablo español me da vergüenza también, qué usted va a pensar "¿ah, por qué habla él tan raro?" [For example, I, when I speak Spanish I'm embarrassed too, that you are going to think, "ah, why does he speak so strange?"]

ILEANA: We understand.

Haidy starts by relating an experience when she felt embarrassed at not knowing a word in English and was laughed at by her peers. She shared in Spanish, "Me cuesta mucho eso" [That's really hard for me]. Genesis then reassured her, first in Spanish and then in English, that she shouldn't pay attention to people who laugh at her. Brian also related in Spanish his own insecurity about his Spanish language use, which served the dual purpose of supporting Haidy and sharing part of his own personal life with the students. Ileana, a student who rarely participated in the conversation, replied, "We understand." One could read the "we" as either their small group, or a more collective "we"—Ileana and her classmates, all of whom face similar struggles with language in school. Without the translanguaging that occurred in this conversation, these kinds of emotional insights, connections, and interpersonal support could not have occurred.

Having supportive peers, as we can see in the above excerpt, is essential in facing challenges and completing academic tasks, and students in Ms. Angeles's class seemed to understand that they had to help each other. This network of peers is critical to developing a sense of belonging and membership in the social order of the school (Johnson, Crosnoe & Elder, 2001). Given the challenges students labeled as SIFE face in order to graduate, it is important that they support one another both academically and socioemotionally. Throughout the teaching of these lessons with culturally and socially relevant texts and the use of translanguaging, we saw students support one another in a variety of ways. They explained English directions to one another in Spanish. They translated words and ideas from the poems into Spanish. They joked and teased one another, making the classroom fun for all students, even those who struggled. We even saw this kind of support for one of the poem's narrators, Donna, who was contemplating dropping out of school:

RESEARCHER (BRIAN): So if you were Donna's friend, what advice would you give her?

LENA: Do not change her mind until she grows old, bigger. If somebody or her parents saw her or help her, "oh you gotta go to school because you have a better future when you grow old," but nobody is telling her, at her house nobody's telling her.

ABIGAIL: You know what I think? When you got money and you pass, you get ambicioso. Como se dice ambicioso?

LENA: Ambitious.

ABIGAIL: Yeah and just think about that.

Lena and Abigail offered Donna support, just as they might one of their peers. Lena tells Donna that she shouldn't make such a big decision until she is a little older, but also understands Donna's position, since "at her house nobody's telling her" to stay in school. Abigail uses both languages to impart her advice, telling Donna to think about the future (making money once she passes and graduates), which should make her feel more ambitious. This kind of advice was representative of the kind of support that students offered both to one another and to the characters in the poems. Because they were all Spanish-speaking Latinos, they were not only able to support one another using Spanish, but also to share their common experiences in a new country and school.

A Missed Opportunity: How Much Is Too Much Structure?

In the lesson that followed the discussion of the different poems, students were given the choice to write their own free verse poem or complete a cloze poem using a handout that was provided to them. Though they were presented with options, most students used the structured cloze poem, which left little room for their own ideas and expressions of emotion. By simply providing words to fill in the blanks, the activity was overly structured and possibly constrained students' production, creativity, and personal expression, as in Figure 7.2. In

For me, school is difficult.

I know it is important, but I don't know why algebra is hard to learn

When I study algebra, I feel boring.

For me, it is easy to learn how to Play basket ball.

But when I study algebra, I feel boring

For me, it is difficult to learn how to the formulas are complicated

I will not give up. You should not give up.

I will Read more in english.

I will put more atention in algebra.

I will all nesesary for graduated.

Only if I do this will I be able to be Profeciona,.

FIGURE 7.2 A Student's "Cloze" Poem

addition, though students consistently translanguaged while talking in their small groups, they wrote their poems primarily in English. Perhaps if students had been encouraged, explicitly taught, and given practice using translanguaging in their writing, as well as more freedom, these poems might have been more interesting and more revealing of their feelings about their school experiences.

This was further exemplified by Ileana, who showed us a book of poems that she worked on during her free time (Figure 7.3). She explained that she had five other notebooks of writing at her house where she wrote in both Spanish and English as a way to express her emotions. Ileana was proud to share her writing with us and other students, such as Haidy, who admired it and asked Ileana during class to see more. It was clear that Ileana had her own translingual literacy practices that the English Language Arts class had not accessed. In fact, she did not even complete the poetry activity during the lesson. This demonstrated to us that cloze poetry writing in English only was perhaps a "missed opportunity" in the lesson and that our attempt to scaffold and structure the poetry writing was constraining rather than supportive.

Developing lessons that tap into students' interests, motivation, and emotions by giving them independence and flexibility to write about their own experiences using their full language repertoire could have been more effective. A more meaningful activity could have provided opportunities for students to make choices that allowed them to take a more active and purposeful role in the poetry writing and could have better engaged them in the writing process. This is especially true for immigrant students who have had an incomplete or interrupted education in their countries of origin. Their education in the U.S. is

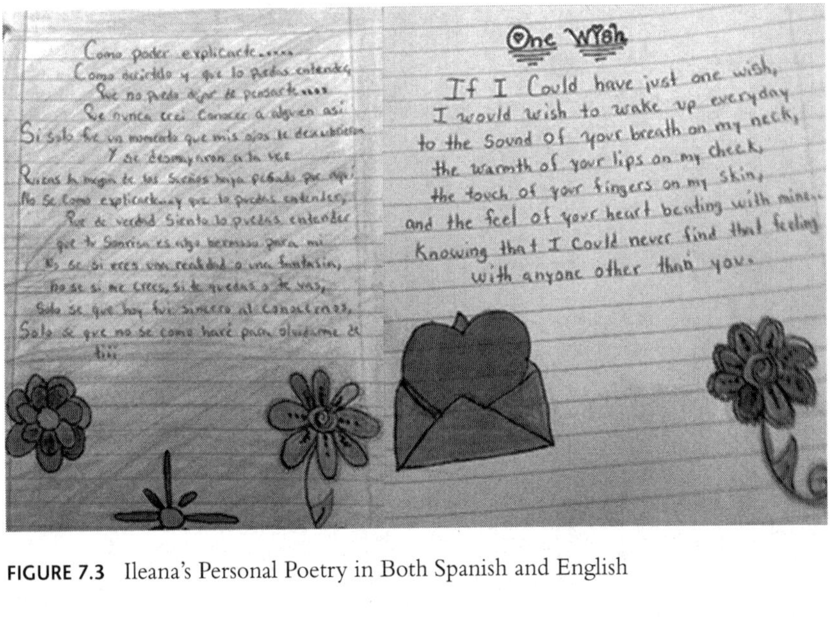

FIGURE 7.3 Ileana's Personal Poetry in Both Spanish and English

often remedial, making up for what they "lack," rather than building on their strengths and their knowledge. Our time in Ms. Angeles's classroom showed us how translanguaging could support students academically and socioemotionally, as well as how much more they were able to do when given the opportunity.

Larger Meanings and Implications

While it was clear that the English Regents exam was a serious obstacle for all of Ms. Angeles's students, we also saw just how much students knew and were able to do with English texts through their use of translanguaging. Rather than force students into the traditional mold of the classroom, Ms. Angeles's classroom, and the lessons we co-facilitated in particular, let students be themselves as they interacted, languaged, and learned on their own terms. This kind of classroom, responsive to students' needs and flexible in its approach to language, contributed to the creation of a "safe space" for these emergent bilinguals.

As we have documented throughout this chapter, translanguaging was a central feature of the discourse in Ms. Angeles's classroom. Students used features of both Spanish and English flexibly; it was the natural form of communication in the classroom space. This kind of linguistic flexibility through translanguaging is especially important in those settings that are traditionally English-only, such as English Language Arts. Rather than police students' language use, we used translanguaging to meet students where they were and used their languages as a bridge to English content. As we have already noted, students used translanguaging in a variety of ways to make meaning from the English poems. They used their whole linguistic repertoire to co-construct meanings of new vocabulary and comprehend the poems themselves. They used features of both languages to participate in conversations and analysis of those poems, which made those conversations more complex and allowed students to demonstrate their understandings. They also used translanguaging to navigate the socioemotional aspects of the work. Because the poems were related to their own lives, students were able to navigate the emotions they brought up and express themselves to one another, which helped them form a supportive community. In short, without translanguaging, students' academic *and* socioemotional needs might have been left unmet.

Conclusion

Emergent bilingual students who are labeled SIFE in a high-stakes testing culture face an array of academic difficulties, which can lead to feelings of frustration, hopelessness, and indifference. As we saw in Haidy and the other students' timelines, the English Language Arts Regents was consistently a low point in their academic experiences. Without an outlet for students to talk about the negative feelings associated with testing and other academic challenges, those feelings can easily overcome any sense of motivation or drive to succeed. We must try to create the best possible environment for these students—one that is flexible and responsive to their needs, interests, and language practices—so they feel they *can* succeed. This means making space for students to open up about their feelings and personal lives as they build the skills they need to tackle academic challenges. These needs can be met through the use of translanguaging, which enables emergent bilingual students to access academic texts in English, as well as express the thoughts and feelings that arise out of interactions with those texts. Without translanguaging, they may not have been able to demonstrate their understandings of, and connections to, the poems, nor share parts of their lives with teachers and others. For emergent bilinguals labeled SIFE, then, translanguaging is *more* than simply a scaffold, more than an entry-point to English. It is a tool they can use to bring their whole selves into the classroom, enabling them to learn—both academically and socioemotionally—in a way they deserve.

TEACHER'S VOICE BY KATRINA MAE ANGELES

Everybody has a story to tell, and each story is worth hearing. This has been my working principle since the beginning of my teaching career. I have gradually learned the importance of meeting students where they are and listening to their stories. They must be at the center of the curriculum. Success in learning from a teacher is dependent upon several essentials like trust, respect, and commitment, all of which hinge on the languages we use to express ourselves emotionally and understand each other. Relationships are strengthened when people understand and interpret accurately the actions and words of one another.

The lessons featured in this chapter were created with these principles in mind. The topic was chosen in order to spark the interest of the students. A familiar experience such as school, something students can relate to, is always a good place to start. Then there is the delivery of the lesson. It took time to establish a translanguaging environment in this class, but it was absolutely necessary in order for any learning to take place. I knew I had a moral obligation to teach students how to read, write, and speak in English. However, that would have been impossible if I had not used translanguaging in my classroom. By allowing students to communicate with one another using their home language, and by communicating with them in their home language myself, I was able to accomplish several things: (1) demonstrate an interest in learning about their lives and language practices to more successfully communicate with them, (2) model how there is no shame in making mistakes when using a language you are still learning, and (3) create a safe space for them to use the language of their choice at any given time during the lesson.

Translanguaging reinforces an important message for our students: that their stories *are* worth telling. It also allows us to be more receptive to the stories they have to tell. It is the way in which we can create common ground in a classroom so that we can facilitate our students' growth. Only after believing that they matter, that their existence is an integral part of how the world functions, can they begin to make something of themselves.

Discussion Questions and Activities

1. In what ways can translanguaging be used to increase both the academic success *and* socioemotional well-being of emergent bilingual students?
2. Considering the missed opportunities discussed by the authors, describe an activity that may have promoted more self-expression in the students' writing.
3. What other instructional strategies or resources could aid students in facing both academic and socioemotional challenges?

References

DeCapua, A., & Marshall, H. W. (2011). Reaching ELLs at risk: Instruction for students with limited or interrupted formal education. *Preventing School Failure: Alternative Education for Children and Youth*, 55(1), 35–41.

DeCapua, A., Smathers, W., & Tang, L. F. (2007). Schooling, interrupted. *Educational Leadership*, 64(6), 40–46.

García, O., Johnson, S., & Seltzer, K. (2016). *The translanguaging classroom: Leveraging student bilingualism for learning.* Philadelphia: Caslon.

García, O., & Leiva, C. (2014). Theorizing and enacting translanguaging for social justice. In A. Creese & A. Blackledge (Eds.), *Heteroglossia as practice and pedagogy* (pp. 199–216). New York: Springer.

Glenn, M. (1982). *Class dismissed: High school poems.* New York: Clarion.

Greenberg, M. T., Weissberg, R. P., O'Brien, M. U., Zins, J. E., Fredericks, L., Resnik, H., & Elias, M. J. (2003). Enhancing school-based prevention and youth development through coordinated social, emotional, and academic learning. *American Psychologist*, 58(6–7), 466.

Johnson, K. M., Crosnoe, R., & Elder, G. H. J. (2001). Students' attachment and academic engagement: The role of race and ethnicity. *Sociology of Education*, 74(4), 318–340.

Menken, K. (2008). *English learners left behind: Standardized testing as language policy.* Clevedon, UK: Multilingual Matters.

Office of English Language Learners. (2013). SIFE: Meeting the challenge [PowerPoint slides]. Retrieved on March 16, 2016, from: http://schools.nyc.gov/NR/rdonlyres/E5E66E15-85DF-4704-957C-9EBC88086664/0/SIFEMeetingtheChallenge_khrev101713.pdf

8

RECLAIMING BILINGUALISM

Translanguaging in a Science Class

Cecilia M. Espinosa and Luz Yadira Herrera with Claudia Montoya Gaudreau

Introduction

Traditionally, and viewed from a policy perspective, languages in a dual language bilingual program are strictly separated, whether it is by subject area, by teacher, or by day. The standard is to allocate only one language to a specific time period, space, or teacher. From this official standpoint, rarely are students invited to bring their entire linguistic repertoire to construct meaning in the different learning events that take place in a classroom. Yet, in daily practice, teachers and students challenge this notion in order to teach and to learn. In this study, we examine the ways in which a dual language bilingual teacher utilizes translanguaging to support student learning, as well as the ways in which bilingual students utilize their complete linguistic repertoire to construct meaning in a middle school science classroom. In this dual language bilingual classroom, students are reclaiming their own bilingualism, studying Spanish, as well as English.

Translanguaging is an emerging and growing concept in the field of bilingualism. Baker (2011) argues that, translanguaging is "the process of making meaning, shaping experiences, gaining understanding and knowledge through the use of two languages" (p. 288). Ofelia García's (2009) conceptualization of translanguaging moves beyond the "two languages" concept to extend its meaning to involve the "multiple discursive practices in which bilinguals engage in order to make sense of their bilingual worlds" (p. 45). The present study is guided by García (2009) and García and Li Wei's (2014) notion of translanguaging and focuses on the students' and their teacher's use of translanguaging strategies in a Spanish-medium science classroom. This study differs from the previous classroom case studies in this book in that it aims to uncover how students and their teacher utilize their bilingual resources in a minoritized language-medium classroom where Spanish is the language of instruction, instead of the usual English-language majority classroom.

The Context

Middle School 1 (MS 1) (pseudonym) is located in a vibrant immigrant community in a large urban neighborhood in New York City. It is a mid-size school with a population of approximately 800 students in grades 6 through 8. About 80% of students receive free or reduced lunch, thus the majority of the students come from low-income households. The school's student population by ethnicity is evenly distributed among three groups (approximately 30% each): Asian, White, and Latino. Black or African-American students account for the other 10% of the population. Approximately 17% of the entire student body is designated as English language learners. The language diversity in this school is remarkable; the top languages of the school are Russian, Chinese (Mandarin, Cantonese, Fukienese), and Spanish, and lower-incidence languages include Uzbek, Arabic, French, Italian, Polish, and Korean. The school leadership is committed to bilingual education as reflected by programming that supports home language development. It offers a dual language bilingual education program (DLBE) in each of the three top languages—Russian, Chinese, and Spanish. The programs could be considered a developmental bilingual program (or one-way dual language) since all of the students in the programs come from homes in which those languages are used in different ways. The emergent bilinguals (EBLs) in these programs fall along different points of the bilingual spectrum, and include students who were born in the U.S., as well as those born in Latin America and the Caribbean, Russia, and China. The DLBE programs offer focused instruction in Russian, Chinese, and Spanish in the content areas of science and social studies, deliberately planned this way because these are subjects that do not require a state standardized exam. Students also receive a daily period of instruction in what is called "Native Language Arts" (NLA). The DLBE program is for students classified as English language learners, as well as those that are English proficient. A freestanding English as a second language (ESL) program is also available to students who are classified as English language learners and speak home languages other than Russian, Chinese, or Spanish or who elect not to participate in the dual language bilingual program.

The student cohort that is the subject of this chapter is in the 6th-grade Spanish DLBE program. They are all Latino students who are predominantly U.S.-born, except for one student who was born in Guatemala and another in the Dominican Republic. This is the first year of the Spanish DLBE program, and, for the most part, this is also the first time that students have received instruction in Spanish. Although Spanish is their home language, their schooling has been subtractive and English only or mostly. This form of subtractive education has robbed students of the opportunity to become literate in Spanish (Valenzuela, 1999), until now. Only one of the 16 students in the class is officially designated as English language learner (ELL); the remaining 15 students either have tested out of the state's English proficiency exam or have never been identified as requiring ELL services. Still, we refer to the students in this chapter as emergent bilinguals (EBLs), since they are, in fact, emerging in their bilingualism and biliteracy in Spanish, as well as strengthening their language skills in English. Whereas much of the research available on translanguaging pedagogy in the U.S. has focused on students who use translanguaging strategies to make meaning in their English-medium classrooms or teachers who use translanguaging to maximize the students' learning in English, this chapter offers a case of the use of translanguaging to make sense and negotiate learning in Spanish.

The teacher, Ms. Montoya, is a bilingual and biliterate native New Yorker born to Peruvian immigrant parents. She is a 17-year veteran teacher, spending most of her career at MS 1. This is the first year that Ms. Montoya teaches in a bilingual program; previously, she taught Spanish as a foreign language to students at the school. Even though it is her first year teaching in the bilingual program, her teaching is often used for professional development for the other dual language bilingual educators in the school. Ms. Montoya is a passionate teacher with a knack for engaging her students through discussion, hands on activities, and multiple opportunities for collaborative group work; what is more, she encourages the use of translanguaging through all of these different avenues.

Ms. Montoya was open and excited to engage in this study with us and welcomed us into her classroom. We met twice to plan the lesson and audio recorded our meetings. We were also in touch via email and phone in order to fine-tune the lesson plan. After the lesson, we collected teacher and student artifacts, took pictures of the students' work, and audiotaped and transcribed the lesson. We also asked the students to complete a questionnaire after the lesson took place, asking them to share their reflections on the lesson.

Planning the Lesson

We designed a science lesson on the three states of matter. During the first planning session, we discussed how to think strategically about the translanguaging strategies for the lesson. Ms. Montoya stressed that her use of translanguaging was going to be based on students' needs and her knowledge of the students. She explained that, at times, students might feel more comfortable in English, but she also nudges them by asking the same question first in English, and then in Spanish. She reminded us that these students are reclaiming Spanish because few have had instruction in Spanish prior to this class. At home most of them speak or hear Spanish. Ms. Montoya bases her teaching on individual children's experiences and their knowledge of the specific content, as well as their language development. We planned on encouraging students to use any language for their responses throughout the lesson in order to make their thinking visible.

We also discussed the literacy strategies in the lesson. Ms. Montoya chose to use the "gist" strategy as a tool the students could use when reading the science text after the experiment. The "gist" strategy allows students to synthesize or react to the content by writing down the main idea or a comment next to what they've just read. In addition, Ms. Montoya explained that the school wanted the teachers to use higher level thinking questions in both languages and she is challenging the students to respond to these types of questions in Spanish.

Ms. Montoya planned to prepare a slide presentation for the recipe to make "oobleck," a substance that can behave like a liquid or a solid depending on the pressure applied to it. As we talked about the ingredients, we searched for words that the students might not know in Spanish. One such word was "cornstarch" (almidón de maíz). We thought that cognates would be important, and we agreed on the use of certain words: "colorante" and not "colorante alimenticio" (food coloring). We also talked about the language objective and the vocabulary the students would need to know. Ms. Montoya led the lesson, while Cecilia and Luz supported the groups of students as they engaged in the hands-on activity and the work with the science text. We start by providing a brief overview of the lesson design.

LESSON OBJECTIVES

- *Content objective:*
  - Students will be able to (SWBAT) demonstrate comprehension of the characteristics of the three states of matter by conducting a scientific experiment in which they will create, observe, and write a response on the different properties of matter.
- *Language objectives:*
  - SWBAT use descriptive language in order to explain the cause and effect and outcomes of the experiment.
  - SWBAT state the main idea from the reading of the text by utilizing the "gist" strategy in a language of their choice.
- *Translanguaging Objective:*

  SWBAT utilize various components of languaging (listening, speaking, drawing, writing, reading, viewing) in order to pose questions, make predictions and connections, and expand on their answers, using their entire language repertoire during the in-class discussions, the post-experiment write-up, and while writing the gist.

(Continued)

(Continued)

- *Reading comprehension/literacy activity:*

  Students will participate in a presentation/discussion of the topic (the three states of matter), a hands-on-activity, and will spend time reading and annotating from the Spanish science textbook.

- *Do Now:*

  ¿Qué pasaría si dejamos un vaso con agua en la parte de afuera de la ventana? en el invierno o en el verano? Explica tu respuesta en 2–3 oraciones. [What would happen if we left a glass of water outside a window? During winter or during the summer? Explain your response in 2–3 sentences.]

- *Vocabulary:*

  viscozo, temperatura, calor, fusión, congelación, colorante, almidón de maíz [viscous, temperature, heat, fusion, freeze, food coloring, cornstarch]

- *Activity:*

  - Can two states of matter occur at the same time? Can it be solid and gas at the same time? Can it be liquid and solid?
  - Students will explore changes in the state of matter by making oobleck.
  - Teacher will display the steps (with visuals) in creating the oobleck on the interactive whiteboard.

- *Handout to record observations:*

  - What do I think will happen? (Prediction)
  - What actually happened?
  - New questions I have.

After the exploration, Ms. Montoya will ask the students to spend time reading from the science text and applying the "gist" strategy using sticky notes in small groups.

- *Formative assessment with translanguaging:*

  - Student oral responses to teacher questions
  - Student work (notebook, gist notes, and handout)

- *Homework:*

  - Find examples of the three different states of matter.

The Lesson: What Happened

In this section, we describe briefly what happened throughout the lesson in order to contextualize it. Then, we focus more extensively on two moments of the lesson:

- Inviting translanguaging: Ms Montoya's discourse and actions.
- Use of the "gist" strategy when reading the science texts.

Ms. Montoya started the lesson with a review. During this time, she guided the students through questions and paraphrasing in explaining their understanding of the states of matter (solid, liquid, and gas). She reviewed the characteristics of each state of matter and encouraged the students to use Spanish, while creating a space where they could use all their language resources to express their understandings. Not only did the students utilize their full linguistic repertoire, but Ms. Montoya did as well. She did so to clarify, pose questions, expand, and paraphrase. The students did it to deepen their understanding, clarify concepts, and explain their learning to others. Ms. Montoya also asked the students to explain the components of an experiment—hypothesis, observation, and analysis. The students also discussed the issues of safety while doing an experiment. During this time, both students and Ms. Montoya utilized all their semiotic resources, including features from English and Spanish, gestures, and visuals. The students also engaged in the "Do Now," which stated: ¿Qué pasaría si dejamos un vaso con agua en la parte de afuera de la ventana? en el invierno o en el verano? Explica tu respuesta en 2–3 oraciones. [What would happen if we left a glass of water outside a window? During winter or during the summer? Explain your response in 2–3 sentences.]

Next, Ms. Montoya introduced a slide presentation with the recipe for making oobleck: "1 part water, 2 parts cornstarch, a few drops of food coloring." The presentation included a list of the ingredients, visuals, and print for each step, all in Spanish. Then Ms. Montoya shared the story of oobleck and its origins from Dr. Seuss's (1949) book, *Bartholomew and the Oobleck*. Before materials were distributed, students predicted what might happen when they mixed the ingredients listed in the handout. In groups of four, the students engaged in the experiment. During this time, Ms. Montoya went from group to group facilitating the dialogue using her entire linguistic repertoire posing questions, making suggestions, explaining, demonstrating, and elaborating on student comments. The students were deeply engaged in exploring the materials. They examined the changes in the texture as they poured water in the cornstarch. The classroom was filled with talk in both languages about what happened when they tried to lift the oobleck and it dripped from their fingers.

Once the experiment was finished and materials were put away, Ms. Montoya asked the students to complete the rest of the handout. Students individually answered: "What happened?" and "What questions do you have?" She reminded them that they were not limited to English or Spanish to respond.

The students then worked in groups of four reading the science text, which was in Spanish. They took turns reading a section and then stopped to discuss their understandings and take notes using the "gist" strategy. During this time, students utilized both languages. Ms. Montoya reminded the students to use a sticky note to address an important point they wanted to remember or a question they had, as they read the text in Spanish. Figures 8.1 and 8.2 show how students in

FIGURE 8.1 Gist in Spanish

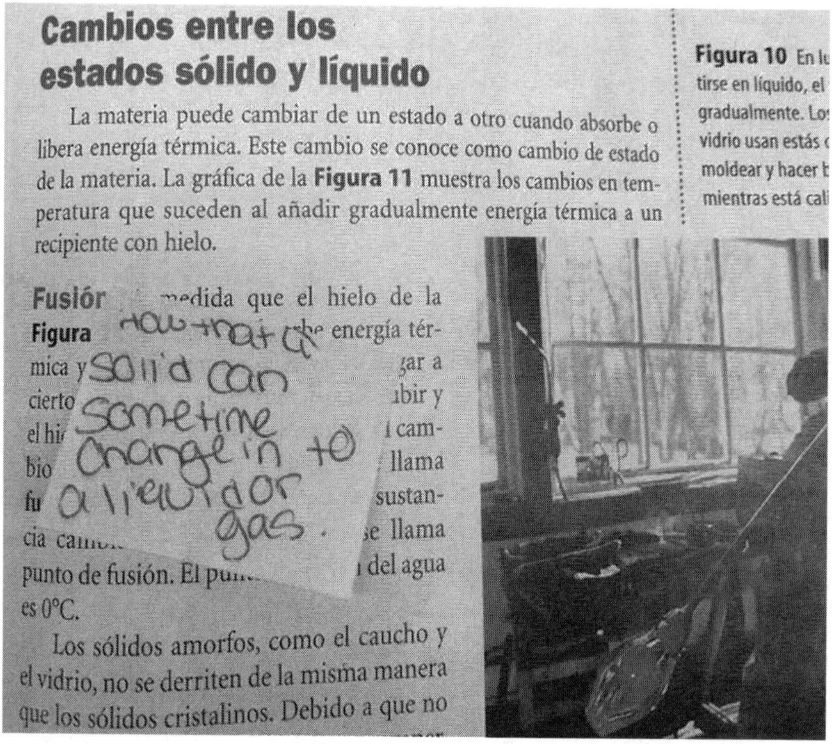

FIGURE 8.2 Gist in English

Ms. Montoya's class used the sticky notes in different ways. In Figure 8.1, the student extracts the main ideas from the text by writing her notes in Spanish, which is the same language as the text. She shows that she is able to use the same language of the text to solidify her understanding of the content. In contrast, the student in the next image (Figure 8.2) uses English to synthesize his understanding of the text in Spanish. Doing so helps him regulate his own comprehension of the text.

We further explore students' language use while writing their gists later in this chapter. We focus next on specific moments of the lesson to take a close look at how Ms. Montoya and the students utilized translanguaging as a strategy to construct meaning collaboratively.

Inviting Translanguaging: Teacher's Discourse and Actions

Ms. Montoya carefully planned and utilized translanguaging in several instances throughout the lesson, always keeping her students' needs in mind. She utilized translanguaging to invite the students to write in the language of their choice. She confirmed, restated, and built upon what they said. She posed questions.

She demonstrated and relied on multimodal translanguaging in order to ensure understanding of the content. She also positioned the students as scientists.

After reading the Do Now and telling students in Spanish to read the question and write the answer, Ms. Montoya tells the class:

> Quiero que escriban en lo que puedan escribir mejor. Si quieren escribir en inglés o en español está bien. O mi parte favorita es cuando lo ponen en inglés y dicen las palabras en español. Lo que sea más fácil para que ustedes puedan dar a entender qué es lo que piensan. [I want you to write in the language you can write better. If you want to write in English or in Spanish, it is OK. Or my favorite part is when you write in English and you say the words in Spanish. Whatever makes it easier for you to show your thinking.]

Here Ms. Montoya is making evident that she wants students to use language to show their thinking, and even though she is encouraging the use of Spanish, students are free to show their understandings and what they can do using their entire language repertoire.

Ms. Montoya understands that for the students to construct meaning in a language they are reclaiming, they must use all their language resources. By doing this, Ms. Montoya ensures her students are "engaging their entire linguistic repertoire and expanding it" (García & Li Wei, 2014, p. 71).

Ms. Montoya continues probing the students' understandings through her questioning techniques that include translanguaging:

MS. MONTOYA: The Sun. OK, let's take it a bit further than that. Un poco más. ¿Qué es la parte del sol? ¿Pero cómo lo afecta? El sol baja, y el vaso ¿Qué pasa? A bit more. [What is the part of the sun? How does it affect it? The sun comes down and the glass . . . What happens?]
Someone else, let's see. Julieta you haven't participated.

JULIETA: With the sun, water gets hot and evaporates into gas.

MS. MONTOYA: That's right! So, what affects it? ¿Qué es lo que lo afecta? The heat. There is another word for heat. Dame otro sinónimo. Think about it. Cuando uno pone agua en hielera ¿Qué pasa? El sol no le da ahí, no se evapora. ¿Qué pasa?
[When one puts water in the icemaker, what happens? The sun does not get there. It does not evaporate. What happens?]

JULIETA: The temperature changes the water.

MS. MONTOYA: That's right! So, that is one thing that affects it, la temperatura.

Ms. Montoya knows that many of her students, including Julieta, are receptive bilinguals. She wants to make sure that they understand the scientific concept she is teaching them and she also wants them to develop productive skills in

Spanish. But she does not challenge Julieta nor does she tell her: "Aquí no se habla inglés." Instead, she accepts Julieta's answer, which responds to her use of her own language repertoire, while allowing Julieta the space to incorporate the features from Spanish into her repertoire.

Ms. Montoya continues probing further the scientific understandings of her students:

MS. MONTOYA: Perfecto. Bien. Solid has what? Can you give me an example? Dame un ejemplo de sólido.
MARCO: A rock.
MS. MONTOYA: Una piedra. Muy bien. [A rock. Very well.] What else?
JULIETA: Un líquido puede tomar una forma sólida. [A liquid can take a solid form.]

In the exchange above, Ms. Montoya probes further by asking the students to think about a specific example, and when Marco, a student, answers "A rock," she simply follows up with "Piedra. Muy bien." Marco's reply is not wrong because it is given in English. What happens next is extremely important. Julieta, the student who had consistently answered in English now turns to Spanish: "Un líquido puede tomar una forma sólida." By giving her students space to use their entire language repertoire and prodding them to come up with features of what is socially defined as Spanish in this class, Julieta, and the others, feel comfortable trying out the features of what to them is a new language in school, although it is, after all, their home language. By engaging in these translanguaging practices, Ms. Montoya aims "for sustainability of the complex language practices of bilinguals in functional interrelationship with the social and academic context in which they are performed" (García & Li Wei, 2014, p. 73).

In the next exchange, Ms. Montoya draws on her linguistic and semiotic repertoire in order to ensure students understand the concept.

MS. MONTOYA: Perfecta respuesta. Si yo tengo agua en este container. [Perfect response. If I have water in this container.] . . .
(She goes to pick up the container) . . .
MS. MONTOYA: Miren acá. Este jarrón, yo tengo el líquido aquí ¿Sí o no? ¿Tiene una forma el líquido? [Look here. I have liquid in this container, Yes or no? Does the liquid have a form?]
STUDENTS (SEVERAL IN UNISON): Sí.
MS. MONTOYA: (still holding the container so everyone can see it): Está adentro de este jarrón, ahora si yo lo vacío ¿Tiene forma? [It is inside this container, now if I empty it, does it have a form?]
SEVERAL STUDENTS: No.
MS. MONTOYA: No ¿verdad? [No, right?]

In this instance, Ms. Montoya provides support through multimodal translanguaging for she uses realia, gestures, and actions in order to support student learning of the content. An example of how she maximizes meaning in the lesson is in supporting students' understanding through showing actual artifacts used in the experiment.

Finally, in the exchange that follows, Ms. Montoya utilizes translanguaging to confirm, restate, and build on what students say, in addition to supporting the positioning of the students as scientists.

MS. MONTOYA: Díganme algo que uno tiene que hacer cuando hace un laboratorio. [Tell me what does one have to do when one does a lab?]

ROBERTO: Safety.

MS. MONTOYA: (repeating what the student said) Safety. Seguridad. ¿Qué más? [What else?]

JAZMÍN: Procedimiento. [Procedure.]

MS. MONTOYA: Procedimiento, muy bien. There is a procedure for everything. Procedimiento. OK, what else do you need before a lab? He said procedimiento—estar seguro, seguridad. Safety first. ¿Qué más? [What else?]

RONALD: Observación. [Observation.]

MS. MONTOYA: Observación. Perfecto. Pero antes de observar lo que está pasando ¿Qué es lo que uno hace? Una . . . [But before doing an observation, what is something one does? A . . .]

MIGUEL: Un hipótesis. [A hypothesis.]

MS. MONTOYA: ¡Una hipótesis, muy bien! Una hipótesis. You have to make a prediction and that is exactly what a hypothesis is. Write the "if" statement. En eso es lo que vamos a trabajar ahora. [This is what we are going to work on now.]

In the exchange above, when Roberto provides the answer in English, "safety," Ms. Montoya doesn't say "Wrong!" She merely provides the word in Spanish, "seguridad." It is precisely Ms. Montoya's stance that the students' linguistic features work together/juntos that gives the other students the assurance to try out the other answers in Spanish, "procedimiento," "observación," "un hipótesis." And when Miguel comes up with what is considered the wrong gender for the Spanish "hipótesis," Ms. Montoya doesn't tell him, "Wrong, you say 'una hipótesis.'" She merely and with excitement confirms the response as "muy bien," and moves on to first restate it as "una hipótesis," focusing instead on the meaning of the scientific use of a hypothesis: "You have to make a prediction and that is exactly what a hypothesis is." Just like scientists have to make predictions, bilingual students who are reappropriating features of a home language that they are not accustomed to using in school also have to predict, try out, and confirm.

Ms. Montoya is allowing them to predict how Spanish works, to try it out, and then she confirms their linguistic predictions.

Finally, by telling students "Write the 'if' statement . . ." she is reminding students of how hypotheses are expressed in English. Ms. Montoya hopes that this would help her students understand how to also write the hypotheses in Spanish, as she strengthens their bilingual scientist identities.

Whereas Ms. Montoya has carefully planned spaces for translanguaging ahead of time, she also makes decisions moment by moment based on her understanding of what students say and their Spanish performances. Her focus is on providing continuity by facilitating the discussion and moving it along, while meeting the students where they are. She relies on her knowledge of particular students to invite them to participate.

Through her discourse and actions, Ms. Montoya invited students to take up translanguaging. The next section focuses on how students negotiated language use during the reading of the science text as they annotated and paraphrased important content of the science text through the use of the gist strategy.

Students Getting the Gist

Getting the "gist" is a common literacy practice used with students to increase their reading comprehension by stopping to purposely think and annotate what they've just read in the margins of the text itself or by using sticky notes. Students write the essence of what they've just read, the main ideas conveyed, or their own short analyses (see Figures 8.1 and 8.2).

Ms. Montoya takes this popular teaching strategy a step further by having students write their gist on sticky notes using their entire linguistic repertoire. In the lesson we observed, Ms. Montoya accesses her students' background knowledge on the three states of matter. After students have had an opportunity to experiment with the different states of matter in the hands-on activity, the students were asked to read a section of the chapter from their science text in Spanish, and to write the gist using sticky notes on the margins. The following vignette shows how students used translanguaging when writing the gist:

Roberto, a U.S.-born student who is in a bilingual class for the first time, reads aloud from the text in Spanish to the rest of the group:

> "Cuando un objeto caliente se acerca a un objeto más frio, la energía térmica se transfiere del objeto caliente al más frio. El movimiento de energía térmica de una sustancia de mayor temperatura a una con menor temperatura se llama calor. Cuando una sustancia se calienta, gana energía térmica. Por lo tanto, sus partículas se mueven

(Continued)

(Continued)

> más rápidamente y su temperatura se eleva. Cuando una sustancia se enfría, pierde energía térmica, lo cual hace que sus partículas se muevan más lentamente y baja la temperatura" (Snyder & Zike, 2008, p. 110). [When a hot object comes close to a cold object, the thermal energy transfers from the hot object to the cold one. The movement of thermal energy from an object with higher to lower temperature is what we call heat. When an object gets hot, it gains thermal energy. That is why its particles move more quickly and its temperature gets higher. When a substance gets cold, it loses thermal energy, and so its particles move slower and the temperature goes down.]

The three other group members listen silently as Roberto reads, tracking the words in their own textbooks. After he finishes reading, he looks up at the group and begins speaking in English:

ROBERTO: So . . . so . . . heat will change the temperature, make it go higher . . .

ANDERSON: It's talking about how heat will change the temperature . . . causes evaporation . . .

ROBERTO: . . . and uh, what's it called?

ANDERSON: Particles!

ROBERTO: The particles will move rapid[ly] . . . and the cold, will make it slow down.

In this short vignette, students in the group listen closely as Roberto reads a passage from the text aloud in Spanish, and afterwards, both he and Anderson begin to make meaning of what they have just encountered in the text through discussion using English. Roberto and Anderson translanguage to clarify what Roberto has just read in Spanish by using English, the language that maximizes comprehension for them. Explaining and discussing in English helps Roberto and Anderson make meaning of the Spanish science-content vocabulary found in the text.

In the writing of the gist, Roberto skillfully demonstrates his ability to draw from all of his language resources in order to write a main point on his sticky note, which then helps him make sense of the paragraph he has read and what the group discussed. He writes: "Heat will actually change the temperature and particles 'se mueven rapidamente' [move rapidly]." The language flexibility that is practiced in Ms. Montoya's classroom allows Roberto to write in ways that help him deeply understand the scientific concept. Learning is enhanced through translanguaging.

Reflecting on the Gist and Translanguaging

In a post-lesson short questionnaire, students discussed how they utilized the gist strategy to help them learn. Several students revealed that they used English when writing the gist of what they read in the science textbook in Spanish:

JASON: I write my notes in English so it is easier for me to remember.

XIMENA: English helps me a little, but because it helps me understand a word a little better.

ALEJANDRO: I write my gist in English. English helps me by showing how I can translate Spanish into English.

Other students remarked that in writing the gist, they used both English and Spanish.

JULIA: I use English and Spanish for my gist. English helps me by understanding it [the point the book is making].

ELENA: When it comes to reading science textbook en español, I use sticky notes to find the gist. I would write the gist in the language I think I understand the most.

Students' perceptions on how they utilize translanguaging reveal how they use this tool in different ways to support their thinking. Students show that they are aware of how they learn best. They are fully equipped to use their entire language repertoire to learn. Julia, for example, uses English when the text is mostly in Spanish in order to increase understanding and deepen her content knowledge. Alejandro uses translanguaging as a tool to deepen cross-linguistic connections and develop a discourse of science. Elena demonstrates her metacognitive awareness in her statement; she shows her level of consciousness in her decision-making process when she utilizes the linguistic resources at her disposal in order to make meaning of the content she is learning. Using translanguaging is a valuable skill when learning language for academic purposes, when students have to take charge of their own learning. The students' responses indicate that translanguaging can serve as a tool for young scholars and thinkers.

Larger Meanings and Implications of the Use of Translanguaging

Through the use of translanguaging strategies in Ms. Montoya's class, the students are developing what Bourdieu (1991) has called "linguistic capital," a competence in the ways that society uses language, by engaging their own internal language capacities. In other words, Ms. Montoya is providing access to scientific vocabulary and ways of talking about science in both languages, thus giving access to "languages of power" (García, 2009, p. 12), so that they can transform their future possibilities as bilingual U.S. Latinos. It is these translanguaging literacy practices that "provide an area for constructing and performing identities" (Merchant & Carrington, 2009, p. 63). But Ms. Montoya does so not by providing them access to this linguistic capital just in English or just in Spanish, but by enabling them to deploy their entire language repertoire, including features of Spanish that they use at home, to build this new and complex linguistic competence.

By translanguaging, the students in Ms. Montoya's class are reclaiming their bilingualism, as they develop their knowledge of science content. Students take up translanguaging precisely because Ms. Montoya herself supports flexible language use through her own practices. In 2001, Lemke reminded us to "integrate science teaching that is responsive to different needs with teaching that addresses the challenges of a heterogeneous and diverse classroom community" (p. 306). As a teacher, Ms. Montoya is familiar with individual students' experiences, strengths, and understandings of the specific content, in this case science, and uses translanguaging to adapt to individual students' needs.

The question of how Ms. Montoya knows when to use translanguaging and for what purposes can be best explained through the idea of "mētis." In his book, *Seeing Like a State*, Scott (1998), explains that, "broadly understood, mētis represents a wide array of practical skills and acquired intelligence in responding to a constantly changing natural and human environment" (p. 313). Citing Scott (1998), Traugh (unpublished) argues that "it is the detailed knowledge of individual persons and of the particular school and classroom contexts in which we teach that are keys to the development of a teacher's mētis, of her/his local and situated knowledge" (p. 21). Ms. Montoya's knowledge of her local context and the individual students' strengths (Carini & Himley, 2010), her mētis, enables her to take up translanguaging to engage students as scientists. In addition, Ms. Montoya gives her students "the agency to negotiate their linguistic and meaning-making repertoires" (García & Li Wei, 2014, p. 75).

The students' bilingualism is supported in this classroom environment and students are able to take ownership of those skills to increase their learning. In this chapter, we examined how students used translanguaging in a variety of ways and for different purposes. Translanguaging was used as a tool for clarification of the larger concepts being reviewed and as a way to deepen understanding of content, as well as in making cross-linguistic connections and references to aid in learning. Additionally, translanguaging was used to gain metacognitive awareness. Although this chapter surveyed a science-content classroom, the translanguaging strategies that students expertly utilized can be applied to enhance their learning in any content. What is more, translanguaging is not only an approach to support students whose English practices are emerging, but also those who are reclaiming a minoritized language. In this lesson, we see how translanguaging is a tool that can be utilized for students learning and strengthening their literacy skills in Spanish.

Conclusion

In this dual language bilingual classroom, Ms. Montoya does not follow a language separation policy in the rigid ways it is traditionally mandated from the top. Instead, Ms. Montoya utilizes her own and the students' entire linguistic repertoire in flexible, dynamic, and intentional ways. She does this in order to maximize interactions, while supporting complex learning and thinking. During her planning, she carefully considers when it will be appropriate to utilize translanguaging. She also utilizes it based on her knowledge of individual student strengths and their learning needs on a moment-by-moment basis. Translanguaging takes place during particular key instances in her lesson. Her focus is always on supporting students to reclaim their bilingualism, while they are learning rigorous science content. Ms. Montoya understands deeply that in order to reclaim their bilingualism, while engaging in deep thinking, students must have ample opportunities to leverage their entire linguistic repertoire (García & Li Wei, 2014). Ms. Montoya aims for sustainability of the complex language practices of her bilingual students, as she helps them develop those language practices valued in school. Translanguaging allows the teacher and the students to mediate complex science learning and language learning.

TEACHER'S VOICE BY CLAUDIA MONTOYA GAUDREAU

As I think back on everything I have done in my educational career, the one thing that stands out the most to me is the use of language. I feel that language is the precursor for all communication, especially in my career. As a teacher, I find that language is the first chance for me to interact with my students and establish a rapport. I am lucky enough to know English and Spanish fluently; having studied in South America was a great help, but my love for language does not end there. I have learned welcoming phrases in different languages from my students that allow me to connect with students and parents. Being comfortable in one's home language is key for newcomers and students that speak an additional language at home. It is very important for students to feel successful in their home language, as well as the language of school.

The use of translanguaging has helped me expand my knowledge of how bilingual students need to take up their entire linguistic repertoire in order to learn and express their knowledge of the content. I find that with translanguaging students are more accepting of others and of the use of their home language for academic purposes. Feeling linguistically secure is important to learn and to continue to develop language expertise.

As a dual language bilingual teacher and foreign language teacher, I see the importance of language for understanding and comprehension.

(Continued)

(Continued)

I allow my students to use their home language and apply it to the work we are doing in the classroom. This gives them the opportunity to shine in either language and use all types of language features.

One of the major challenges that I have encountered in taking up translanguaging is that students feel that they need to perform perfectly in both languages, the one being taught and their home language. This stems from the fear they have of being incorrect in using language, something that schools have implanted in them. Many times students do not feel confident enough to answer in a class with students from various language backgrounds. They may also not be comfortable using language with the teacher(s) they have in the classroom. Through translanguaging, students come to value language as a communicative tool, rather than a precise code that is either right or wrong.

Since translanguaging is a new concept, it may take time for the teachers to get accustomed to allowing students to use all their language resources to learn. Curriculum mapping may be one big aspect of lesson planning, but taking into consideration the students, their different levels and modalities of learning, is another. We teach in a world where differentiation of educational content is imperative and necessary. Translanguaging allows me to meet students where they are, and it also helps students expand their linguistic repertoire.

Discussion Questions and Activities

1. Discuss what it means to reclaim one's bilingualism. What is the role of translanguaging in this process?
2. Observe in a classroom of emergent bilinguals and, if possible, ask for permission to record a portion of a lesson in a content area, such as math, science, or social studies. As you review the recording, consider the following questions:

    a. What do you notice about how language is used?
    b. Are there missed opportunities for teaching and learning because of the way in which language is being used in the classroom?
    c. How would you have used translanguaging in this content classroom to develop the students' language performances, to deepen their learning, and to include all students?

3. Design a lesson in a content area in which you can invite students to use their entire linguistic repertoire, creating the space for them to reclaim their bilingualism.

    a. In what ways could students utilize their agency to reclaim their bilingualism using the spaces you've provided in your lesson plan?

b. In what ways do these experiences provide access to deeper understandings of the content?

References

Baker, C. (2011). *Foundations of bilingual education and bilingualism*, 5th edn. Clevedon, UK: Multilingual Matters.

Bourdieu, P. (1991). *Language and symbolic power* (ed. J. B. Thompson). Cambridge, MA: Harvard University Press.

Carini, P., & Himley, M. (2010). *Jenny's story: Taking the long view of the child, prospect's philosophy in action.* New York: Teachers College Press.

García, O. (2009). *Bilingual education in the 21st century: A global perspective.* Malden, MA: Wiley-Blackwell.

García, O., & Li Wei (2014). *Translanguaging: Language, bilingualism and education.* Basingstoke, Hampshire, UK: Palgrave Macmillan.

Lemke, J. L. (2001). Articulating communities: Sociocultural perspectives on science education. *Journal of Research on Science Teaching*, 38(3), 296–316.

Merchant, G., & Carrington, V. (2009). Literacy and identity. *Literacy*, 43(2), 63–64.

Scott, J. (1998). *Seeing like a state: How certain schemes to improve the human condition have failed.* New Haven: Yale University Press.

Seuss, Dr. (1949). *Bartholomew and the oobleck.* New York: Random House Books.

Snyder, S. L., & Zike, D. (2008). *Ciencia para New York, Grado 6.* New York: Glencoe, McGraw Hill.

Traugh, C. (unpublished) Using descriptive inquiry to support school-based teacher learning. Bank Street College of Education, New York.

Valenzuela, A. (1999). *Subtractive schooling: U.S. Mexican youth and the politics of caring.* Albany, NY: State University of New York Press.

PART III

Implications for Policy and Practice

9

A TRANSLANGUAGING EDUCATION POLICY

Disruptions and Creating Spaces of Possibility

Ofelia García and Tatyana Kleyn

Introduction

In chapter 2, we briefly described the language policy context of U.S. education. Chapters 3 through 8 demonstrate the potential and the limitations of translanguaging work in what Bartlett and García (2011) have called "subtractive times." Despite the constraints posed by present language education policies in the U.S., translanguaging has major implications to transform the teaching and learning of emergent bilingual students.

This chapter uncovers the tensions between the modernist/structuralist language policies followed in U.S. schools today, and the more *critical poststructuralist position* of translanguaging theory. By putting both of these tendencies alongside each other—one responding to *external* standards and state ideologies, the other to the *internal* linguistic realities of the emergent bilingual children—we create spaces of possibilities. This chapter describes how taking up translanguaging theory transforms our vision of bilingual students and the ways in which we educate them. We do so by referencing examples from the case studies presented in chapters 3 through 8, demonstrating how a translanguaging lens can transform traditional subtractive language education policies and practices.

Translanguaging Education Policy

As the U.S. population has become more linguistically diverse, language education policy has become more restrictive and increasingly guarded by the federal government. As we saw in chapter 2, since the 1980s and the establishment of the U.S. Department of Education during the Reagan era, the federal government has found ways to encourage states to ramp up English-only education for the growing number of immigrants. With the growing opposition to bilingual education, many bilingual programs have closed and some have been relabeled as "dual language" by federal and state educational authorities.

Challenges remain to educate all emergent bilinguals so that they can engage deeply with content, develop language and literacy for academic purposes, and develop identities that position them as successful students and people. Whereas educators working outside of a translanguaging theoretical framework try to grapple with these challenges by promoting English only (and in bilingual programs strict spaces for English and the language other than English in their "standard" versions), and mostly dismiss the students' varied home language practices, the educators that we portray in chapters 3 through 8 have found ways of working with the students' entire language repertoires and have developed pedagogical practices to do precisely this.

These educators are bolstering bilingual students' performance by taking up translanguaging theory, a critical activity that disrupts and opens up spaces within the existing language education policies that are imposed. It develops, by working in the space between top-down policies and the local practices of teachers and students, what we might call a *translanguaging education policy.* A translanguaging education policy keeps two dimensions in perspective—the *internal* repertoire of the bilingual child and the *external* societal language that might be the aim of a policy. Although a translanguaging education policy might retain the externally imposed program labels of ESL or bilingual, at its core it starts and works with the internal complete language repertoire of the bilingual child. A translanguaging education policy supports and keeps the students' entire language repertoire paramount, as it also makes students aware of when and how to suppress certain features of their repertoire (or activate them) to adjust to, and sometimes resist, external language education policies. That is, students and teachers are never left alone by a translanguaging education policy. Instead, it works alongside students and teachers to propel them to greater learning and teaching. And yet a translanguaging education policy is inherently critical of many established policies and works to transcend them to increase opportunities for language-minoritized students as it promotes social justice.

It is important to work alongside education officials to resist and expand policies so they become more inclusive of emergent bilinguals. But while the clock ticks slowly at educational bureaucracies and change is often slow in coming, our stances and practices cannot be put to the side, but must be adapted to meet the realities that teachers and students are facing. External language policies that educators are expected to enact can inform educators' work, but translanguaging education policy follows Menken and García's (2010) support for teachers in negotiating and disrupting the policies that are handed down to them. Adopting a critical theoretical lens and bringing together established top-down language education policy and students' language practices transforms theory, practices, and policies. Translanguaging education policy emerges out of this third space (Gutiérrez, Baquedano-López & Tejeda, 1999; Soja, 1996).

Below we discuss 10 ways in which a translanguaging lens disrupts traditional ways of thinking about education and language policies, as seen through the case studies presented in chapters 3 through 8:

1. Disrupting distinctive roles of policymakers, teachers, and researchers
2. Disrupting traditional understandings of language
3. Disrupting monolingualism and traditional bilingualism
4. Disrupting categorization of students
5. Disrupting the distance between home and school
6. Disrupting purposes of learning for bilingual students
7. Disrupting traditional language education models
8. Disrupting traditional content areas
9. Disrupting scripted curricula
10. Disrupting inequities, hierarchies, and circles of power

These disruptions then produce the generative space in which a translanguaging education policy emerges.

Disrupting Distinctive Roles of Policymakers, Teachers, and Researchers

Effective change in schools cannot happen without establishing and developing trust among the different stakeholders in the education community—teachers, administrators, families, students, policymakers, and researchers. Outsiders looking to effect transformations, especially a university-based team like that of CUNY-NYSIEB, need to first be accepted as members of the school community. To do so requires that university personnel and school faculty become equal participants and see themselves as co-learners (Li Wei, 2014). From teachers, university-based educators learn about the policies facing schools and how those are being enacted in practice on the ground. From the university-based teams, teachers learn about theories, research, and educational innovations that they might not be practicing. Through the collaboration, teachers develop trust in themselves as creative thinkers and innovators of practices. They learn about theoretical positions, such as translanguaging, which go against what they have often been taught to think and do. In this way, spaces of possibilities are opened up that renovate the teachers' stances/beliefs and thus their practice.

The case studies in chapters 3 through 8 portray specific lessons that a university-based team co-planned or co-taught with classroom teachers. In some cases, the teams helped teachers plan the lessons, always according to their students' needs and their curricular demands. That is, none of the lessons in the case studies were "model" lessons. Rather, they were the same lessons the teachers carried out day in and day out, but enhanced with understandings of translanguaging developed through extensive dialogue with the university-based team.

And the research that was carried out was not set up as an "experiment." Instead, it was part and parcel of the larger work that was being done in that classroom. Thus, the collaboration allowed the "rough edges of work" to be revealed, rather than the unquestioned expertise of teachers, researchers, or policymakers.

What is important in this collaborative co-planning/co-teaching/co-researching activity is that the risk-taking among participants was shared equally. Whereas the teachers opened up their classrooms to the university-based team's glance, the team showed their own vulnerabilities as they tried out translanguaging strategies in the teachers' actual classrooms. The collaboration was then unusual for a traditional researcher–teacher model, in which only the teacher opens herself up to criticism. Translanguaging was not presented as a bounded theoretical construct, impervious to the school policies at hand, but in tension with the realities in which it was executed.

The lessons in chapters 3 through 8 are not to be followed or recreated blindly, for they are meant to show how particular teachers in their specific contexts leveraged the translanguaging of their students. They do not simply portray a "how to" guide for incorporating translanguaging strategies. Rather, the lessons highlight the tensions for researchers, teachers, and students in opening up spaces for different languaging practices in an educational context that has preselected only certain language practices as legitimate. The burden then of doing the critical work that surrounds translanguaging is equally distributed, as both teachers and researchers join forces not just to co-plan, co-teach, and co-research, but also to co-disrupt educational practices in ways that open up possibilities and that generate a translanguaging education policy that is workable in the present educational conditions. In so doing, teachers and researchers become language policymakers.

Disrupting Traditional Understandings of Language

As we said in chapter 1, translanguaging deconstructs the traditional concept of language, bringing back the linguistic performances of people regardless of the linguistic features accepted as "academic language" (for a critique of the concept of academic language, see Valdés, forthcoming). Translanguaging also goes beyond the definitions of named languages such as English, Spanish, and others. It brings to light the fact that people, in our case bilingual students, often operate with a linguistic system that has features that go beyond named languages. This is particularly visible in the case studies included in Part II of this book.

From an external school viewpoint, we might say that all the case studies in this book, except the one presented by Espinosa and Herrera, were of classrooms where English development was the goal. Yet, what we see taking place in all of the case studies, even in those classrooms that claim to be teaching English Language Arts, is that a translanguaging education policy transcends named languages, ensuring that students access their entire language repertoire in the process of learning, even when the goal is expert performance in a named language for academic purposes. Both teachers and students use language features other than those considered within the bounds of what society names one language or another.

The teachers in all the case studies understand the school's linguistic goals for instruction. And these goals differ depending on the school's context and the teacher's own stance. In the lessons portrayed by Ebe and Woodley, the goal is clearly performance in English. For those in which Kleyn, Collins and Cioè-Peña, and Seltzer and Collins worked, the goal is performance especially in English, but also in Spanish. For the teacher in the classroom described by Espinosa and Herrera, the goal is performance in Spanish. However, the use of translanguaging in all these classrooms would cause an observer to question which language was indeed that of instruction. In all cases, the teachers are leveraging the students' full language repertoires, encouraging them to use features that do not correspond to what is named as only English or only Spanish or another language.

Taking up a translanguaging lens means that all named languages are deconstructed and questioned. New York City, with the intermingling of speakers from so many places with so many histories, is the perfect laboratory in which to do this, for named languages have truly become deterritorialized. Teachers first notice the indeterminacy of other language practices among their students, for example, those of students who speak Haitian Creole or Fulani or even Chinese or Spanish. When teachers first start to work with Haitians or speakers of Fulani or Chinese, they are troubled by the lack of consistency in naming the languages the students speak. Haitian students make up a sizable minority in New York. What do Haitian students call what they speak? Haitian or Haitian Creole? And is it a language or a creole or a patois? Eventually teachers start understanding the racism and linguicism involved in calling what Haitians speak a "patois." And then they take the next step, for even saying that a language is a "creole" makes it a mongrel, a hybridized version of the real language, neither French nor an African language. Aren't all languages in some ways creoles, with features that belong to other times and historically to other people, they might ask? *Why* do we call the ways in which enslaved or colonized people speak creoles and not languages? Who made the decision not to give these ways of speaking status as language? De Graff has said (1999) that creoles are languages, but carrying it one step further, we might say that all languages are in some ways creoles. So if creole is not a useful designation, is language? We begin to see that naming these practices "creoles" puts most Haitians in a subordinate position to the small powerful minority that speaks what is called the "French language" in Haiti.

Many students in New York City, where most of the case studies took place, speak what some call Fula, others Fulani, yet others Pulaar or Pula. At first, teachers demand one label. Eventually, as they deconstruct the concept of language, they learn to accept the many designations for the language features and ways of using language that students from Guinea speak. The question then emerges: Who coined these terms for these ways of speaking? *Why* were these practices named and who named them differently? The role of missionaries in naming ways of speaking in the continent of Africa is then elucidated. And we are left with the understanding that all these dynamic language practices of people were named to enable some power over those who needed to be subjugated to Western practices, religious as well as linguistic.

Chinese-speaking students also make up a majority of language-minoritized students in New York. In the school in which Espinosa and Herrera conducted their study, Chinese students in the dual language bilingual Chinese/English program are speakers of Fukienese, and some of Cantonese, and not of Mandarin, the language of instruction in the classroom. Teachers become conscious of the fact that "Chinese" is a social construction, for students speak in ways that are not mutually intelligible in what are named Mandarin, Cantonese, Fukienese, etc. And yet, Chinese usage calls all of them dialects of "Chinese." How are they all Chinese? Is a common script enough to call divergent language features and uses with one name? *Why* have the Chinese adopted this position? Teachers begin to understand that the power of Mandarin Chinese is elevated through this naming game.

Spanish speakers make up the bulk of language-minoritized students in New York City. Speakers with very different economic and sociopolitical histories live and speak to each other in the city. By putting the language features of the many U.S. Latinos alongside each other, teachers also start understanding that the concept of "Spanish," as taught in school, is also a social construction. They start realizing that the language practices of Spanish conquistadores could not have been what we consider today "Spanish," since the first grammar of what we learned to call "Spanish" was written by Antonio de Nebrija in 1492, the year of the encounter. The efforts to "standardize" Spanish in the 16th century, to rein in the linguistic practices of people—what we now call Romance in the Iberian peninsula, and what we now call Quechua, Guaraní, Nahua, Otomí, etc., in Latin America—has been a way to exert power over conquered and colonized people.

In the same way, teachers who take up a translanguaging lens then start to understand that English has also been constructed from the ways of speaking that the Anglo-Saxons brought to the British Isles around AD 450. When in 1066 William the Conqueror from Normandy defeated King Harold, the ways in which the kings spoke changed, reflecting what society at the time referred to as French. Eventually this way of speaking spread to the courts, the church, the upper classes, and eventually the commoners. Clearly what we know today as English has also been constructed. It is not just that there are "Englishes" (Kachru, 1992; Kachru, Kachru & Nelson, 2009), it is that every "English-speaking" person has features that are their own and that are not equally shared among all speakers. We learn to speak in social interaction, and so speakers from New York or speakers in the same family share features that overlap. However, speakers in Scotland and New York or speakers who do not share any social affiliation will have features in their "English" that do not overlap. This is why many times speakers of "English" on television are given subtitles so that they are understood. Teachers learn to appreciate that English is also a social external construction that differs from the internal linguistic features that a speaker has, which are often more complex and divergent than those codified as English in school.

What teachers learn to understand in the inquiry about named languages is the power behind their construction. Although power is acknowledged, it is not dismissed. That is, teachers learn that their teaching has to respond to the internal use of language by the child, but always in relationship to the external named language that has been constructed. Unless these two aspects of language are in conversation, the power of named languages will continue to be exercised among language-minoritized populations.

A translanguaging education policy evens out the playing field among all so-called "languages." It legitimizes all the language features of individual speakers that are important both for communication and for identity.

Disrupting Monolingualism and Multilingualism

Traditionally people are categorized as bilingual/multilingual or bidialectal/multidialectal. But if the unit of analysis is the linguistic features of the individual's language repertoire, rather than the named language(s) as constituted by political states or nations, then we can say that all of us are multilingual, or better yet that all of us translanguage or are translanguagers, using features of our individual linguistic repertoires according to the communicative situation we have at hand. Translanguaging theory focuses not on named languages, but on the language practices of individuals that are always varied and unique. Translanguaging education policy is thus inclusive of all linguistic differences, although it does not dissolve the social realities of being considered monolingual, bilingual, or multilingual. Although translanguaging education policy is inclusive of all linguistic differences, it is particularly relevant for bilingual/multilingual individuals. There is no contradiction between considering "language" from the individual speakers' perspective and acknowledging the importance of monolingual/bilingual identity constructions, both individually and socially.

Teachers are traditionally categorized as monolingual or bilingual, usually based on the types of programs in which they teach, more so than on their own language practices. Some of the case studies feature bilingual teachers who have been trained to use what is considered their two languages in instruction. But others are assigned the role of "monolingual" teachers. We have seen that the translanguaged classrooms of Mr. Brown (Woodley) and Ms. Chapman-Santiago (Ebe) are taught by teachers who are said to be monolingual. Yet, these teachers have considerable expertise in using features of their students' linguistic repertoire to teach (sometimes because they have learned them or use them themselves, other times because they seek them from other students or teachers, or from parents, or from technologies like Google Translate). Therefore, translanguaging education policy means that all teachers take up the students' individual features and leverage their diversity of practices. It is an inclusive policy, appropriate for all teachers.

As we will see when we next discuss the categorization of students, the emphasis on labeling students because they have perceived "language problems" (i.e., the lack of English proficiency), means that the students' bilingualism is left unrecognized. In most schools, the potential of multilingual speakers, those who truly have a complex expanded linguistic repertoire and perform well using all their features, is completely disregarded. As long as the student can perform academic tasks with features from what is considered English, their other features are ignored. Translanguaging education policy doesn't leave any features behind, but leverages them to learn deeply, regardless of whether the outward performance is with those features that the school demands at that time. A translanguaging education policy takes this difference into account and works precisely to recognize the multicompetence (Cook, 2008, 2012) that all students have in using linguistic features other than those sanctioned in schools.

Disrupting Categorization of Students

In the United States, where our multiple case studies take place, students are strictly categorized according to ethnicity, linguistic proficiency, ability, and other characteristics. Reflecting the majority of bilingual students in the U.S., most of the students in our case studies were Latinos. And because of the U.S. emphasis on "curing" what is considered the "English language learner problem," students in most of our case study classrooms were all designated as "English language learners." Taking up translanguaging education policy means that teachers disrupt all student categories. Students in U.S. schools are categorized simply as English language learner (ELL), long-term ELL, former ELL, student with incomplete/interrupted formal education (SIFE), and fluent English proficient (FEP). And students with disabilities are often separated from the rest of the students and categorized even further. Just as there has been movement in the recent past to address the continuum of abilities/disabilities in the population by acknowledging dis/abilities, we must recognize the complicated continuum of language performance in different contexts by deconstructing student categories, that is, by seeing students as individuals with their own capacities, rather than as just members of categories in the class. The teachers in our case studies disrupt the given categories of students by taking up a translanguaging lens, thus opening up possibilities of emergence, growth, and development for all students.

The classroom portrayed in the chapter by Kleyn is the only one that is officially an integrated co-teaching classroom (ICT), with some students in this classroom officially labeled as having disabilities and having an individualized education plan (IEP). Many of these same students are the ones that perform very well when the teacher adopts translanguaging. In the rest of the classrooms of our case studies, the differences between students are palpable, although the program structures do not capture these differences.

In the chapter by Seltzer and Collins, the students in the English Language Arts high school classroom are all identified as having incomplete or interrupted education (SIFE). And yet, there is enormous variability among them. Perhaps the only experience they have in common is living in poverty and their recent arrival in the United States. Students are only considered SIFE if they are immigrants. Because of laws concerning required attendance, it is unusual for students in the United States to have interrupted education. But certainly many bilingual students born in the U.S. have received a poor and incomplete education. But then schools categorize them as "long-term English language learners," when many of these students, having been in U.S. schools for many years, cannot perform in any language but English. What is the difference then between students categorized as SIFE and those categorized as long-term English language learners? Once students enter a category, it is difficult to move them out. Teachers who take up translanguaging look at students as individuals, and not as categories, enabling them to actually differentiate for *all* their students. This, of course, should be standard educational practice for all students, not just for bilingual students.

Being categorized as an "English language learner" may just mean receiving remedial instruction, assistance reserved for those who are not privileged learners. In this book, we have taken up the term "emergent bilingual," which we argue points to the student's potential rather than their limitations, and acknowledges their bilingualism even if they are being taught through English (see García & Kleifgen, 2010). But as we see in the case portrayed by Espinosa and Herrera, emergent bilinguals are also those who are developing Spanish. And there is no end point between being an emergent bilingual and a "fluent" bilingual because our bilingualism is always emerging for certain tasks. So in a way we are all emergent bilinguals!

The teachers in our case studies consider students' language performances as having potential, and not simply as inadequate in English or Spanish or any other named language. The students' use of their language repertoire was assessed based on how well they could perform the linguistic tasks required by the Common Core State Standards (finding text-based evidence, making inferences, expressing complex thoughts, etc.) and not just solely on how well they understood, spoke, read, or wrote English (or Spanish or another language), although, as required by regulations, they were also assessed with standardized summative assessments in one language or the other, and sometimes in both.

Translanguaging complicates understandings of language proficiency and how we categorize students as being proficient in a given language or learners of it.

Teachers who take up translanguaging education policy know that language proficiency can only be evaluated through performance in different tasks—listening, speaking, reading, writing, signing (for deaf bilingual students)—but also for different purposes. There is no overall measure of language proficiency. Language performance for specific tasks and purposes are assessed differently depending on whether the evaluator is monolingual or bilingual, a parent, or a peer and depending on the task being performed and its purpose. García, Johnson, and Seltzer (2016) have referred to this continuum of language performances as Dynamic Translanguaging Progressions. The teachers in our case studies have learned to differentiate between the different components of language proficiency and the different tasks and purposes for which language is used. For some purposes, the linguistic features used in what is considered one or the other language is not important. For others it is. Across lessons, the student's linguistic performance using all features of his or her repertoire is a better measure of the student's language use than when the student is restricted to only certain features. Translanguaging education policy enables teachers to assess linguistic *performance*, rather than simply categorizing students based on an overall measure of proficiency in the use of certain linguistic forms.

The category of Latinos also has to be deconstructed through a translanguaging policy lens. U.S. Latino language shows great variability of features associated with English and Spanish. Zentella (1997) has clearly shown how the Latina girls in the bloque she studied had features from vernacular Englishes such as, for example, those used by some African-American speakers. Some of the Latino students in our case studies also have features in their linguistic repertoire from what are known as indigenous languages. The phonological, lexical, and syntactic features of their Spanish thus also varies according to the geographic context from which the children (or their parents and grandparents) hail, or the social class to which they belong. Even newcomer students from the same region, for example, speakers of what is often called "Caribbean Spanish," have features that differ greatly, depending on social class and social opportunities, including previous education. A translanguaging education policy enables teachers to acknowledge the great linguistic diversity that exists, while avoiding making any overarching generalizations about groups. As such, the data teachers collect from assessments (both standardized and teacher-made summative, as well as formative) must also be individualized. Just as translanguaging enables educators to go beyond language categories, it makes teachers cognizant of other individual social features that are imbricated with language such as social class, race, gender, opportunities, histories, and abilities. Teachers in our case studies are able to recognize the individual features of the students' language repertoire and of their entire semiotic meaning-making system that is so strongly implicated in the social world.

In many of the classrooms in our case studies, there are students categorized as African Americans, with some being descendants of enslaved people, and others hailing mainly from the Anglophone Caribbean and the African continent. Those who have enslaved ancestors are often categorized as speakers of African-American vernacular English (AAVE), Black English, or Ebonics. Although the labels may vary, these are named as either languages or varieties of English. But teachers who take up translanguaging also question these constructions. Do all students who are racially categorized as "African American" have a distinct variety? Teachers who work with translanguaging begin to understand that all students, including those whom we might consider English monolinguals, and especially those who speak what are considered English vernaculars or varieties, have linguistic features that characterize their language practices. Not all of these features overlap with those who have the same racial characteristics. This huge variability has to do with our social interactions and not simply with the color of our skin. A translanguaging education policy encompasses all students, regardless of whether they are considered monolingual or bilingual or whether they are considered bi/multidialectal.

In the classrooms in our case studies, there are also White students. Often only students of color are perceived as having different language features. And yet, what we see in these schools (see especially the classroom studied by Woodley) is that there is also enormous language variability among White students having to do with social class and educational experience, heritage, places of origin, and histories. Many of the students in the classroom that Woodley studies are of Polish background, some have arrived in the U.S. recently, others have been in the U.S. for a long time. But many of these White students are also bilingual. A translanguaging education policy is inclusive of all differences, including racial ones, transcending categories that are socially taught to children as early as kindergarten. For example, one day García was in a kindergarten classroom in the school in which Woodley's study took place and commended kindergarteners in a group that were working through Uzbek and Spanish in understanding an English-language text that the teacher had just read. García asked whether everyone in the class was bilingual. Quickly one of the Dominican girls went to get two other girls. She then said to García in Spanish: "Ves, estas dos no son bilingües. [You see, these two are not bilingual.] They are blond." The two blond girls then went on to explain that they spoke Ukrainian and Russian. It was an important lesson for all the children in the classroom. A translanguaging education policy deconstructs these categorizations that racialize the language practices of bilinguals (see Flores & Rosa, 2015).

Disrupting Distance Between Home and School Language Practices

The families of emergent bilinguals are often viewed through a similar deficit lens of "not speaking English" and "not being able to assist their children with homework." Bilingual families are overlooked by educators who do not see the wealth of resources, knowledge, language, and experiences they bring (Moll et al., 1992). Ebe's case study shows how the teacher took a counterperspective to this ideology. The teacher sent home an assignment in "English Language Arts" with which immigrant parents, many with beginning English proficiency, could help their children. This was possible for a number of reasons. The first was that the poem was on a universal topic with which all students and families could engage and make culturally relevant connections—New Year's celebrations. The second was that the poem included translanguaging as a literary device. Words and ideas that students identified as being of cultural significance were written in the students' home languages. Finally, because the poems were bilingual, family members who were not proficient in English could play a larger role than usual in editing the home language vocabulary used and sharing cultural and home-country information with which their children may not have been familiar.

A translanguaging education policy does more than simply "bridge" the home and the school; it dissolves the conception of these as different spaces. That is why García, Johnson, and Seltzer (2016) prefer to talk about the translanguaging corriente. The current, its dynamic flow, affects the nature of the bed of the river, with elements of what are perceived as two separate banks intermingling. The levels of the riverbanks, that is, what is seen above the water line, is also always in a state of flux. Thus, the two banks of the river are an illusion, what an observer sees at a particular time. In the same way, the language practices of school and homes of bilingual children are externally perceived as being English in school, and the language other than English at home. In reality, when perceived not externally (above the water line) but internally (below the water line), those practices are much more intermingled, dynamic, and complex. In U.S. homes where family members speak languages other than English, practices associated with English are also prevalent. Likewise, in schools with many bilingual children, practices associated with other languages abound. A translanguaging education policy takes the *internal under-the-water-line* view (how bilinguals themselves utilize the features of their single linguistic system), and not simply the *external* one of two separate riverbanks (how society views the languages of bilinguals as two separate systems).

Disrupting Purposes of Learning and Ways of Teaching

Most often, the preoccupation of educators of bilingual students, and especially of emergent bilinguals, is how well they perform in English only. A translanguaging education policy posits that performing academically with features of what is considered the standard dominant language, in our case English, is important for students. It is important for their lives as students and for occupational and career opportunities. This does not mean, however, that this is the *only* purpose of a translanguaging education policy. The *main* goal is to engage students deeply in meaning-making and comprehension and develop them as critical sociolinguists (Rymes & Leone, 2014), able to meaningfully participate in inquiry about the reasons why bilingual practices have been delegitimized and the ways in which this has been carried out. In so doing, language-minoritized students are engaged emotionally, as well as cognitively and politically, with their education, as they develop secure linguistic identities. A translanguaging education policy disrupts ways of learning and ways of teaching to demand and construct equal educational opportunities for all students, particularly those who have been marginalized by U.S classrooms, schools, and society.

The ways in which translanguaging opens up equal opportunity spaces takes many forms. In many of the classrooms in our case studies, the teacher used translanguaging to help her emergent bilingual students access an English-only curriculum (see for example Kleyn's case study). That is, translanguaging was used to build *comprehension*. As Collins and Cioè-Peña say about their case-study lesson, translanguaging "allowed students to build content knowledge around an unfamiliar topic and understand a complex text of a primary historical source." Students are simply able "to do [more] with English texts" and participate in more complex discussions about these texts (Seltzer and Collins' chapter). By leveraging translanguaging, students and teachers in our case studies explain and clarify vocabulary and new concepts.

Another way in which translanguaging opens up spaces of equal opportunity is by recognizing the value of oral language. Oracy has been shown to be very important to literacy development, especially for emergent bilinguals (Escamilla et al., 2014; Snow et al., 2005; Tharp & Gallimore, 1991). But often in biliteracy studies, attention to oracy in one language is only related to written performances in just that same language. And when students are asked to discuss a text orally or to write about a text, they're expected to use the language of the text. Translanguaging in the study of literacy goes beyond languages of texts, as students use their full oral linguistic repertoires to deepen conversations, reflect, and make connections. For example, Seltzer and Collins describe how students translanguage as they *engage in complex conversations* about English language texts.

Translanguaging education policy also goes beyond a focus on *how* language is used, to emphasize *why* language is being used. Our case studies show how translanguaging helps students *critically analyze* language and understand how it is lodged with power. In decentering language from its powerful position in school, students become citizen sociolinguists (Rymes & Leone, 2014). They are able to play with language, as in Kleyn's case study, as well as explore the way authors use translanguaging in writing for literary effect (see Ebe's case study). Through translanguaging, students also become cognizant of other language practices and of the power of their multilingual classmates (see, for example, Woodley's and Ebe's chapters). Translanguaging enables students to show off all their language practices, rather than conceal them in the name of English learning. In so doing, practices that have not been traditionally legitimated in school are given importance, transforming the school space and expanding it.

In most of the case studies, translanguaging equalizes the playing field for minoritized students by helping them feel more connected and *emotionally engaged*. The teacher, Hulda Yau, in Kleyn's study, says that students "come alive a little bit more." As in Espinosa and Herrera's case study, translanguaging enables students to take charge of their own learning. This happens because a translanguaging education policy emphasizes the teaching of individuals, not of entire groups that are viewed homogeneously. As García and Sylvan (2011) say, it enables us to see the singularities in the pluralities. Claudia Montoya, the teacher in Espinosa and Herrera's case study, explained this by saying: "We teach in a world where differentiation of educational content is imperative and necessary. Translanguaging allows me to meet students where they are." All learning is about being able to appropriate knowledge. Translanguaging helps students share and express *feelings* (see, for example, the lesson portrayed by Ebe). The socioemotional aspect is especially visible in the lessons with the students labeled "SIFE" described in the Seltzer and Collins chapter, where the students translanguage to support one another, as the texts bring up difficult emotions. Translanguaging, as Seltzer and Collins say: "Is a means of understanding, expressing, and building relationships."

Translanguaging education policy also means that students are always supported in their language practices, even when those practices are not reflected in the school curriculum and their home languages are not explicitly taught. That is why in Espinosa and Herrera's case study, translanguaging enables the *reclaiming of minoritized languages*, in this case Spanish. And in Ebe's and Woodley's cases, we see that translanguaging becomes a way to enable students to continue to develop their home language, even when the teacher does not speak it. We are not saying that it is enough to open up opportunities to use the home language during instruction in a majority language. Students need to be supported in extending their language repertoire so that they can use their home language features in academic settings and in majority contexts. However, translanguaging is an important alternative to monolingual instruction, offering students an initial possibility to become critical users of parts of their repertoire that schools do not formally use.

In becoming, as Kleyn calls it, "the new normal," translanguaging builds students' comprehension, engagement, criticality, emotional attachments and feelings, and self-confident identities—all essential in learning. Translanguaging disrupts traditional ways of learning and teaching to promote social justice and equal educational opportunity.

Disrupting Traditional Language Education Models

The case studies included in this book show how translanguaging works for children, not for educational "models." A translanguaging education policy is not just for bilingual education or English-medium education, but it must work across the educational contexts in which students are taught.

A translanguaging education policy enables schools to go *beyond* the unnatural separation of languages sustained by various *educational models.* Some of the classrooms in our case studies are considered mainstream, others are part of bilingual programs, others part of ESL programs. For example, the classrooms portrayed in Ebe's and Woodley's chapters are labeled mainstream English-only classrooms, although their students are highly multilingual. At times, the ESL push-in teacher takes over or co-instructs the lesson, making this more of an ESL classroom. And, as we see in the case studies, the teachers' translanguaging practices mean that their classrooms are true multilingual contexts. The teachers' and students' translanguaging help students develop not only their own bilingualism, but also familiarity with the multilingualism of the class, a critical awareness of multilingualism in society, and a linguistic flexibility that will surely serve them well in the future.

The lessons portrayed in the chapters by Kleyn, Collins and Cioè-Peña, and Seltzer and Collins are given in the context of bilingual programs, all officially transitional in nature. And yet, their translanguaging education policy gives attention to all the linguistic features of their bilingual students, including those that are named as Spanish. Thus, there is nothing transitional about these classrooms, as the students' entire linguistic repertoire is flexed and used. In this way, the language features of what is considered Spanish are also being supported, sustained within the students' linguistic repertoire and extended so they can be used for academic purposes. Instead of being transitional, translanguaging transforms these classrooms into developmental maintenance-oriented bilingual programs. In doing so, they do not support Spanish as a distinct category separated from English, but as part and parcel of the bilingual students' linguistic repertoire. Rather than functionally allocate languages, these classrooms help bilingual students use all the features of their repertoire in functional interrelationship, as it grows in complexity and is sustained bilingually, and not simply monolingually (for the difference between the concept of language maintenance and language sustainability, see García, 2011).

Although the students with interrupted formal education that are in the English Language Arts classroom described by Seltzer and Collins are in a program labeled transitional bilingual education, we know that their low literacy in Spanish and their lack of experience with the school script means that the teacher is not teaching for students to simply transition to English. Translanguaging in these classrooms encourages the development of language use for purposes of schooling—finding text-based evidence in reading, writing argumentative essays, etc. If we want these students to develop English literacy, it is important to develop their ability to use their own language features for school academic tasks, an experience that they have not had in previous schooling.

The lesson portrayed in the chapter by Espinosa and Herrera is the only one that takes place in a program called "dual language." Although many of these "dual language" programs are "two-way," meaning that there are students of two distinct language groups, this one is what is known as "one-way," understood generally as a classroom that contains students from one language group. Teachers who take up translanguaging, however, understand that there is nothing simply one-way about this program. Certainly all the students are Latinos, but they do not all share common characteristics, either culturally, politically, socially, or linguistically. Students' linguistic performances in this classroom fall along all points of the bilingual spectrum. And even though this is supposedly a "dual language" model in which the two languages are strictly separated, the teacher adopts a translanguaging education policy which honors all the children's practices in order to develop more academic performances in what is known as Spanish and English. Despite the strict language allocation policy followed in this school, the teacher takes up translanguaging as a way to ensure that the new language features students are acquiring are appropriated and incorporated into their language repertoire, rather than just added on as a separate set of features that students would then never own.

Translanguaging theory applied to models of language education makes us question the idea of "models" of foreign language/world language education, bilingual education, and English as a second language education. Translanguaging considers foremost the bilingual students' different language repertoires and operates by taking into account the linguistically diverse global context in which we are living.

Translanguaging enables us to enact ESL teaching as more than English only, and bilingual teaching as more than English plus. Bilingualism is not additive; it is not a simple sum—English plus another language. The minoritized language does not have to be simply maintained (Fishman, 1966) as an autonomous static language connected to traditional aspects of "purity," standardization and nation-building (Blommaert, 2010; Dervin & Liddicoat, 2013; Heller, 1999; Kramsch, 2010; Makoni & Pennycook, 2007). Cole and Meadows (2013) have called efforts to protect national languages from contamination from other languages "nationalist essentialism." These top-down policies have little to do with the ways in which people "sustain" language practices in multilingual contexts, always in functional interactions with others. The translanguaging work of the classrooms described goes beyond the notion of "models," as handed down by educational authorities. They start from the recognition that the bilingualism of students and teachers is dynamic, irrespective of how their type of program is categorized externally.

Most emergent bilingual students today are being educated in some form of English-medium program. For example, in New York City almost 80% of emergent bilinguals are in "English as a new language" programs (New York City Department of Education, 2013–2014). But as our case studies make evident, a translanguaging education policy works for all bilingual children, regardless of models.

Disrupting Traditional Content Areas

A translanguaging education policy transcends academic content areas. It is not just for language-related subjects. Translanguaging liberates disciplines from academic structures that are socioeducationally constructed. Knowledge exists in an interconnected world and language is an important way in which these connections are made. If emergent bilingual students are expected to perform well in one language before starting to acquire knowledge, they will remain marginalized (Cummins, 1979). If instruction is strictly in a decontextualized discipline or subject, then interdisciplinary connections will not be readily made, preventing students from becoming inquisitive.

Teachers in our case studies work in interdisciplinary spaces. The social studies lesson portrayed in the chapter by Collins and Cioè-Peña, and the science lesson in Espinosa and Herrera, went beyond the traditional disciplines to encompass the language that was necessary to make sense of the subject matter and the larger understandings required to understand phenomena in the social and scientific world. But of the six lessons that we have included here, only the two referenced above are about content other than language. Educators are quick to acknowledge the usefulness of translanguaging when teaching in a language that students don't understand, but recognition of translanguaging as much more than a linguistic scaffold to learn content is slower to come by.

It is also more controversial to use translanguaging when the goal is the development of the features that are considered "standard" and that make up what is then seen as "academic language." Educators are often told that they should "stick" to the "language" of the allocation policy so that students have opportunities to practice the use of that language. This indeed has been the conventional wisdom in foreign language education and bilingual education. But in the recent past, scholars have questioned this so-called "direct approach," softening national and state language boundaries and supporting "flexible instructional strategies" in teaching additional languages (see, for example, Cummins, 2007, for bilingual education; Turnbull & Dailey-O'Cain, 2009, for second and foreign language education). Indeed, this is what happens in our case studies where educators are teaching "English Language Arts." In effect, what we see is translanguaging being used to develop students' general language performances—their ability to read, write, infer, express complex thoughts, write argumentative essays, etc. A translanguaging education policy transforms English Language Arts instruction (or Language Arts in any named language) into language arts instruction, enabling teachers and students to focus on how language is used for the purposes and functions required in the human, social, and scientific world, rather than just simply on English vocabulary and structure.

Four of the six lessons portrayed in our case studies (in the chapters by Ebe, Woodley, Kleyn, Seltzer, and Collins) take place in classes labeled as English Language Arts. Yet much more is being learned when translanguaging becomes part of instruction in the *arts* of language. Translanguaging transforms not only our understandings of language, but also of the function of language in society. By infusing the critical aspects of a translanguaging education policy in lessons categorized as "language arts," students and teachers engage in critical metalinguistic awareness, an important ability especially for language-minoritized students and their teachers. This means that both students and teachers become advocates of a translanguaging education policy that creates more equitable educational circumstances for language-minoritized students. Students in these translanguaging arts classrooms are learning more than language, they are becoming experts in sociopolitical aspects of the societies in which they live, and by doing so are more knowledgeable of the world and of the academic disciplines that schools maintain.

Disrupting Scripted Curricula and Prescribed Texts

As we have said before, many of the schools and teachers described in our case studies are under mandate to follow scripted curricula. In the classroom that Kleyn studied, teachers used the Core Knowledge Curriculum; in the classroom that Woodley studied, the ReadyGen curriculum was used; and in Ebe's field site, the Expeditionary Curriculum was chosen. Translanguaging, as we saw in those three case studies, completely transformed the scripted curricula, opening up important spaces for student engagement. Woodley cites the teacher, Andrew Brown, reflecting on his use of translanguaging to deliver the curriculum: "Now that they are hearing more from other students, and every class is about many perspectives, they're clearly more involved."

The lesson taught and studied in the chapter by Collins and Cioè-Peña included the teaching of The Declaration of Independence, a unique historical text. The dynamic translanguaging work of students and teachers brought this text into the present. The words and syntax of the declaration gained their independence, becoming uprooted from their original historical context and applied to a multilingual present.

These examples show us how teachers of emergent bilinguals do not turn their backs on texts and curricula handed down to them, but approach them with their students in mind. They go beyond the set guidelines or descriptions to bring content alive through the flexibility and creativity of translanguaging, as the students' understandings and interests are brought forward.

Disrupting Inequities, Hierarchies, and Circles of Power

By starting with the children and what they can do, and not with external notions of educational policy, a translanguaging education policy disrupts the inequities and established hierarchies exerted by educational systems that keep power in the hands of the few. The responsibility for education is returned to the language-minoritized community, including students, families, and educators.

The language-minoritized community is then given authority and power over the education of their own children. In this way, they legitimize their own translanguaging practices and normalize bilingualism as a community and societal resource for learning.

A translanguaging education policy emerges in the space between the language education policy imposed upon teachers and the actual language practices of the language-minoritized children that *must* be legitimized if we are to provide them with an equitable education. For a translanguaging education policy to be enacted in all schools, we must stop talking about these children as in need, limited, simply as English learners, or minoritized. Instead, we must see them as resourceful individuals who language in complex ways that may not be valued by schools or policies.

What the case studies in chapters 3 to 8 show is that despite the hard work and commitment of educators to enact a translanguaging education policy, the construction of just and equitable education spaces is difficult to achieve. It is often in conflict with the traditional education policies of schools. And the fire of translanguaging education policy burns in limited spaces and classrooms. Without oxygen from the outside and without recognition of its importance, its potential will be extinguished.

Although translanguaging disrupts, it is unable, by itself, to create the conditions for social justice and equality in education that our children demand. Disruptions are not constructions. And so we have to ask ourselves, what would be needed in order for society to construct a true translanguaging education policy?

Conclusion

This chapter has shown how the translanguaging education policy that educators in our case studies adopted was able to disrupt some of the most common myths in the education of language-minoritized students:

1. That language education policy is handed down by knowledgeable policymakers to be faithfully implemented by educators and students;
2. That what these students need is academic language, especially in the dominant language, in our case, English;
3. That monolingualism means one language and bilingualism means two;
4. That students should be categorized and dichotomized;
5. That the home and the school are not connected;
6. That the purpose of learning is to acquire the dominant language;
7. That there are educational "models" that can be followed to teach these children;
8. That one can teach content areas and language without relationship to each other;

9. That a scripted curriculum provides the elements that students need to be successful;
10. That only those with White and English privilege can be truly educated.

Despite the potential of a translanguaging education policy to disrupt these myths, the chapter ends with a caveat. For this potential to be actualized and normalized, we need changes in how society views language-minoritized communities. What our case studies show and celebrate is the enormous amount of work and effort that educators exert to disrupt traditional language education policies. As a society, we are a long way off from normalizing the translanguaging practices that are reflections of bilingual-minoritized communities.

References

Bartlett, L., & García, O. (2011). *Additive schooling in subtractive times: Bilingual education and Dominican immigrant youth in the Heights.* Nashville, TN: Vanderbilt University Press.

Blommaert, J. (2010). *The sociolinguistics of globalization.* Cambridge: Cambridge University Press.

Cole, D., & Meadows, B. (2013). Avoiding the essentialist trap in intercultural education: Using CDA to read naturalist ideologies in the classroom. In F. Dervin & A. J. Liddicoat (Eds.), *Linguistics for intercultural education* (pp. 29–47). Amsterdam: John Benjamins.

Cook, V. J. (2008). *Second language learning and language teaching.* London: Arnold.

Cook, V. J. (2012). Multi-competence. In C. Chapelle (Ed.), *The encyclopedia of applied linguistics* (pp. 3768–3774). Oxford: Wiley-Blackwell.

Cummins, J. (1979). Linguistic interdependence and the educational development of bilingual children. *Review of Educational Research*, 49, 222–251.

Cummins, J. (2007). Rethinking monolingual instructional strategies in multilingual classrooms. *The Canadian Journal of Applied Linguistics*, 10(2), 221–240.

De Graff, M. (1999). *Language creation and language change: Creolization, diachrony, and development.* Boston: MIT Press.

Dervin, F., & Liddicoat, A. J. (Eds.). (2013). *Linguistics for intercultural education.* Amsterdam: John Benjamin.

Escamilla, K., Hopewell, S., Butvilofsky, S., Sparrow, W., Soltero-González, L., Ruiz-Figueroa, O., & Escamilla, M. (2014). *Biliteracy from the start: Literacy squared in action.* Philadelphia: Caslon Publishing.

Fishman, J. A. (1966). *Language loyalty in the United States.* The Hague: Mouton.

Flores, N., & Rosa, J. (2015). Undoing appropriateness: Raciolinguistic ideologies and language diversity in education. *Harvard Educational Review*, 85, 149–171.

García, O. (2011). From language garden to sustainable languaging: Bilingual education in a global world. *Perspective: A publication of the National Association for Bilingual Education, Sept/Oct*, 5–10.

García, O., Johnson, J., & Seltzer, K. (2016). *The translanguaging classroom: Leveraging student bilingualism for learning.* Philadelphia, PA: Caslon.

García, O., & Kleifgen, J. (2010). *Educating emergent bilinguals: Policies, programs and practices for English language learners.* New York: Teachers College Press.

García, O., & Sylvan, C. (2011). Pedagogies and practices in multilingual classrooms: Singularities in pluralities. *Modern Language Journal*, 95(3), 385–400.

Gutiérrez, K. D., Baquedano-López, P., & Tejeda, C. (1999). Rethinking diversity: Hybridity and hybrid language practices in the third space. *Mind, Culture and Activity*, 6, 286–303.

Heller, M. (1999). *Linguistic minorities and modernity: A sociolinguistic ethnography*. London: Longman.

Kachru, B. (1992). World Englishes: Approaches, issues and resources. *Language Teaching*, 25, 1–14.

Kachru, B., Kachru, Y., & Nelson, C. (Eds.). (2009). *The handbook of world Englishes*. Malden, MA: Wiley/Blackwell.

Kramsch, C. (2010). *The multilingual subject*. Oxford: Oxford University Press.

Li Wei. (2014). Who's teaching whom? Co-learning in multilingual classrooms. In S. May (Ed.), *The multilingual turn: Implications for SLA, TESOL and bilingual education* (pp. 167–190). New York and London: Routledge.

Makoni, S., & Pennycook, A. (2007). *Disinventing and reconstituting languages*. Clevedon, UK: Multilingual Matters.

Menken, K., & García, O. (2010). *Negotiating language policies in schools: Educators as policy makers*. New York: Routledge.

Moll, L. C., Díaz, S., Estrada, E., & Lopes, L. (1992). Making contexts: The social construction of lessons in two languages. In M. Saravia-Shore & S. F. Arvizu (Eds.), *Cross-cultural literacy: Ethnographies of communication in multiethnic classrooms* (pp. 339–366). New York: Garland.

New York City Department of Education (NYCDOE). (2013–2014). *Demographic report*. New York: Department of English language Learners and Student Support.

Rymes, B., & Leone, A. R. (2014). Citizen sociolinguistics: A new media methodology for understanding language and social life. *Working Papers in Educational Linguistics*, 29(2), 25–43.

Snow, C. E., Griffin, P., Burns, M. S., & the NAE Subcommittee on Teaching Reading. (2005). *Knowledge to support the teaching of reading: Preparing teachers for a changing world*. San Francisco: Jossey-Bass.

Soja, E. W. (1996). *Thirdspace: Journeys to Los Angeles and other real-and-imagined places*. Malden, MA and Oxford: Blackwell.

Tharp, R., & Gallimore, R. (1991). *The instructional conversation: Teaching and language in social activity*. Santa Cruz, CA: The National Center for Research on Cultural Diversity and Second Language Learning.

Turnbull, M., & Dailey-O'Cain, J. (2009). *First language use in second and foreign language learning*. Toronto: Multilingual Matters.

Valdés, G. (forthcoming). Entry visa denied: The construction of symbolic language borders in educational settings. In O. García, N. Flores, & M. Spotti (Eds.), *Handbook of language and society*. New York and Oxford: Oxford University Press.

Zentella, A. C. (1997). *Growing up bilingual*. Malden, MA: Blackwell.

10

SETTING THE PATH

Implications for Teachers and Teacher Educators

Tatyana Kleyn

The case studies in this book show translanguaging enacted in specific classrooms with unique students during a discrete lesson or series of lessons. These settings range from elementary to middle to high school, cover most content areas, and are found in the spectrum of programs that serve emergent bilinguals, including general education classrooms. Although each case is distinct, there are lessons that can be learned for both schools and teacher education programs. This chapter, divided into two sections, outlines the implications for elementary, middle, and high school teachers on the one hand and teacher educators on the other, in order to create contexts and instructional approaches that are inclusive of students' language and cultural practices as a way to ensure they receive an education that is socially just and pedagogically sound. The first part of this chapter, focused on teachers in schools, references the case studies in chapters 3 through 8. The second part, which addresses the implications for teacher education, looks beyond the case studies.

Implications for Elementary, Middle School, and High School Educators

As evidenced in the case study chapters, there are big and small ways that teachers can plan instruction and steer classroom moments that are responsive to, and reflective of, students' language repertoires. We start from larger lessons that should be applied to all settings, regardless of grade level, content area, and/or program type and then move into more specific areas. We provide these implications with the understanding that they may not be ideal for every setting; nevertheless, we offer them as suggestions to improve the ways bilingual students, and specifically emergent bilinguals, are given access to learning and to having a voice in the classroom.

Lessons for All Teachers

Translanguaging—as evidenced throughout this book—has a place in *all* educational settings. It may be enacted differently with distinct goals, but its purposeful role for students who are emergent bilingual, experienced bilinguals, and even monolinguals (for the moment) cannot be ignored.

- Translanguaging is for all language learning. It is not just for supporting students as they learn English or the named language of power in their national context. Therefore, translanguaging has a place in bilingual education (Collins and Cioè-Peña; Espinosa and Herrera; Kleyn[1]) and English as a second (or new or additional) language programs, just as it is equally powerful in world or foreign language programs and general education classes (Ebe; Seltzer and Collins; Woodley). When looking deeply at the students in almost any given classroom, one cannot accurately describe any such learning environment as monolingual or monodialectical. Instead, teachers can uncover the multilingualism of their classrooms to make visible the range of language practices that students have. When these multilingual practices are made to be a natural part of their learning environment, they enrich the children's education.
- Building a classroom community that is inclusive of all students' languages and cultures is important. Students cannot and should not be asked to leave their home language and cultural practices at the door. Instead, the school must allow and encourage students' full selves to be a part of the teaching and learning process. Rather than feeling ashamed of speaking a language other than English, they should feel pride in this and see how it is a resource for learning. We saw examples of inclusion and pride with the students in Ms. Chapman-Santiago's class, where students read aloud in named languages most of their peers didn't speak (Ebe). We also saw this in Mr. Brown's class, whose students not only continue to learn in their home language, but also learn the languages of their peers (Woodley). If students do not find themselves in a classroom where multilingualism is the "new normal" (as Ms. Yau stated), then any efforts to translanguage will be in vain.
- Planning includes more than just content knowledge; it is also comprised of knowing students and their linguistic strengths and challenges. This information can be attained via formal and informal assessments, such as listening, observing, and asking both students and their families. For students who are emergent bilinguals, there are often a number of formal assessments for their English development each year. However, their home language may not be given as much, or any, attention. And for students who do not qualify for language services, their home languages may be completely disregarded or invisible to their educators, unless teachers take explicit measures to fully know and understand their students.
- Get to know students as people who may have experienced traumatic and/or difficult situations and may be in need of socioemotional support. Give

students opportunities to share impactful moments with you. The Life Timeline activity (Seltzer and Collins) is a way for students to reflect on their positive and difficult milestones and for their teachers to learn about their students as a way to better know them, support them, and make connections to their experiences.

- Identify and analyze translanguaging as a literacy device. This allows students to see that the flexible and fluid use of languages is a natural way for bilinguals to communicate orally and in writing. Ebe's case study shows how students not only engage in reading a poem with translanguaging (in a language they are not familiar with), but go on to write their own poems following this model. This type of exposure legitimizes the language practices of bilinguals in and out of the classroom and for academic and formal purposes.
- The linguistic landscape of the classroom and the school should be reflective of students' home languages and cultures, as well as the content students are learning. This means ensuring that multilingual bulletin boards, signs, labels, posters, and charts are clearly displayed around the classroom. It also means having multilingual books, dictionaries, and iPads so that students can access resources in other languages. The classroom linguistic landscape should also include maps and photographs that show cultural diversity, as well as multilingual student work. While this may be easier in classrooms where teachers and students speak the same languages, Ebe's and Woodley's chapters demonstrate the power of using translation technology, as well as students, staff, and families as resources to circumvent these challenges (even if the text is not 100% accurate).
- Students must understand the expectations and rationale for inclusion of more than one language within each lesson. This should be stated explicitly—both in terms of the process or how students will be moving through the lesson and the final product or the piece of work they will develop. This was demonstrated in Collins and Cioè-Peña's lesson, in which students were given directions and then instructed about the languages they could access during the class discussion, group work, and their writing responses.
- Strike a balance between planning for translanguaging and allowing for flexibility. Plan for translanguaging for both students and teacher(s) with intentionality and a purpose related to the lesson's content and language objectives. We have seen many examples of this. Teachers may explain the content in two languages (Espinosa and Herrera) or explain difficult concepts in a language understood by the students (Spanish, in Kleyn's case). Teachers can also have students discuss the content in their home language groups (Ebe), or ask students to translate their vocabulary words into Spanish (Kleyn). Some teachers work with the content bilingually, but have students present in one designated language (Collins and Cioè-Peña). However,

when students require additional support or can only explain themselves in a given language—which may not be the language of that segment of the lesson—allowing for the inclusion of their full linguistic repertoire with the larger goals of learning and full participation in mind is the type of flexibility that optimizes learning.

- Take the time to ask students about their experiences with translanguaging within a given lesson or in general. Have them reflect on their content and language learning and the role that translanguaging played. Also, ask them about the differences they experience between being asked to learn through only the dominant language as opposed to the languages that are spoken in the classroom. Connect these topics to how they identify as students and members of a society. Use this information to inform future lessons and units, as well as to help think through how the culture of the classroom is inclusive and accepting of students' linguistic repertoires.
- Many settings require teachers to use scripted curricula that are generally created for English monolingual students. Consult these materials, but make adjustments based on the students' language practices, cultural backgrounds, and academic and linguistic learning needs. Students should still be working towards the same learning objectives, but how they get there can be tailored to their profiles. For example, Ms. Yau carefully reviews the scripted lessons her school mandates and adds cultural connections, makes spaces for students to discuss in their home language, and takes time to explain concepts she knows are new to her grupito (Kleyn).
- Take a common strategy and give it a translanguaging twist. For example, Ms. Montoya has students annotate their text to increase their reading comprehension (Espinosa and Herrera). This gist strategy is expanded by allowing students to make connections and ask questions about a text in Spanish using their entire repertoire with the larger goal of comprehending the science text.

Lessons for Educators in Bilingual Programs

Bilingual programs are spaces where translanguaging can thrive by design. Usually the teacher is bilingual and the students are becoming bilingual and biliterate. Although in the United States there are two types of bilingual programs—dual language bilingual or developmental maintenance bilingual and transitional bilingual—both are ripe for leveraging all the students' language resources for content learning and linguistic development. The case studies took us into three bilingual classrooms—Ms. Yau's transitional bilingual classroom (Kleyn), which included students with learning disabilities; a transitional bilingual middle school classroom (Collins and Cioè-Peña); and Ms. Montoya's dual language bilingual class (Espinosa and Herrera) where students were learning science in Spanish with English supports. Taken together, these three case studies offer insights into how translanguaging can deepen learning and provide support to students in bilingual programs.

- Develop a clear allocation policy for the two languages, but ensure that there are spaces for dynamic bilingualism that respond to students' bilingual learning. Macro-level structures that create spaces to use one language or the other are common in all bilingual programs, but especially in DLBE languages are often strictly divided by day, time, content area, and/or teachers. These language allocation structures are in place to ensure students have many opportunities to develop both languages without one dominating the other for a number of reasons (i.e., resources, power of English teacher or student comfort, language of standardized tests). However, heavy-handed segregation of languages limits the potential of bilinguals to see connections across languages or to leverage their full linguistic repertoire to access content and develop language practices. We see this flexibility in program design in many of our case studies. For example, Ms. Yau created translanguaging spaces for students to discuss the English read-aloud in Spanish and have students identify cognates (Kleyn). Ms. Montoya used English and Spanish to explain scientific concepts when it was necessary to ensure that students did not miss out on scientific concepts while reclaiming their home language (Espinosa and Herrera). In Collins and Cioè-Peña's lesson, students were given ample opportunity to work through an English document using their full linguistic resources. Each teacher stayed true to the macro structure of their language allocation policy, while being flexible to the needs of the students in micro-moments of learning interaction.
- Use parallel or translated texts when appropriate to facilitate students' comprehension of complex words, sentences, and concepts. This is especially useful when a topic is being introduced, but throughout a unit it can give students access to vocabulary in both languages. For example, in one case study students were given the text of the Declaration of Independence in English and Spanish and were shown a short video clip about the document in both languages (Collins and Cioè-Peña). This approach allows students to not only access content and become more self-sufficient, but provides them the opportunity to see named languages side by side to notice similarities and differences between them.
- Allow students to be evaluated using their full linguistic repertoire, especially if the goal is to assess content learning rather than a given language. Many of the case studies show how teachers accept all students' answers if they show comprehension, reflection, and thought. For example, Ms. Yau had an English sentence starter for her grupito to complete about the story they listened to, but accepted answers that were in English, Spanish, or both languages (Kleyn). Rather than allowing students to use only part of the language repertoire, students could access all their resources to express themselves and complete the assessment for their teacher to gauge their learning and her teaching.

Lessons for English-Medium Classrooms

Many of these English-medium classes are multilingual when it comes to the students, yet the goal is for them to learn English, in classes labeled as English as a second language (ESL) or English as a new language (ENL), or to learn content in English in general education classes. Most emergent bilinguals in ESL/ENL programs spend the majority of their days in general education settings, where they need comparable supports. Here we build on the cases of Woodley's elementary general education classroom, the English Language Arts classes of Ebe at the middle school, and Seltzer and Collins at the high school level.

- Provide translations of lesson objective(s), key words, directions, and concepts when appropriate. This helps students get a general sense of the focus of the lesson. When students are exposed to vocabulary words in their home languages, it can serve the dual purpose of allowing some students to more easily understand new terms, while providing others with the opportunity to learn these words in their home language. This was the case in Mr. Brown's class, where students not only discuss words in their home language, but they question the concept of exact translations (Woodley).
- Place students in home language partnerships or groups to discuss concepts and/or directions together. Having peers come to a common understanding of a given task or notion allows for an entry point into the content of the lesson. Ms. Chapman-Santiago did this with her multilingual class to get students talking about the key ideas at the very start of the lesson (Ebe). When students do not have a home language partner, they can still be permitted to use their home language and have access to a bilingual dictionary or online translations.
- Provide students with opportunities to question and correct electronically translated texts. It is common knowledge that translation programs are very useful, but far from perfect. To remedy this situation, students in Mr. Brown's class are positioned as home language experts as they are called to the interactive whiteboard, on which the electronic translations appear, in order to make any necessary changes (Woodley). During this process, students are also exposed to different languages and writing systems.
- Allow students to make presentations or read aloud to the class in their home languages or bilingually. In Ms. Chapman-Santiago's class, students read directions aloud in multiple languages, even when their peers may not understand them (Ebe). These public spaces for all languages legitimize their value and position the students as having a valuable resource that is part of learning.
- When texts are in English, be sure to make culturally relevant connections. Given that language and culture are intertwined, using a student's cultural lens is another way to help them access content. Seltzer and Collins's case

study shows that when texts are tied to students' experiences, they are more easily able to connect with them and be engaged in meaningful discussion.

- Integrate home and school practices by requiring that students' funds of knowledge be leveraged in school and home. Ms. Chapman-Santiago has students share their New Year's poem with their families to attain additional information and to support their home language practices (Ebe). This type of assignment positions families as sources of knowledge and linguistic resources for their children and enables the home and school contexts to form an integrated learning context for the child.
- For specific assignments, have students create final products that are translanguaged. Poems such as those created in Ms. Chapman-Santiago's class are excellent for this (Ebe). This gives students a chance to share their home language with their peers and breaks down the misconception that English is the only language to be used in classrooms that are not officially labeled as bilingual.

Lessons Across Content Areas

The case studies in this book include lessons in different content areas that lend themselves to distinct foci when it comes to translanguaging. Although some of the suggestions overlap with those presented for the different programs, we feel it is important to consider how translanguaging can be applied across subject areas.

English Language Arts

The majority of the case studies in this book were English Language Arts classes (Ebe; Kleyn; Seltzer and Collins). The integration of languages other than English speaks to the role of translanguaging in such classes to learn English, as well as additional languages and literacy concepts that are not specific to any named language. Therefore, English Language Arts classes need not be solely in English, and if they are, they may be taking away from the learning opportunities of bilingual students.

- Make spaces for students to share their writing, even if it was produced at home—in whichever language—in school. This was not the case in Seltzer and Collins's chapter, where the authors discovered one student's prolific writing in her journal, yet there was no place for it in the English Language Arts classroom. Had her journal writing been acknowledged, it could have served as a springboard to develop her writing in school.
- Look for texts that are reflective of students' realities, whether they are written in English, their home language, or bilingually. These connections will

serve as points of entry to connect to larger concepts. Seltzer and Collins's case study shows how they found short stories that were reflective of their students' experiences. Ebe's case study has students reading a poem that is outside of their cultural framework, but is then connected to their own realities. Although Kleyn's case study shows little apparent connection to students' backgrounds, the teacher makes the connections to the students' lives in order to make the text accessible to her students.
- Have students analyze how authors use translanguaging in their writing and the purposes for it. Ms. Chapman-Santiago asks students to engage in this type of analytical exercise with the New Year's poem that included Vietnamese (Ebe). Many bilingual writers engage in translanguaging to reflect their natural communication patterns. For a list of Latino literature aimed at children and youth, see the guide created by Vanessa Pérez Rosario (2015) and select the texts that best connect to students' experience and the standards.

Science

The case study of Espinosa and Herrera take us into a middle school science classroom where students are learning about different states of matter. The official language of the class is Spanish, but as students have limited experience using Spanish in academic contexts, they rely on their full linguistic repertoire to access scientific content.

- Cognates between English and Spanish (and other languages) are common to content areas. Decide on key words/terminology that will be used and ask students to identify cognates—and false cognates—between the two languages. While students may be able to state the terms across two languages, they may not necessarily know their meaning, so it would be important to discuss both the words and their meanings.
- Students are better able to understand science by doing science rather than simply reading about it. This is true for all students, but especially those who are learning science in an additional language or a language they are reclaiming. Ms. Montoya has students engage in working with a material that changes physical form (Espinosa and Herrera). This gives students a direct experience with the concept. These hands-on experiments are an important precursor to reading and writing about a concept, especially in a new language.

Social Studies

The topics students learn about in social studies lend themselves to connection to cultures and languages. In this book, we were able to see how Woodley's case introduces upper elementary school children to slavery in the U.S., whereas

Collins and Cioè-Peña have middle schoolers explore the Declaration of Independence. Both topics require in-depth understanding of the history of the United States.

- Be sure to make cross-cultural connections, especially when students have been part of an education system in a different country where they were exposed to different histories and perspectives. Mr. Brown allows space for students to make connections to oppression that occurs in their home country (Woodley). Making connections to key documents and laws in students' countries of origin is another way to help them understand the purpose of guiding documents in the U.S. (Collins and Cioè-Peña).
- It is critical that all students be exposed to primary documents to ensure they experience the documents' authentic language and understand their full intention. However, students must receive plenty of support in accessing these documents via translanguaging and other strategies. The Declaration of Independence was provided to students in Spanish as well as in its original format in Collins's and Cioè-Peña's lesson. Students discussed the document in small groups and were given permission to use their full linguistic repertoire to make sense of a difficult text.

The suggestions we provide across programs and content areas can assist emergent bilingual students in experiencing a multilingual education, regardless of setting and across subject areas. But this can only be done if teachers are prepared to make these formative changes in their instructional and assessment pedagogy. For this reason, we now turn to recommendations for teacher education programs and their faculty.

Implications for Teacher Education

In order for teachers to make translanguaging a natural part of their practices, it must become an embedded component of their teacher education programs. In this way, educators would enter their classrooms from day one with a solid foundation of the importance of including all students' home language practices in their instruction and an understanding of how to do it. This section lays out the necessary components for teacher education programs to prepare their candidates[2] to work effectively with linguistically and culturally diverse students across grade levels and content areas.

We build off the canon of literature developed by researchers and teacher educators to prepare candidates for culturally and linguistically diverse classrooms (Burns & Richards, 2009; de Jong & Harper, 2005; Friedman, 2002; Hawkins, 2004; Levine, Howard & Moss, 2014; Tedick, 2005; Trumbull & Farr, 2005; Valdés et al., 2005; Walqui, 2008). In 2000, Sonia Nieto sounded the alarm to view diversity of students from a social justice stance within teacher education programs. She asserted that, "many programs have been steeped in negative assumptions about diverse populations based on deficit theories. These theories include the perspective that students from non-dominant groups are genetically or culturally inferior, or that they bring little of value to their education" (p. 181). At the same time, Wong-Fillmore and Snow (2000) issued a report that stressed the need for prospective and practicing teachers to develop a background in language, or what they refer to as educational linguistics, as a way to teach literacy to emergent bilinguals. They pushed for teacher education programs to include topics such as how languages work and differ across cultures, sociolinguistics, language development, and ways to teach with linguistic diversity in mind. A similar call for linguistically responsive teacher education—with a focus on mainstream teachers—was put out by Lucas, Villegas, and Freedson-Gonzalez in 2008. They called for preparing teachers to differentiate instruction for students still developing English proficiencies, learn more about the background of students labeled as English language learners, analyze assignments for their linguistic demands, and teach them. Lucas et al. suggest developing a stand-alone course for general education teacher candidates, infusion of differentiation for emergent bilinguals across courses (which would require professional development of faculty), and contact with emergent bilingual students throughout their program. More recently, Freeman and Freeman (2014, 2015) have put out two related volumes—one on preparing preservice teachers and the other on educating inservice teachers—to address the linguistic diversity of schools that is often overlooked or skimmed over in teacher education programs. Each of these volumes brings together teacher educators from across the nation to share their work and research in preparing teachers to better serve their current and future emergent bilinguals.

The recommendations we provide here are grounded in many of the works cited here. However, we take these recommendations one step further in order to consider how to create classrooms where students' full linguistic repertoire is welcomed and viewed as a resource for content and language learning. The goals of these recommendations also go beyond the pedagogical, to the socially just, where students are viewed and valued for who they are in a most holistic way.

Start With Faculty

Before teacher candidates can become equipped to enact translanguaging pedagogies, their education professors must at least have a baseline understanding of dynamic bilingualism and translanguaging so that they can be included in all courses that address equity, literacies, and methodology. While it may be faculty in bilingual education and TESOL that have the most developed expertise in this area, faculty across disciplines must consider how their candidates will support emergent bilinguals.

In order to make bilingualism and translanguaging central in teacher education, all education faculty need to expand their knowledge base in the following ways:

- Professional development, provided by faculty with a strong foundation in translanguaging, is one way to build capacity and go beyond discipline borders that are often experienced in very rigid ways in higher education. This can be done during regularly scheduled meetings to ensure full attendance, special professional development sessions, or as part of a retreat where more time can be devoted to the topic.
- Sessions for faculty should provide an overview of translanguaging, a list of resources for further development, and time to review their syllabi and consider how translanguaging can be embedded into existing courses.
- Co-teaching is a more in-depth approach to educating both faculty and candidates about translanguaging (Kleyn & Valle, 2014). Two instructors can teach one course (which is challenging within a higher education content, but not impossible), with one taking on the role of developing translanguaging understandings and connections to the course content. Once a faculty member outside of bilingual education and TESOL has co-taught and learned about translanguaging and has made it a part of their class, another instructional faculty dyad could be created to build capacity. (To read more about co-teaching at the college level to prepare teachers to work with emergent bilinguals and students with disabilities, see Kleyn & Valle, 2014).

Informed faculty that collaborate across disciplines is a first step to developing a teaching force that understands translanguaging as a natural and important approach for teaching bilingual students. We now turn to the type of coursework that would further prepare teachers to make their practices inclusive of students' languages and cultures.

Develop Course Content Focused on Bilingual Learners

Although it is important to infuse translanguaging into most education courses, there should also be coursework about language systems, language acquisition, and bilingualism (García & Kleyn, 2012). This requires specialized classes that build a foundation about bilingual education and bilingualism in education and the students who participate in these programs. We view the following cornerstones as vital for all teacher candidates to understand:

- Language is a social practice that is learned through authentic experiences (García, 2009). This is in contrast to how traditional language learning has been conceptualized as set of discreet skills—to be memorized and repeated, often in isolation.

- Languages and language varieties are situated within political contexts that create hierarchies of languages and their speakers. Schools then can become microcosms that reproduce larger linguistic prejudices. However, starting from bilingualism in education can push back on these inequitable stances.
- A student's home language is a strength that should be leveraged, rather than a deficit to be silenced (Ruiz, 1984). By building on home language practices, students are better positioned to learn an additional language and learn content in general. Teacher candidates can begin to internalize this by being placed in the position of having a lesson taught through a new language. This can be contrasted by repeating the same lesson, but with the ability to access their full linguistic repertoire. They can then reflect on how this changes their ability to learn, even in the new language.

It is the combination of readings, time spent with bilingual students and their families, and experiences in schools that will help candidates solidify core concepts about bilingualism, especially in education. Next, we delve into how to set up a classroom culture that is inviting of cultural and linguistic differences.

Build an Inclusive and Inviting Classroom Culture in Teacher Education Classes

Understanding the reasons why translanguaging is critical to student learning is important, but this cannot be done until a culture of inclusion for all languages and cultures is established. Otherwise, it will be viewed as a remedial approach rather than a normal communicative practice of bilinguals. Within different teacher education classes, candidates need to:

- Observe how bilingual interact in natural environments. Contrast this with how schools enact language education policies and/or how language(s) are permitted or prohibited in a classroom.
- Analyze schools and classrooms for their linguistic landscapes. Which languages are included and which are excluded? Why? What message does that send students and their families about the values placed on their background?
- Design lessons for students to think about the benefits of being bilingual (Reyes & Kleyn, 2010). As adults, it may seem obvious that knowing two or more languages is better than one, but the message students receive from the mainstream media is that only one language counts and it is the language of power.
- Observe teachers to see where they fall along the continuum of inviting or discouraging students to use their full linguistic repertoire. Consider how this impacts the classroom culture of inclusion and whether the students are viewed through a holistic lens.

- Create a list of the big and small ways teachers invite and give permission for students to bring in their home languages and cultures for learning.

Setting up a welcoming classroom culture in teacher education classes will set the path for the extent to which students will feel free or restricted in bringing their whole selves into the classroom. Once an inclusive culture is in place, planning for translanguaging is the obvious next step.

Encourage Teacher Candidates to Plan for Translanguaging

Purposeful planning is required to maximize the power of translanguaging. Providing candidates with opportunities to develop and modify unit and lesson plans will put them on a path to making translanguaging a central—rather than peripheral—part of how they plan for instruction.

- If a program has set templates for unit and lesson planning, ensure that space is created for translanguaging. Have candidates create authentic unit plans on required topics that naturally embed translanguaging either as part of the learning process, the final product, or both.
- Many schools are required to use scripted curricula, which are often created with a monolingual student in mind. To make the instruction better suited for emergent bilinguals, have candidates review the curriculum and note its approach to multilingualism and multiculturalism. Then, make modifications to the lessons by identifying spaces for translanguaging, as well as making cultural connections.
- Multilingual resources are important for helping students to not only access content, but also view issues from different perspectives and worldviews. In designing units, candidates should seek out a range of resources from text and trade books to websites and videos that are in different languages and also those that include translanguaging within them.
- All units include formative and summative assessments; however, too often these are restricted to just one language. Candidates should create assessments where translanguaging is leveraged as a way for students to fully demonstrate their learning. This should not be limited to tests, but must branch out to portfolios, presentations, projects, and other authentic assessments.
- Access the multiple resources developed by CUNY-NYSIEB (http://www.nysieb.ws.gc.cuny.edu/cuny-nysieb-publications/) and other sources to assist in planning for units that encourage and include students' home languages.

Learning to plan for translanguaging—from lessons to resources to assessments—is an important part of a teacher education program. Having such opportunities in a range of classrooms will equip candidates to include translanguaging in their own instructional approaches, which must be tied to the standards set forth by local and national policymakers.

Connect Translanguaging With National and Local Standards

Standards for different content areas and grade levels are commonplace across the globe. Yet, the role of students' home languages in meeting these standards is often omitted, or the assumption is that these standards are to be met through the national language. The danger in only allowing students to reach standards monolingually is that students are unable to grasp content in a complex manner when part of their linguistic resources for meaning-making are silenced.

Within the U.S., the Common Core State Standards have become the driving force of education across many states. Valdés, Menken, and Castro (2015) explore the many questions that arise for educators of emergent bilinguals when top-down standards meet diverse students and multilingual classrooms. To ensure that national or local standards do not translate into teaching solely through one language, it is important for future teachers to analyze the standards that drive instruction in their region with a lens for the presence or absence of languages other than English and their role in teaching and learning. As part of the review, candidates should ask:

- How do the standards make reference to non-dominant languages and what is the (hidden) meaning behind this?
- Are students' home languages included or excluded? What is the implication for translanguaging?
- When language(s) are addressed, is it as a system of discreet skills or is it approached as a social practice?
- How would spaces for translanguaging support students' learning and meeting the standards?
- To what extent do these standards reflect the multilingual and multicultural realities of our society? What would you add or change to make the standards more meaningful for bilingual students?

Reviewing standards through the lens of linguistic and cultural inclusiveness highlights the value placed on diverse learners and the role of translanguaging in assisting students to meet and go beyond the prescribed standards. It is important to see how translanguaging unfolds in classrooms with students and its dis/connection to standards.

Set Translanguaging in Action

Reading about the theoretical underpinnings and pedagogical strategies of translanguaging is important, but insufficient, if we want teachers to make it a part of their regular practices. Therefore, as part of their education program, future teachers should be able to experience, observe, and try out translanguaging in a variety of ways.

- Classes within teacher education programs should be designed with spaces for translanguaging. This can be via encouraging teacher candidates to complete course readings in multiple languages, forming small groups with same language speakers, and exposing all students to bi- or multilingual presentations. The professor's modeling of translanguaging is critical to how candidates experience and enact it in their own classrooms.

- Require candidates to teach lessons where they enact translanguaging pedagogies in a variety of programs and content areas. This should be done throughout their teacher education programs from the early stages to their final internship experiences.
- If possible, watch video recorded lessons taught by teacher candidates individually, in small groups, or as a class. These clips can also be compiled to make a video library that can be accessed by faculty and students within the teacher education program.
- Trying out or watching translanguaging is important, but it must be connected to analysis that considers student learning of content, languages, and larger issues of identity, inclusion, and voice.

Moving from theorizing to experiencing to enacting translanguaging is an important step in having candidates move out of their comfort zone of monolingualism as the instructional norm. However, translanguaging pedagogies cannot be identical, as they are dependent on the programs and students within each classroom.

Understand the Role of Translanguaging in Different Settings

As the chapters in this book illustrate, translanguaging is an approach that can be applied in different types of classrooms, although each has their unique considerations. Although the underlying goals of translanguaging stay consistent, how it is applied in diverse settings changes. Taking a closer look at translanguaging across contexts and with diverse learners is useful for teacher candidates during their teacher education program. We recommend a careful consideration of the following programs, student profiles, and teachers:

- *Bilingual Education Programs:* Although all bilingual programs use two languages for instruction, their goals and structures differ. Candidates would benefit from observing different bilingual classrooms to analyze the degree to which they allow for a dynamic and fluid use of languages or maintain two discreet and isolated monolingual spaces, as well as the rationale for each. Being able to recognize when translanguaging is used and when the two languages are used independently is as important for future teachers as it is for bilingual individuals.
- *English as a New/Second/Additional Language (ESL, ENL, EAL):* Programs that aim to teach students English may be made up of speakers of many languages. Therefore, the approach to translanguaging would differ from that in a bilingual class, where the students and teachers are all enacting

bilingualism in just two languages. Candidates who are going to teach in English-medium classrooms for emergent bilinguals should consider what a teacher and students could do to leverage different students' home languages as a resource to learn English or another language.

- *Content and Language Integrated Learning (CLIL):* An approach that is widely used in Europe, CLIL classrooms are ripe for translanguaging so that content learning can be supported, while students learn in and through an additional language.
- *Foreign/World Language Programs:* The traditional assumption about foreign/world language programs is that students need to be completely immersed in the new language. However, translanguaging is a viable approach for both learning majority and minoritized languages. It is not and should not be viewed only as a bridge to the dominant language, but also as a multiway street to learning and integrating language practices.
- *General Education/Bilingualism in Education:* One should not conflate general education classrooms with monolingual classes. Often students in these settings bring a rich linguistic diversity that can also be included in their teaching and learning. Translanguaging allows for bilingualism within general education; it should not be solely used in bilingual education.
- *Across Content Areas:* Translanguaging may look different when students are learning math, science, social studies, or language arts, among other areas. Candidates can consider similarities and differences in the use of translanguaging when teaching these subjects.
- *Across Grade Levels:* Students are at different developmental stages and therefore translanguaging may take on a different focus in an early elementary classroom as opposed to a secondary class.
- *Students Across the Home Language/Literacy Continuum:* Emergent bilinguals come to school with different educational trajectories. Some enter school with a solid home language literacy foundation, whereas others may be in a formal learning environment for the first time, never having had the opportunity to read and write in their home language. While translanguaging is useful for both groups, it may be enacted another way with different students.
- *Students With Disabilities:* There are ways that translanguaging facilitates learning and participation for bilingual students with disabilities. Consider how allowing for the use of home languages provides students with disabilities a voice in the classroom.
- *English (or Dominant Language) Monolingual Students:* Translanguaging is not only for bilinguals. All students can benefit from being exposed to different languages and cultures. How is using translanguaging with English monolingual students different from its use with bilingual students who speak minoritized languages?
- *Multilingual Classes With Monolingual Teachers:* Although some teachers speak the home languages of their bilingual students, this is not always the case.

How does a teacher who is either monolingual or does not speak the same languages as her students still set up a classroom where these languages are welcomed and used for learning?

Depending on their course of study, candidates would be well prepared to investigate translanguaging in each of the areas that is related to their field. Finally, we consider the role of translanguaging as a way to re-envision education for students who have yet to experience an equitable and holistic education.

Enacting a Translanguaging Social Justice Stance

While a large part of this book deals with the pedagogy of translanguaging, the underlying reason for pushing this approach is to provide an equitable education for emergent bilingual students—a subgroup of students whose education has been unnecessarily monolingual and dismissive of the linguistic and cultural resources they bring to schools. It will not be until these students are viewed through a holistic lens that values their languages and backgrounds that we will have an education system that does right by all students. Teacher candidates across programs must delve into difficult and uncomfortable conversations about the resistance to language practices other than those legitimated in schools. What sociopolitical and economic reasons are there for keeping the language practices of minoritized populations out of schools? What racialized ideologies are dominating the silencing of these language practices? Specifically, we recommend discussion with students and teacher candidates about the topics of

- Voice—What is the role of translanguaging in providing voice to emergent bilinguals? If students are denied the use of their home language, what are the implications educationally, emotionally, and politically?
- Freedom—To what extent is linguistic freedom provided to students who speak a home language that differs from the national language? Are the human and linguistic rights of these students being met? If not, what changes need to occur at the national, local, and school levels?
- Access—How is access to learning content, a new language, and continuing to develop a home language provided or denied to emergent bilinguals, and why? What role can translanguaging play in making learning more accessible?

Asking these questions will help situate translanguaging within a larger context of equity and social justice for minoritized students. If translanguaging is solely viewed as a method, then its full potential and goals will never be realized.

The eight areas described above play a crucial role in setting teacher candidates on the path of providing students an education that is inclusive and just. Teacher education programs that pay attention to linguistically diverse students across all differences, and position translanguaging as an approach all faculty and candidates must be familiar with will be taking an important step in preparing teachers for our superdiverse world.

Conclusion

Although translanguaging is a natural way in which bilingual individuals communicate, it has not typically been the norm in the education of bilingual students. To redefine the norm and position translanguaging as a common practice in all classrooms, we can start by learning from the case studies presented here and extrapolating the lessons to teachers in different programs, grade levels, and content areas. In this way, practicing teachers will continue to improve their approaches to working with multilingual students who are often learning content and language simultaneously. But in order for translanguaging to become a valid pedagogical approach for all teachers, it must be introduced and taught to preservice teachers in their universities. The multipronged approach presented in this chapter will ensure that students receive an education that is fully inclusive of all their linguistic and cultural practices.

Notes

1. We provide the names of the authors of relevant chapters in parentheses.
2. Within this chapter, we use "candidates" to refer to preservice and inservice teachers who are studying within a teacher education program at the tertiary level. We reserve the term "students" for those in the K–12 system to more easily distinguish between these two groups.

References

Burns, A., & Richards, J. C. (Eds.). (2009). *Cambridge guide to second language teacher education.* New York: Cambridge University Press.

De Jong, E. J., & Harper, C. A. (2005). Preparing mainstream teachers for English language learners: Is being a good teacher good enough? *Teacher Education Quarterly*, 32(2), 101–124.

Freeman, Y. S., & Freeman, D. (Eds.). (2014). *Research perspectives in preparing preservice teachers to work effectively with emergent bilinguals.* Bingely, UK: Emerald Group Publishing.

Freeman, Y. S., & Freeman, D. (Eds.). (2015). *Research perspectives in preparing inservice teachers to work effectively with emergent bilinguals.* Bingely, UK: Emerald Group Publishing.

Friedman, A. A. (2002). What we would have liked to know: Preservice teachers' perspectives on effective teacher preparation. In Z. E. Beykont (Ed.), *The power of culture: Teaching across language difference* (pp. 193–217). Cambridge, MA: Harvard Education.

García, O. (2009). *Bilingual education in the 21st century: A global perspective.* Malden, MA and Oxford, UK: Wiley/Blackwell.

García, O., & Kleyn, T. (2012). Teacher education for multilingual education. In Carole A. Chapelle (Ed.), *The encyclopedia of applied linguistics* (pp. 5543–5548). Oxford, UK: Wiley-Blackwell.

Hawkins, M. R. (Ed.). (2004). *Language learning and teacher education: A sociocultural approach*. Clevedon, UK: Multilingual Matters.

Kleyn, T., & Valle, J. (2014). Modeling collaborative teaching in teacher education: Preparing preservice teachers to teach ALL students. In Y. Freeman & D. Freeman (Eds.), *Research perspectives in preparing preservice teachers to work effectively with emergent bilinguals* (pp. 137–164). Bingely, UK: Emerald Group Publishing.

Levine, T. H., Howard, E. R., & Moss, D. M. (Eds.). (2014). *Preparing classroom teachers to succeed with second language learners: Lessons from a faculty learning community*. New York: Routledge.

Lucas, T., Villegas, A. M., & Freedson-Gonzalez, M. (2008). Linguistically responsive teacher education: Preparing classroom teachers to teach English language learners. *Journal of Teacher Education*, 59(4), 361–373.

Nieto, S. (2000). Placing equity front and center: Some thoughts on transforming teacher education for a new century. *Journal of Teacher Education*, 51(3), 180–187. DOI: 10.1177/0022487100051003004

Pérez Rosario, V. (2014). *The CUNY-NYSIEB guide to translanguaging in Latino literature*. New York: CUNY-NYSIEB, The Graduate Center, The City University of New York. Retrieved on March 16, 2016, from: www.nysieb.ws.gc.cuny.edu/files/2015/02/CUNY-NYSIEB-Latino-Literature-Guide-Final-January-2015.pdf

Reyes, S. A., & Kleyn, T. (2010). *Teaching in two languages. A guide for K-12 bilingual educators*. Thousand Oaks, CA: Corwin.

Ruiz, R. (1984). Orientations in language planning. *NABE Journal*, 8(2), 15–34.

Tedick, T. J. (Ed.). (2005). *Second language teacher education: International perspectives*. Mahwah, NJ: Erlbaum.

Trumbull, E., & Farr, B. (2005). *Language and learning: What teachers need to know*. Norwood, MA: Christopher-Gordon.

Valdés, G., Bunch, G., Snow, C., & Lee, C. (2005). Enhancing the development of students' language(s). In L. Darling-Hammond & J. Bransford (Eds.), *Preparing teachers for a changing world: What teachers should learn and be able to do* (pp. 126–168). San Francisco: Jossey-Bass.

Valdés, G., Menken, K., & Castro, M. (Eds.). (2015). *Common core, bilingual and English learners: A guide for educators*. Philadelphia, PA: Caslon Publishing.

Walqui, A. (2008). The development of teacher expertise to work with adolescent English learners: A model and a few priorities. In L. S. Verplaetse & N. Migliacci (Eds.), *Inclusive pedagogy for English language learners: A handbook of research-informed practices* (pp. 103–125). New York: Lawrence Erlbaum.

Wong-Fillmore, L., & Snow, C. (2000). *What teachers need to know about language*. Washington, DC: Center for Applied Linguistics.

CONCLUSION

Ofelia García and Tatyana Kleyn

This book describes how translanguaging theory views the language use and education of emergent bilingual students (chapter 1), reviews how an educational project translated the theory into practice in many schools and engaged in Transformative Action Research (chapter 2), and portrays actual classroom lessons in which translanguaging is used by educators and students to teach and learn (chapters 3 through 8). By bringing together the theory and the practices which it elicits, the book transforms the ways in which we have understood language education policy, focusing instead on what we call a translanguaging education policy (chapter 9) and its implication for educators and teacher education (chapter 10). Thus, the book is an attempt to transform the theory, practice, and policy that have dominated traditional understandings of language education for minoritized students.

Although the book posits new theoretical understandings for how bilinguals use language and are educated and advances novel pedagogical practices, it does not ignore the constraints under which educators function in schools that continue to operate as a means of social reproduction (Bowles & Gintis, 1976). And yet, by inserting translanguaging into the life of schools, spaces of possibility are created that disrupt the myths with which education in the United States has operated.

With its critical stance on the education of language-minoritized students, as well as its poststructuralist outlook on language and society, translanguaging transforms traditional understandings and practices. A more equitable educational space is created through translanguaging, one that is capable of transcending the social reproduction aspects of schooling and generating social transformations that promote social justice.

This book is also a testament to the hard work of a few teachers and schools and to an energetic team of scholars and teacher educators who believed that transformation was possible, and who refused to abandon bilingual children to the remedial education environments in which they were generally being serviced. As this book goes to press, the educational project that made this work possible in the last four years is coming to an end. But the seeds that were planted, the collaborative structures that were set up in the schools and among CUNY (and later SUNY) faculty and students, and the pedagogical practices that were taken up by teachers will continue to bear fruit in the years to come.

Different language policies may come and go. As this book goes to press, the Common Core State Standards are being increasingly questioned, No Child Left Behind has been replaced by the Every Student Succeeds Act (ESSA), and the policies of the New York State Education Department are forever changing. What cannot change is the strong relationship between teachers and students, their trust in each other, their caring sense, their efforts to teach and learn, and their sense of wonder in each other's lives. Without trust and care among teachers and students, policies will not succeed. Translanguaging is the thread that binds together homes and schools and teachers and students, in caring trust. Translanguaging insists that the values and practices of minority homes must be on an equal footing as those of majority ones. As we have seen, translanguaging disrupts the familiar in order to construct new realities and transform the ways in which we speak, teach, and learn, thus advancing a more just society for all.

Reference

Bowles, S., & Gintis, H. (1976). *Schooling in capitalist America.* New York: Basic Books.

AFTERWORD

Kate Menken and María Teresa (Maite) Sánchez

The six case studies presented in this volume make an extremely significant contribution to research and practice in education. In addition to offering greater understandings of translanguaging as pedagogy to a field hungry for this information, one can readily observe the work of teachers willing to *trans*gress traditional monolingual practices within schools, each starting small earthquakes that together are tantamount to major educational change.

Our purpose in this afterword is to situate these cases of translanguaging moments in the context of broader schoolwide change, the larger earthquakes their work engenders, by discussing the significance of school leadership within the work of CUNY-NYSIEB schools. It is evident that the case studies feature exemplary teachers, driven to try something radically different for their emergent bilingual students than the instruction that is typically offered. These are experienced teachers who have understood the need to change the ways education has traditionally been done in their schools in order to better engage their emergent bilingual students and nurture their success in school. When these teachers began their involvement with CUNY-NYSIEB and learned about dynamic bilingualism and translanguaging, something clearly resonated with them, making them eager to learn more and implement changes in their classrooms. This book covers these teachers' journeys and encourages any teacher to try translanguaging approaches in their classrooms—because any teacher can do it! Some of the teachers began with translanguaging pedagogy alone, whereas others were part of a community that fostered multilingual practices. We would encourage teachers anywhere to try it out, even if they are the first in their building to do so. Nevertheless, there is another story about the broader context in which these teachers work, which we explore here.

As it happens, all of the teachers in this volume were fortunate to have had the support of their principals to engage in this work. This is significant because it means that principals afforded their teachers the time needed to engage with discussions and practices of dynamic bilingualism and translanguaging. These teachers were clearly self-directed in their desire to learn more and devoted the time and energy to do so, but they were also supported by their school administration. For instance, the principals approved the teachers' release time to meet with their CUNY-NYSIEB Support Team during school hours and to attend professional development sessions for the project. We now turn our attention to these school leaders and their own process of change over the course of their involvement in CUNY-NYSIEB.

As in many places, school principals in New York are called upon to determine educational programming and language policy for their emergent bilingual students, yet very few have received the preparation they need to make those determinations (Menken & Solorza, 2013). New York is like the vast majority of U.S. states in this regard, in that the state licensure requirements do not mandate any preparation for principals or other school leaders (e.g., assistant principals, supervisors, or superintendents) about how to educate emergent bilinguals. This makes it very difficult for school administrators to make decisions for their emergent bilinguals. It is for this reason that at its inception CUNY-NYSIEB focused on increasing the knowledge base of school administrators about bilingualism and language learning.

Like the educators whose teaching is documented in this book, the learning curve was great for principals and other school administrators as well, especially because the majority of administrators did not previously have any background in bilingualism or the education of emergent bilinguals. The schools described in this volume underwent major change, as it was not only the teachers, but also the principals and other school administrators who adopted new approaches to linguistic and cultural diversity rooted in the CUNY-NYSIEB vision and principles. One of the most significant changes to take place was an overall shift in mindset, and school principals describe how their own language ideologies changed as a result of their involvement in the project, as they moved from seeing bilingualism as a deficit to seeing it as a resource.

The principal of the school where one of the teachers in this volume works explains this paradigm shift as follows:

> Well I don't have an ESL background at all, so I would think, my thoughts were that the ESL teachers went in four times a week, eight times a week, whatever it was, and taught the children English, and taught them, almost like being a one-way street. Now I think of it that there's so much more to it, and that the use of the home language should be encouraged and used as much as we can to help them gain English. But also, just because they don't know English doesn't mean they can't think and can't express themselves, and so that I think is really important for us to realize as a school.
>
> *(Ms. B, School Principal)*

In this passage, this school principal describes how her views about language learning changed as a result of her involvement in CUNY-NYSIEB. Her limited expertise in the education of emergent bilinguals prior to the project led to a number of misconceptions regarding how the programs for these students are to be structured, grounded in a belief that they should be taught solely through the medium of English. It is worth noting that this principal's views at the outset of her involvement in CUNY-NYSIEB were shared among many of the school administrators we have worked with, many of whom also initially believed that instruction should be English-only and that the home language could not support a child learning English. But as this interview excerpt shows, Ms. B began instead to see the students more holistically and recognize their knowledge and skills. In our recent analysis of interviews conducted with principals and other administrators in CUNY-NYSIEB schools, we have found that this change in stance is common across school leaders involved in the project.

Central to this change process is how leadership within CUNY-NYSIEB schools has been redefined. Interestingly, we have found that changes in school leadership structures in these schools went hand-in-hand with broader language policy and pedagogical shifts, as documented by Ascenzi-Moreno, Hesson, and Menken (2016). Because teachers, especially those of ESL and bilingual education, are often the ones in their buildings with the most expertise in the education of emergent bilinguals, they began to be called upon in CUNY-NYSIEB schools to be directly involved in making schoolwide decisions for these students. A school principal and assistant principal describe the involvement of teachers in the development of the school's CUNY-NYSIEB plan, in which they outlined proposed changes in the education of emergent bilinguals aligned to the project's vision and principles, along with the tasks and timeframes to implement those changes:

PRINCIPAL: Well they [teachers] have been really immersed and involved in creating the plan, and they have taken a leadership role in implementing the plan, I think very much so. So, I think they're really essential.

ASSISTANT PRINCIPAL: They're the ones who are doing it.

At the start of the project, these school leaders spoke about themselves as the center of school decision making but, by the end, began to see the teachers as the leaders of school change efforts. The school administrators in this interview describe how teachers—who in this case were a mixture of ESL, general education, and literacy teachers—took on major leadership roles in developing, adopting, and implementing the school's CUNY-NYSIEB plan. Thus, top-down leadership arrangements with the principal as the sole decision maker fell out of favor for CUNY-NYSIEB work, as across schools more hierarchical leadership was abandoned in favor of collaborative models in which teachers became school leaders and worked alongside administrators.

In schools like the one described in the preceding paragraph, the principals readily adopted and promoted CUNY-NYSIEB's vision and principles and actively encouraged experimentation with translanguaging. In others, schoolwide changes emanated from several teachers who began experimenting with translanguaging pedagogy in their classrooms. After witnessing the successes of these pioneering teachers firsthand, it caught on, and principals became more actively supportive. Regardless, all the teachers in the case studies are emblematic of collaborative school leadership because the pedagogical changes they made in their classrooms led to expanded roles and responsibilities in their schools. In one case, the teacher has gone on to assume leadership responsibilities in her district around translanguaging pedagogy as well. What is more, the project now targets school leaders more broadly, which is inclusive of school principals and other school administrators, as well as teacher leaders, as the primary arbiters of change.

Working in tandem, teachers and school administrators adopted a number of powerful changes in CUNY-NYSIEB schools worth noting here. Many classroom teachers have begun engaging the students' full linguistic repertoire in instruction through translanguaging pedagogy like those documented in this volume, and many schools have likewise changed their linguistic landscape by incorporating all of their students' languages in the hallways, on classroom walls, and in the materials used in instruction (see García & Menken, 2015; García & Sánchez, 2015, for further discussion). In addition to adopting translanguaging pedagogy in classrooms, some schools have begun to offer new classes taught through the medium of students' home languages, for instance in what the schools term "Native Language Arts" classes. Some schools have made additional programming shifts for emergent bilinguals. For example, some ESL and transitional bilingual education programs have been replaced with dual language bilingual education programs, the program model in New York with the greatest opportunity to develop bilingualism and biliteracy.

The work of the teachers in the case studies took place within a context of overall school reform as their schools moved from monolingual or monoglossic to multilingual. While any teacher could try experimenting with translanguaging pedagogy in their classroom, regardless of the initial level of support from their administrators, we expect that the successes they experience from doing so would start small earthquakes that would foster schoolwide change. Moreover, in order to improve the education of emergent bilinguals, we must all work collaboratively as we nourish a vision for these students that appreciates them completely, and is full of hope and opportunity.

Kate Menken
Co-Principal Investigator, CUNY-NYSIEB
María Teresa (Maite) Sánchez
Project Director, CUNY-NYSIEB

References

Ascenzi-Moreno, L., Hesson, S., & Menken, K. (2016). School leadership along the trajectory from monolingual to multilingual. *Language and Education*, 30(3), 197–218. DOI: 10.1080/09500782.2015.1093499

García, O., & Menken, K. (2015). Cultivating an ecology of multilingualism in schools. In B. Spolsky, O. Inbar-Lourie, & M. Tannenbaum (Eds.), *Challenges for language education and policy: Making space for people* (pp. 95–108). New York: Routledge.

García, O., & Sánchez, M. (2015). Transforming schools with emergent bilinguals: The CUNY-NYSIEB project. In I. Dirim, I. Gogolin, D. Knorr, M. Krüger-Potratz, D. Lengyel, H. Reich, & W. Weiße (Eds.), *Intercultural education: Festchrift for Ulla Neumann* (pp. 80–94). Berlin, Germany: Waxmann-Verlag.

Menken, K., & Solorza, C. (2013). Where have all the bilingual programs gone?!: Why prepared school leaders are essential for bilingual education. *Journal of Multilingual Education Research*, 4, 9–39.

CONTRIBUTORS

María Cioè-Peña, M.S.Ed., is a doctoral student in the Urban Education program at the CUNY Graduate Center where she is a Presidential MAGNET Fellow. Her research interests include bilingual special education policy and pedagogy, and parental involvement. She received a master's degree in Teaching Children with Disabilities from Long Island University. She worked at the NYC Department of Education as a bilingual special education teacher at preschool and elementary levels for nine years. María is a Research Assistant on the CUNY-NYSIEB project.

Brian A. Collins is an Assistant Professor of Bilingual Education at Hunter College, CUNY. His research focuses on the bilingual language development of children of immigrants in the U.S. and how language competences interface among dimensions of children's social, psychological, and academic well-being. His work gives careful consideration to contextual factors in the home and school environment and factors unique to children of immigrants. Dr. Collins has been an Associate Investigator on the CUNY-NYSIEB project and is committed to connecting his research to educators, clinicians, and specialists who work with bilingual children.

Ann E. Ebe began her work in schools as a bilingual elementary school teacher, reading specialist, and administrator. She has worked in schools and universities in California, Arizona, Hong Kong, Massachusetts, and, most recently, New York. She served as Director of Bilingual Education and was an Associate Professor of Literacy Education in the Graduate School of Education at Hunter College in New York City. Dr. Ebe now lives in Mexico City where she is working with schools. Her primary research interests include exploring translanguaging in classrooms, the reading process of bilingual students, and the selection of culturally relevant texts. She has been an Associate Investigator on the CUNY-NYSIEB project.

Cecilia M. Espinosa was born in Ecuador. Before completing her Ph.D., she was a bilingual-multiage classroom teacher and a director of a dual language program in Phoenix, Arizona. She is currently an Associate Professor of Early Childhood/ Childhood Education at Lehman College, CUNY. Her work has been deeply influenced by the Prospect Center for Education and Research and the New York City Writing Project (NYCWP). She has been an Associate Investigator with CUNY-NYSIEB. Her research interests include collaborative research, biliteracy development, descriptive processes, teacher inquiry, children's literature in Spanish, translanguaging, and the role of teacher learning communities in their professional development.

Ofelia García is Professor in the Ph.D. programs of Urban Education and of Hispanic and Luso-Brazilian Literatures and Languages at The Graduate Center, City University of New York. She has been Professor of Bilingual Education at Columbia University's Teachers College, Dean of the School of Education at the Brooklyn Campus of Long Island University, and Professor of Education at The City College of New York. García has published widely in the areas of bilingualism, bilingual education, sociology of language, and language policy. She is the General Editor of the *International Journal of the Sociology of Language* and the co-editor of *Language Policy* (with H. Kelly-Holmes). Among her best-known books are *Bilingual Education in the 21st Century: A Global Perspective* and *Translanguaging: Language, Bilingualism and Education* (with Li Wei), which received the 2015 British Association of Applied Linguistics Award. She was a founder of CUNY-NYSIEB and has served as Co-Principal Investigator.

Luz Yadira Herrera is a doctoral candidate in Urban Education in the CUNY Graduate Center and an Enhanced Chancellor's Fellow. She is an Adjunct Instructor in the Puerto Rican and Latino Studies Department at Brooklyn College, previously teaching in the Bilingual Education and TESOL Programs at The City College of New York. Herrera is also a Research Assistant for CUNY-NYSIEB. Herrera taught emergent bilinguals in a New York City public school for seven years. Her dissertation research is on the impact of translanguaging in the classroom as it relates to advancing social justice in education.

Tatyana Kleyn is Associate Professor and Director of the Bilingual Education and TESOL programs at the City College of New York. She received an Ed.D. from Teachers College, Columbia University. From 2014 to 2015, Tatyana served as president of the New York State Association for Bilingual Education and was a Fulbright Scholar in Oaxaca, Mexico. Tatyana is author of *Immigration: The Ultimate Teen Guide* and co-author of *Teaching in Two Languages: A Guide for K–12 Bilingual Educators* (with Adelman Reyes). Tatyana is the director of the documentaries *Living Undocumented: High School, College and Beyond* and *Una Vida, Dos Países: Children and Youth (Back) in Mexico.* She was an elementary school teacher in Honduras and Atlanta, Georgia. Tatyana has been Associate Investigator for CUNY-NYSIEB and served as Interim Co-Principal Investigator in 2013–2014.

Kate Menken is an Associate Professor of Linguistics at Queens College of the City University of New York (CUNY) and a Research Fellow at the Research Institute for the Study of Language in Urban Society at the CUNY Graduate Center. She is Co-Principal Investigator of the CUNY-New York State Initiative for Emergent Bilinguals (NYSIEB) project and chaired the Bilingual Education Special Interest Group of the American Educational Research Association. She holds an Ed.D. from Teachers College, Columbia University. Her research interests include language education policy, bilingual education, and emergent bilinguals in secondary schools. Recent books are *English Learners Left Behind: Standardized Testing as Language Policy* (Multilingual Matters, 2008), *Negotiating Language Policies in Schools: Educators as Policymakers* (co-edited with Ofelia García, Routledge, 2010), and *Common Core, Bilingual and English Language Learners: A Resource for Educators* (co-edited with Guadalupe Valdés and Mariana Castro, Caslon, 2015).

Ricardo Otheguy is Professor of Linguistics at the Graduate Center of the City University of New York. His work in theoretical and applied linguistics has appeared in major international journals. His publications in theoretical linguistics are in the areas of language contact, functional grammar, and the Spanish of the United States; in applied linguistics, his publications are in the area of bilingual education and the teaching of Spanish as a home language and as a second or foreign language. Otheguy has developed textbook materials for the teaching of Spanish to Latino students in the United States, as well as materials for teaching Spanish as a second language. Otheguy has been the Principal Investigator of CUNY-NYSIEB since its inception.

María Teresa (Maite) Sánchez is the Project Director of the CUNY-New York State Initiative for Emergent Bilinguals (CUNY-NYSIEB). She holds a Ph.D. from Boston College. Her research interests include language education policy, and bilingual education and instruction for emergent bilinguals in different educational settings. She has co-authored several publications related to emergent bilinguals including "Supporting emergent bilinguals in New York: Understanding successful school practices" (2014), "District- and school-level collaboration between English language learners and special educators in the pre-referral and referral process" (2012), and "Undermining teacher competencies: Another look at the impact of restrictive language policies" (2010).

Kate Seltzer is a Ph.D. candidate in Urban Education at the CUNY Graduate Center, a Research Assistant on the CUNY-NYSIEB project, and an Instructor in the Bilingual & TESOL programs at the City College of New York. Her dissertation focuses on challenging and interrupting the traditional ideologies and practices of high school English Language Arts classrooms in order to reflect and foster the complex communicative languages practices of linguistically marginalized students. She is the co-author of *Translanguaging: A CUNY-NYSIEB Guide for Educators* and several other publications on classroom translanguaging, including the new book *The Translanguaging Classroom: Leveraging Student Bilingualism for Learning* with Ofelia García and Susana Ibarra Johnson.

Heather H. Woodley is Clinical Assistant Professor of TESOL, Bilingual and Foreign Language Education in Multilingual Multicultural Studies at NYU Steinhardt. Her research and teaching take a critical approach to improving school experiences for emergent bilinguals, and her publications explore multilingual classroom practices and arts as social justice education. She was a Research Assistant with CUNY-NYSIEB and a classroom teacher in the Bronx and Washington, DC. She received a 2014 Outstanding Dissertation Award from the National Association of Bilingual Education, was a Fulbright Scholar in Morocco, and earned her Ph.D. in Urban Education at The Graduate Center, CUNY.

The Teachers

Katrina Mae Angeles has been a teacher since she was very young. As a junior in high school, she was a facilitator for the Academic Proficiency Program of Prosec Inc. and later became an English Literature teacher in the high school from which she graduated. She holds a master's degree in Teaching English to Speakers of Other Languages from New York University. After graduating, she taught English as a New Language in a high school in New York City for eight years, and is currently teaching in a high school in Long Island, New York. Always happy to collaborate with others for the benefit of her students, she participated in the CUNY-NYSIEB project for three years, focusing specifically on students with interrupted formal education.

Andrew Brown has been working as a NYC public school teacher since 2008. He received his master's degree in Elementary Education from the C.W. Post campus of Long Island University in 2003 and recently received his TESOL certification from St. John's University. He is the 5th-grade English as a New Language (ENL) teacher at P.S. 153 in Maspeth, Queens, and began incorporating translanguaging in his classroom since he joined CUNY-NYSIEB. He is currently taking Spanish classes with the goal of becoming a bilingual teacher.

Charene Chapman-Santiago has been a NYC public school teacher and humanities coach since 2002. She entered the education field as a New York

City Teaching Fellow after working in the entertainment field following her graduation from New York University. Her M.A. in Education is from Pace University and she holds an Advanced Degree in Educational Supervision and Administration from the College of Saint Rose. Chapman-Santiago wears many hats at Ebbets Field Middle School in Brooklyn where she presently teaches. Since she started participating in CUNY-NYSIEB, she has become the point person and model teacher of translanguaging. She presented her translanguaging work at the New York State Association for Bilingual Education (NYSABE) conference and has been videotaped integrating translanguaging in her classroom for professional development purposes.

Claudia Montoya Gaudreau has been a NYC public school teacher since 1998. She holds an Early Childhood–Elementary School Teacher B.A. with a minor in Spanish and English Literature and a Reading Literacy M.A. from Brooklyn College, CUNY. Montoya helped launch the Spanish dual language bilingual program at IS 228 Intermediate School for Magnet Studies in Brooklyn in 2013. She has participated in the CUNY-NYSIEB project and has implemented translanguaging in her dual language bilingual classroom, where students are reclaiming their bilingualism.

Hulda Yau has been working for the Rochester City School District (RCSD) since 2003 and is a 2nd-grade bilingual teacher in an integrated classroom. Hulda holds a Master of Science in Education from the State University of New York at Brockport and has New York State certificates in the areas of PreK–6, Spanish 7–12, and a Bilingual Education Extension. She has worked with CUNY-NYSIEB since 2014 and through this collaboration has presented on translanguaging at the 2015 NYSABE conference and St. John Fisher College and for teachers in the RSCD. She facilitates a descriptive inquiry group at Henry Hudson School and is the lead teacher-scholar in a research study to examine the impact of translanguaging strategies on a variety of student outcomes.

INDEX